Power Boating
FOR
DUMMIES®

by Randy Vance

WILEY

John Wiley & Sons, Inc.

Power Boating For Dummies®

Published by
John Wiley & Sons, Inc.
111 River St.
Hoboken, NJ 07030-5774
www.wiley.com

WILEY

About the Author

Randy Vance has been boating since he was 8 years old. From family boat to personal runabout at age 20, he's bought and sold nearly a dozen boats in his boating career.

With his family, Randy ran a small resort and marina on Lake of the Ozarks in Missouri for more than 20 years. During that time, he was a popular outdoors columnist in local papers and magazines and hosted or appeared on many radio and television programs covering topics of boating and fishing. Later, Randy began a public relations career at Bass Pro Shops, employing his enjoyment of boating, outdoors, and writing in one happy position. After a short stint at the failing Outboard Marine Corporation, *Boating Life* magazine publisher John McEver asked Randy to take the helm of his magazine — a position Randy has enjoyed with co-editors Robert Stephens and Sue Whitney since 2000. *Boating Life* magazine and some of Randy's articles have won awards in many publishing circles.

During his tenure at *Boating Life,* Randy has had the pleasure of piloting thousands of boats in hundreds of different places and conditions. Mexico, the Exumas, Dry Tortugas, Alaska's Admiralty Island, Sweden, and Bimini, Bahamas, are among his favorite boating destinations.

Randy, his wife Linda, and youngest daughter Amy, along with three champion Cotons du Tulear and a stray Jack Russell Terrier, enjoy a 25-foot Bluewater offshore boat with twin Evinrude outboards. Most often you'll find him offshore at Cape Canaveral or just outside of Springhill, Florida, or Punta Gorda, Florida.

Randy and his daughter Amy are in the midst of the long and arduous process of researching his next book *Restoring Old Boats For Dummies. . .* just joking; they're attempting to bring a 1978 Glastron GT 150 back to its former glory. The GT 150 was made famous in the 1973 James Bond movie *Live and Let Die* when it jumped a levee over the head of a local sheriff.

Randy's son Justin and wife Shasta are currently raising the next crop of boating Vances in Phoenix, Arizona, a desert state surprisingly blessed with beautiful boating waters. Randy's daughter and fellow boater Megan Chacon is raising another boating infant named Brody while husband Gabe Chacon gets his mariner's fix aboard the U.S.S. Lincoln, stationed in Seattle, Washington, when he's not boating.

Boating creates strong bonds among those who participate, and Randy's primary pleasure has been bringing new boaters into the sport.

Dedication

To my wife and kids, who are ready to boat any time I jingle the keys.

Acknowledgments

This book would not be possible if it were not for the "What Next?" That was the name my family gave the 15-foot outboard-powered Starcraft that Dad bought in 1963. We launched it the first time in Huntsville, Alabama, and left the drain plug out. It sank on the ramp. We raised it that same day and went skiing. A few years later, when I could barely see over the helm, my dad let me drive it from the launch ramp to our rented cabin on the lake. Later, renting that boat at our family resort helped put me through college. For me, boating has always been what was next and sometimes what came first.

Howard Vance, my grandfather, was a guy who boated to fish. Somewhere, I have a photo of him in his captain's hat beaming from the helm of his Kayot pontoon boat. He infected me with the bug of fishing from a boat. When a boat wasn't available, my grandpa Leonard Young kept the fishing bug stoked: I'd visit him at his Kentucky farm and find a bucket of minnows in the stock pond and a bass rod leaning up against the pump house when I arrived.

But just as this book wouldn't have been possible without those responsible for my boating origins, it wouldn't be credible without the boating experiences I've enjoyed later in life with other greater boaters.

Midland Michigan outdoors columnist Steve Griffin and I paddled a blue canoe through the Quetico Provincial Park. That darned canoe would go every way but where you pointed it. We taped a new name on its freeboard: "Blue Bitch." We laughed our heads off the rest of the week, and I learned a valuable lesson: No matter how bad a boat is, it's good for friendship.

Bob Orth, my father-in-law, approaches boating with the systematic logic of a pilot — which he was for some time. For him, planning, preparation, and careful execution of every aspect of boating is the challenge and fun of the game. Mike Folkerts is Commodore of the Alaska branch of the United States Coast Guard Auxiliary. A week of boating with his team and watching them work together like a well-oiled machine taught me much about the way families and friends learn to enjoy each other while boating. Mike's crew also moved the needle on my safety gauge a little closer to the U.S. Coast Guard ideals. Curt Jarson and I have adventured to the Bahamas often, and from him I learned both the finesse of setting up a boat to run through rough water and the mental discipline of "holding on loosely" while other boaters handle my boat.

Many other people in the boat building and marine publishing arena, friends, peers, and competitors have influenced my boating almost always for the better. I could not have written this book were it not for the friendship I share with all of you.

Perhaps most instrumental in creating this book are my teammates at *Boating Life* magazine, Robert Stephens, Sue Whitney, and John McEver, who all covered my butt while, in my spare time, I pulled many loose ends together in *Power Boating For Dummies*.

What makes *For Dummies* books so easy and fun to read is their carefully formatted style that lets readers grab concepts one tidbit at a time, sort of like browsing a buffet line to select the goodies you want when the mood strikes. I might never have captured that style in this book if it were not for veteran *For Dummies* author Chris Bigelow.

Publisher's Acknowledgments

We're proud of this book; please send us your comments through our Dummies online registration form located at http://dummies.custhelp.com. For other comments, please contact our Customer Care Department within the U.S. at 877-762-2974, outside the U.S. at 317-572-3993, or fax 317-572-4002.

Some of the people who helped bring this book to market include the following:

Acquisitions, Editorial, and Media Development

Development Editor: Christopher Bigelow

Senior Project Editor: Christina Guthrie

Acquisitions Editor: Michael Lewis

Senior Copy Editor: Elizabeth Rea

Assistant Editor: Erin Calligan Mooney

Editorial Program Coordinator: Joe Niesen

Technical Editor: Lenny Rudow

Editorial Manager: Christine Meloy Beck

Editorial Assistants: Jennette ElNaggar, David Lutton

Art Coordinator: Alicia B. South

Cover Photos: iStock

Cartoons: Rich Tennant (www.the5thwave.com)

Composition Services

Project Coordinator: Katie Key

Layout and Graphics: Reuben W. Davis, Sarah Philippart, Christin Swinford

Special Art: Interior illustrations by Precision Graphics (www.precisiongraphics.com)

Proofreaders: Laura L. Bowman, John Greenough

Indexer: Steve Rath

Publishing and Editorial for Consumer Dummies

    Kathleen Nebenhaus, Vice President and Publisher

    David Palmer, Associate Publisher

    Kristin Ferguson-Wagstaffe, Product Development Director

Publishing for Technology Dummies

    Andy Cummings, Vice President and Publisher

Composition Services

    Debbie Stailey, Director of Composition Services

Contents at a Glance

Table of Contents

Introduction

· ·

I've been power boating for 45 years and even sailed a little, too. In that time, I've had the pleasure of guiding fishermen, teaching my kids and friends to water-ski, and in many ways ushering new boaters into the fun and adventure of a lifestyle I wouldn't consider life much fun without. In all that time, I've written newspaper columns and magazine articles on the how-to's of power boating. For nine years I've been the editor-in-chief of *Boating Life* magazine.

Through my work and play, I've learned that new boaters don't get into trouble from the complexity of boating but from their preconceived notions of how boating should be done. In *Power Boating For Dummies,* I do my best to protect you from trouble by helping you know just what to expect from a boat before you ever get your hands on the controls.

Among non-boaters and especially among sailing boaters, there's often an unjustified assumption that power boaters are goof-offs who bungle along with beer in hand as they pilot crafts they know nothing about. Well, every group has a few outlaws, and I've had the fortune of watching diligent water cops take them out of the game. But I've also had the pleasure of helping others who want to get better at boating to avoid the stereotype.

Power boaters are responsible people seeking family unity, friendship, and personal growth in a pastime that requires the ultimate in teamwork. In all cases, power boaters want to get outdoors in a place filled with like-minded individuals and enjoy nature, each other's company, and maybe a little bit of adventure. But most of all, power boaters don't want their fun to depend on something as fickle as the wind! If you're in this group, this book is for you.

About This Book

Power Boating For Dummies is a comprehensive guide to practically every-thing you need to know about buying, owning, operating, and maintaining a boat to about 35 feet in length. However, you'll find that the information and recommendations in this book also give you great foundational knowledge for handling larger boats as well.

If you read this book before ever stepping foot on a boat, I walk you through the process of imagining what kind of boating you may like to do. If you have some boating experience but haven't yet looked into buying your own boat, I escort you through that process as well. If you already have a boat but want to know more about how to pilot it, equip it, store it, tow it, handle emergencies on it, or dine onboard it, this is the book for you. Even if you already have some experience captaining your own boat, this book could help fill in some gaps in your knowledge and give you some new ideas for improving your boating experience.

Of course, no single book could tell you all there is to know about boating; here are a few facts you need to investigate on your own:

- ✔ **Boating rules vary by state.** When it comes to boating, every U.S. state has its own jurisdictional quirks regarding safety, equipment, and licensing, among other things. Although I give you some tips about how to find out about your local regulations, you need to do some investigating on your own to be fully informed.

- ✔ **Boat brands and specifications vary by manufacturer.** Boats are all similar, but none are the same. In my years as a boater, I've owned a dozen different boats and several different kinds of boats. As editor-in-chief of *Boating Life* magazine, I've driven literally thousands of boats. In this book, I've tried to make some reliable generalizations that hold true for nearly all makes and styles of boats. Of course, you should find out all the specifics about your own boat, starting by thoroughly studying the owner's manual.

- ✔ **Boating activities and preferences vary by geography.** I've boated in enough places to know that people tend to boat different ways in different regions. For instance, brand loyalty to certain boats or motors can be so fierce in some regions that you'll just want to go with the flow, in case you ever want to resell your boat in that area. I recommend that you fully immerse yourself in your local boating culture to learn the local lore.

Conventions Used in This Book

As you know if you've ever watched a movie or read a book about sailors or pirates or other nautical types, the marine world is filled with specialized jargon. Many of these terms are commonly used in power boating as well, especially words for boating gear and the parts of a boat.

Long-time boaters sometimes develop a little bit of snobbery about their mastery of boat jargon. As the editor-in-chief of _Boating Life_ magazine, I regularly receive snide letters about our occasional inadvertent failure to adhere to every dictate of boating jargon. I respond to such letters in online video format at `www.boatinglife.com` in a piece called Naughty-cal Terminology, so check it out!

For this book, I've sprinkled in some boating jargon, but I put those terms in _italics_ and define them upon first mention in every chapter, so you won't get lost even if you skip around in the book. Here are some other conventions you should be aware of:

- Keywords in bulleted lists appear in **boldface** for ease of reading and reference.
- Web sites and e-mail addresses appear in `monofont`, so they stand out better on the page.

What You're Not to Read

Of course I'd love for you to read every word of this book — I worked so hard on it and all. However, if you're pressed for time or would rather be out on your boat than reading every bit of this book, you can skip some parts and not miss a beat.

Throughout the book, you'll see sidebars, which appear in gray boxes. The topics of these sidebars are ancillary to the overall topic of a particular section or chapter, but again, you won't miss out on critical information if you decide not to read them.

Foolish Assumptions

In writing this book, I assumed you were either a newbie to boating or some-one with some experience who wanted to hone your skills in a systematic way. You're on the verge of getting into the sport, or you've been in it just long enough to thump a dock real hard with your boat or get embarrassed because you missed the trailer when you were loading up. Thanks to the cool _For Dummies_ format, you can jump in, grab just the information you want and need, and get out there to try it out while it's fresh in your mind.

That's what I was thinking when I wrote this book. That and one other thing: Everybody makes mistakes in everything, including boating. I've been boating for 45 years, but I still make embarrassing mistakes. In this book, I don't try to hide my blunders if I think you can learn from them. Some people won't play games they can't play perfectly. I hope you're not that way, because you'll quickly abandon boating if you are.

How This Book Is Organized

The format of *Power Boating For Dummies* helps you find exactly what you want to know and gives the information to you in bite-sized pieces. Here's a quick rundown of how this particular book is organized, so you know where to look for exactly what you need.

Part 1: Getting On the Right Boating Track

Part I is about getting geared up for boating. In it, I assume you don't yet have a boat or the gear you need to operate it safely. I explain how to determine what kind of boat is right for you and how to go about shopping for it, plus the goodies that make it fun and safe to operate.

Part 11: Safely Operating Your Boat

In this part, I assume you've never driven a boat, or if you have, you've found the experience completely foreign and frightening.

If you can set aside what you may already know about boat operation, tell yourself that driving a car is not like driving a boat, and read the chapters in this part from a perspective of complete ignorance, you'll quickly get your handling skills up to snuff and be better than 90 percent of boaters out there.

Part 111: With Much Boating Fun Comes Much Responsibility

There's more to boating than just racing toward the open water to kick back, soak up some rays, maybe do a little fishing, and splash around in the refreshing waters. In this part, I help you become a more responsible boater, starting with the rules and regulations of boating. To boat safely, you need to know the boating laws in your state and locality. And you can't be a safe boater unless you take a boating safety course approved by your state.

This part also explores navigation tools, navigating your boat in all sorts of conditions, and dealing with common boating emergencies.

Part IV: Keeping Your Boat Shipshape

Part of the boating lifestyle is routine boat maintenance. Many boaters embrace this wholly, taking on the tasks of detailed mechanical repairs as well as the money-saving and relatively easy task of changing their boat's engine oil. This section gives you lots of practical tactics for servicing your boat and doing minor repairs and replacements. I also help you decide what you can tackle yourself and what you should leave to a mechanic.

Part V: Enjoying Your Boat

This part covers topics that ensure a good time on the water. I start with boat storage because taking care of your boat when you're not on it is key to a long and happy boating life together. You want your boat to be ready when you are, don't you?

Most boaters love company as much as they love solitude. My boat seldom leaves the dock without guests onboard, which led me to include a chapter on dining onboard. An important part of entertaining on your boat is making sure everyone's well fed! And half the fun of my boating experiences is meeting new people in marinas and at waterfront attractions. Boating clubs and other organizations are a great way to get the most out of your boating experiences.

Part VI: The Part of Tens

I love this characteristic part of *For Dummies* books. In this book, it contains short, memorable lists of ten tactics to separate yourself from amateur boaters, ten key items to keep onboard, and ten checks to do when buying a boat to protect yourself from buying a lemon.

Icons Used in This Book

As you flip through this book (or any other *For Dummies* book, for that matter), you'll notice that certain paragraphs have icons attached to them. They're another handy reference tool for you to highlight various types of information. Following are descriptions of each of the icons used in *Power Boating For Dummies:*

This icon calls attention to handy tactics that make it easier to accomplish the tasks under discussion.

Think of this icon like the emblem on your lawn mower that shows a few fingers leaving the hand as the blade passes by. Heeding warnings will keep you out of trouble, pain, or embarrassment.

This icon highlights simple, helpful notes as well as reminders to keep in mind as you hit the water or engage in other boating-related tasks.

Where to Go from Here

Where you go from here is entirely up to you. If you're looking for a specific topic, the table of contents and the index are your friends. Find the topic you want, flip to that chapter or section, and get the inside scoop. Watch for the handy cross-references I provide to other parts of the book that contain related information.

You don't need to read this book cover to cover if you don't want to. Look at *Power Boating For Dummies* as a candy store: Just pick out the morsels you know you want, and go ahead and try out any unfamiliar items that look enticing! Of course, you can always be a traditional-type and read the entire book from start to finish; no one will think less of you.

Part I
Getting On the Right Boating Track

The 5th Wave — By Rich Tennant

In this part . . .

About 250,000 new power boats and about 1 million used ones are sold every year — and that's just in the United States. With so many boats on the market, how can you be sure to get the right one for you? In this part, I explain how to decide what you want to do with a boat. I identify the different kinds of boats that are available and what they do best. I also give you advice on figuring out what boat is right for your favorite boating waters and stocking it with safety and playtime accessories for optimal enjoyment on the water.

Chapter 1

Powering Up to Be a Boater

∙ ∙

In This Chapter

▶ Getting to know your boat-y self

▶ Landing the boat of your dreams

▶ Leading your boat to water

▶ Keeping your boat running with routine maintenance

∙ ∙

*W*hat attracts you to the idea of boating? Is it speeding through the water with a water-skier in tow? Is it fishing for hours out in the middle of a lake or ocean? Is it going on overnight cruises to other ports? Whatever draws you to this pastime, there's no doubt that power boating is a commitment. First you plunk down the cash for a boat and motor, and then you carve the time out of your schedule to use it. But how do you know if you'll like it?

You can't know for sure until you give it the old college try, and some boaters give up the game soon after taking it up. But it's a different story for most boaters I know — by now, they're on their third or fourth boat. Personally, I'm on my ninth boat, and I would give up cable TV, my gym membership, my truck, and air conditioning before I'd give up my boat.

In this chapter, I guide you through the process of deciding whether power boating is for you and give you an overview of what you need to know in order to acquire, use, and care for a power boat.

You Might Be a Boater If . . .

Boaters are like birds of a feather. As you get to know them, you'll find they come from all walks of life, but the better you get to know them, the more you find they're bonded to boating because boating causes them to bond with each other.

Here's why I love boating: As my kids have approached their teen years — my third is now 17 — the pressure has been astronomical for them to pull away from my wife and me and get into other activities with friends beyond our sphere of influence. But if I ask my daughter if she wants to take a couple of friends out in the boat on a given Saturday, I almost always get the pleasure of her company along with her friends, and I get to play a part in turning them all into rabid boaters, too. My daughter didn't want a 13th birthday party at a country club, an expensive restaurant, or Disney World. She wanted it at the lake with the boat, burgers on the grill, and hip-hop on the stereo, laughing herself silly with her friends as we hauled them around the lake on the tube.

That's my story, but you may have different motivating factors. You may be a boater if

- When you cross a bridge over a lake or river, you can't help but wonder about all the boats below, all the people in them, and what it would be like to be with them.

- You almost always book your vacations around water.

- You feel a burning desire to go where most people don't go.

- When you go to the beach, you wade or swim out as far as you can and then want to go farther.

- You want to meet other people in interesting places and do fun and relaxing things.

- You find yourself sitting on the dock fishing, knowing that if you could just get out on the water you'd find an incredibly great fishing hole.

- You want to learn new skills. (In boating, there's always something fun and interesting to learn or a new challenge to master.)

- You've taken rides in friends' boats and envy their freedom and excitement.

- You love to snow ski but don't know what to do in the summer.

Weighing the Costs of Boating

For many people considering boating, the major hurdles are the financial cost as well as the time commitment. To commit yourself to boating, you may need to scale back on some other activities and entertainments — but believe me, it's worth it. Hey, the grass in my yard grows a little longer in the summer thanks to the boat, and yours probably will too. Some of the costs of boating aren't in cash but in time spent doing other things.

As far as the costs of boating that you measure in cash, the comparisons I give in this section show that you may already be spending more cash for less fun with other activities, making boating a better form of entertainment.

Costs of landlubber family activities

If you worry that boating is too expensive, consider the following estimated costs for other fun family activities:

- ✔ **Attending baseball games:** Counting tickets, food, drinks, and stadium parking, I figure each outing costs about $300 for a family of four, and many baseball-loving families like to attend games several times a year.

- ✔ **Visiting theme parks:** Considering entrance fees, parking, food, and souvenirs, I estimate a family of four spends at least $500 for a theme park outing.

- ✔ **Seeing movies:** With tickets, popcorn, and drinks, a movie outing for a family of four costs about $80. If you see several movies a year, that adds up fast.

- ✔ **Playing golf:** Not counting golf club dues or equipment, one golfer can easily spend $200 and more on just one golf outing, counting greens and cart fees, lost balls, and post-game refreshments.

Costs of boating as a family

Compared to other family activities, boating can work out to be a relatively cheap form of family fun if you look at your costs per outing.

Suppose you're thinking about spending $20,000 on a new boat — and keep in mind that you can spend much less than that, especially on a pre-owned boat. If you finance it for ten years, as many people do, you'll pay about $200 per month. If you make a good deal, the dealer may throw in extras like a wakeboard, rope, life jackets, and a big, bright-colored tube to tow the kids around on. (I talk more about buying a boat in Chapter 3.)

Assume you're able to get out on your boat 12 times per year. Here's how your cost per boating outing could shake out:

Amortize the annual payment over 12 trips	$200
Gas up with 30 gallons	$100
Load the cooler with food and drinks	$25
Amortize your annual maintenance, storage, and other costs	$50
Cost per outing	**$375**

Wow, by my estimate, a boat outing for a family of four costs less than a day at a theme park and only slightly more than a night at the ballgame! And if you go out more often than 12 times a year, your amortization goes down accordingly, making boating an even better family entertainment deal. What's more, when your kids get a taste of Saturday wakeboarding, tubing, or fishing, you'll have an easier time getting them out on your boat than you may have convincing them to participate in some other family activities. As a bonus, it doesn't cost anything extra if they want to bring along a friend.

Considering Different Kinds of Boats

The most motivated boaters are anglers. Boat dealers sell about three times as many fishing boats as all other types of boats combined. But plenty of other people buy boats for water-skiing, racing, pleasure cruising, and other activities and reasons. Knowing why you want to boat and what you want to do when you boat helps narrow down the many, many different types of boats to the one you want.

At www.boatinglife.com, you'll find a search engine that lists about 100 different kinds of boats and hundreds of boat brands. The drop-down menus at this site seem to get longer every time I click them. To use the search engine, select the style of boat you want. Select the size of boat, and then your price range. The database sorts through hundreds of boats and gives you a short list of brands and models that may appeal to you.

You don't need to know all about all the kinds and brands of boats on the market today, but familiarizing yourself with the general categories can help you figure out which kind best fits your hopes, dreams, and needs. (I talk in detail about kinds of boats and boating activities in Chapter 2.)

✔ **Boats for watersports and/or day cruising:** Watersports like water-skiing, wakeboarding (which is just a popular, hip form of water-skiing), and tubing are popular boating activities. Also popular is day cruising, which is just bumming around on the water, maybe tooling over to a waterfront burger joint or moseying over to a popular sandbar for impromptu parties. If any of these activities sound like the kind of boating you want to do, you should look into the following kinds of runabouts and day boats:

- **Bowriders and deck boats** are open boats with comfortable seating. They're sort of like convertible sports cars on the water. People buy them to tour, water-ski, wakeboard, hang out and swim, or go on evening cruises to popular waterfront restaurants.

- **Pontoon boats** are large flat platforms floating on hollow aluminum cylinders called *pontoons.* They hold more passengers per square foot than any other style of boat. Some are equipped with so much horsepower that they can pull skiers, or they can just idle along as the passengers enjoy the breeze and the view.

✔ **Boats for fishing:** Fishermen are addicted to their sport and usually devote themselves to the pursuit of one particular species of fish, like bass, walleye, or saltwater fish from bays or open oceans. If you're constantly casting a lure as far from the dock or shore as you can, hoping to get closer to a bite, you're in the market for one of these kinds of boats:

- **Bass boats and walleye boats** have special characteristics such as casting decks, livewells, and trolling motors that make them ideal for pursuing those species of fish.

- **Bay boats and flats boats** are built to run in very shallow salt water to allow you to catch fish there. Boaters often use these boats just to explore every nook, cranny, cove, and beach they can find.

- **Offshore fishing boats** are for catching big game like sailfish, marlin, dorado, wahoo, and tuna. They're also popular for just riding around and beaching up with friends at sandbars. These sturdy boats are especially seaworthy and easy to hose out, thanks to fiberglass decks that usually drain right overboard.

- **Fish and ski boats** are becoming incredibly popular because they give boaters the versatility of a sporty ski boat and a well-appointed fishing boat with livewells and a trolling motor. For many boaters, this is a great "first boat" that lets them explore their passions.

✔ **Boats for overnight cruising:** The romance of living on the water lures many people into boating. Like a motor home on the water, a cruising boat has all the amenities of home in a more compact package. It has sleeping bunks called *berths,* a bathroom called a *head,* and kitchen facilities in the *galley*.

Getting Trained and Licensed

Before you buy your first boat, you need to be ready to use it. Besides getting started on mastering the obvious skill of safely piloting a boat, you need to acquire a few other tidbits of knowledge as you set out on your boating adventure.

Captaining a boat isn't really as hard as driving a car. But it's so different that new boaters get into trouble when they try to handle a boat the same way they handle a car. Boating safety training helps ward off some of the accidents that come from such misconceptions.

Some states require a boating license, whereas others just ask for proof that you completed an online or classroom safety course. Keep in mind that in some states, penalty points for boating offenses could be tallied against your driver's license. You can learn all about your state's boating laws by visiting www.nasbla.org, but here's some general information to get you started:

✔ **Boating licenses:** In states that require licensing, you'll need to take a test, often at the same place you test for an auto or motorcycle license. There aren't many such states, but the best way find them is to visit the Web site of the National Association of State Boating Law Administrators at www.nasbla.org.

✔ **Boating safety courses:** Most states require new boaters to take a safety course. Some states sponsor or fund a specific course, and others allow you to choose from a variety of safety courses. While boating, you're required to keep a certification of completion from such a course with you. A great source for boating training information is www.boatus.com.

✔ **The United States Coast Guard Auxiliary:** This organization is probably the best place to learn to boat well and safely. Chapters of the Auxiliary exist in every region; you can find one at nws.cgaux.org/flotilla finder/index.html. (For more information on the U.S. Coast Guard Auxiliary, see Chapter 18.)

Navigating the Boat-Buying Scene

Ready to take the plunge? Buying a boat may seem as if it should be easier than buying a car, but buying a boat is, in some ways, more complicated. More boat brands exist than car brands, and you can't go to a boat showroom and find rows and rows of all the models and multiple colors and options all in one place — unless you go to a boat show.

In this section I explain some things to keep in mind when shopping for a boat, with a focus on buying new versus buying pre-owned.

Buying a new boat

Buying a new boat is a little easier than buying a pre-owned boat, unless you count the challenging down payment. New boats come with warranties that take care of defects for one to three years and sometimes, excluding the engine, even for ten years or the lifetime of the boat. That provides a lot of peace of mind! In Chapter 3, I explain in detail the tricks of the trade for buying a new boat, but for now here are some highlights:

✔ **Shop around.** You may find three Chevy dealers in your community, but you'll find only one Sea Ray dealer. So, when you shop around, you have to shop similar boats against each other because you can't shop identical models and brands.

✔ **Buy locally.** If you opt to shop one Sea Ray dealer against another one out of town, you may get a better deal from the out-of-town dealer, but keep in mind that the local guy won't service your warranty. Unlike auto dealers, a particular boat-brand dealer doesn't have to provide warranty service for his brand of boat if you bought it from someone else. He might do it, but he doesn't have to.

✔ **Perform sea trials.** Sea trials are like test drives but with a more specific mission. During a sea trial, you should be working from a checklist of specific things to watch out for (see the Cheat Sheet in the front of this book as well as Chapter 3). If you're not familiar with boats, hire a boat surveyor to help you (I tell you how in Chapter 2).

✔ **Line up insurance.** Check with your auto insurance provider to secure boat insurance *before* you close the deal for your boat. Your auto provider may not even sell boat insurance, and you should find that out ahead of time. You don't want to spend a few days hunting for insurance coverage after you've already bought the boat.

✔ **Seek financing.** Finance your boat like you would finance a house. Get qualified for a loan before you shop so that you know just how much boat you can buy.

Buying a pre-owned boat

Buying a pre-owned boat involves many of the same steps as buying a new boat, but sea trials and mechanical inspections are more important because you don't usually get a warranty with your pre-owned boat. Three-fourths of all boats sold each year are pre-owned, and you can find plenty of good deals on somebody else's boat! Follow these general recommendations:

✔ **Shop around.** Most pre-owned boats are sold "from a driveway," as the industry likes to say. Shopping online and in the newspaper is the best way to find a pre-owned boat. Buying locally isn't as important as it is with a new boat because you have to pay normal mechanic rates to get your boat fixed, and any boat mechanic will do the job for you.

✔ **Perform sea trials.** Mandatory, mandatory. Use the Cheat Sheet at the front of this book and Chapter 3 as your sea trial guide, and get a professional to go over the boat you're falling in love with before you tie the knot.

✔ **Check the engine.** If your boat surveyor isn't a mechanic and can't render an opinion on the engine, hire a qualified marine mechanic to check out the engine. A mechanic can catch obvious signs of neglect that can lead to catastrophic engine failure.

✔ **Check the trailer.** Have a mechanic inspect the trailer, too. He should pull off at least one wheel and check the bearings and brakes. If the boat and trailer have been sitting unused for a year or more, you should anticipate a flat tire. Tires left sitting without "exercise" tend to delaminate or get flat spots that cause them to fail on the highway.

Getting Your Boat On and Off the Water

As part of acquiring your boat, you get to choose where to keep it. (In Chapter 16, I discuss your options in detail.) Some boaters like the convenience and romance of renting a slip in a marina. Others pay for dry storage at a marina or other facility.

Many boaters, however, get a trailer for their boat so they can keep it in the garage or backyard and tow it to the water as needed. This seems pretty simple, unless you've never pulled a trailer before. Trailering a boat is a challenge, but it gets easier when you know what to expect.

Following are some key points to know about getting your boat around on dry land. (I explain all this in much more detail in Chapter 6 on launching and loading your boat.)

✔ Chances are that your boat will come with a trailer. If it doesn't come with one as standard equipment, the manufacturer or dealer will recommend one as an option. Follow their advice on a trailer, and don't scrimp on this purchase if you want to keep your boat safe for a long time.

✔ Your land vehicle has a towing capacity, and your new boat must weigh well within that capacity to be legally and safely towed on a trailer by that vehicle. I recommend that you check on these capacities with an experienced hitch installer like U-Haul or your vehicle's dealer.

✔ Towing your boat safely means going more slowly, doubling the distance between your vehicle and the vehicle ahead of you (to allow for your increased stopping time), and taking turns wide so you don't damage your trailer's tires on a curb.

✔ Backing up is the hardest thing to do with a trailer. Take it out into a broad open parking lot — say, at a mall that's closed on Sunday evening. Practice backing up until you get the feel for it. The best thing is to go veeewweeeeey swooooweey, as Elmer Fudd would say.

✔ Launching your boat is tricky but not hard. The first mistake you may make is to leave the boat's drain plug out — your boat will sink at the ramp if you do that! Put in the plug the minute you get to the boat ramp, and then tie a rope to the bow (front) of your boat. Remove the transom straps that hold the boat's back to the trailer, and back it into the water very slowly. When the water covers the trailer's wheels, you're probably in far enough to float your boat. Grasp that rope you tied to the front of the boat and disconnect the bow strap on the front of the boat. Push the boat off the trailer, if it doesn't slide off on its own.

✔ Loading your boat is trickier than launching because aiming the boat at the trailer is harder than pushing it off. Again, go very slowly when driving the boat onto the trailer. Hook your winch strap on the front of the trailer to the silver eyebolt on the boat's *bow*.

Any time you leave the driver's seat of your land vehicle while you're on a boat ramp, make darned sure your car's gearshift is in Park and your emergency brake is set as hard as you can set it. Fail this, and you could see your whole rig roll into the water.

Getting Your Boat Around on the Water

If you're into old movies, maybe you've seen *Cool Hand Luke,* starring Paul Newman. Luke is basically a good-hearted guy (albeit one in prison) with a lack of interest in adjusting his behavior to the expectations of society. The warden finally sums it up with one famous line often repeated by people today when things go wrong: "What we've got here is failure to communicate."

Failure to communicate is the most common cause for stress between members of boating families. Part of the communication problem comes from the expectation that boating is like driving — just on the water. As I say throughout this book, boating is not like driving a car! The two vehicles steer, accelerate, stop, and go in an entirely different manner. Here are some considerations for getting your boat around on the water:

- ✔ **Double-check the safety equipment.** Lack of proper safety equipment is probably the most common citation written by the U.S. Coast Guard. Make sure you have a properly sized life jacket for every passenger and a USCG-approved throwable flotation device that you can toss if someone falls overboard. Many states also require you to carry flares to attract attention in case of an emergency. (I talk about safety gear in Chapter 4 and handling boating emergencies in Chapter 12.)

- ✔ **Steady as she goes.** You've heard this phrase a million times in naval war movies, but the biggest mistake new boaters make is to go too fast too soon. The second biggest mistake they make is assuming that all water is deep enough to drive the boat in. Chances are, if you don't carefully study a chart of the waters before you boat, you'll run aground and break something in the first few weeks of boating. (For more details on charts and navigating, see Chapter 10.)

- ✔ **Dock as slowly as you can.** New boaters are way too used to scooting their cars into the garage and stepping on the brakes to stop just short of smacking the wall. Boats don't have brakes! This is really hard for new boaters to remember. In Chapter 8, I give lots of easy docking tips so you can figure out how to dock without crashing. But if you go boating before you read it, at least keep this in mind: Don't approach the dock any faster than you want to hit it.

Getting Your Hands Dirty

Carmakers are getting better and better at making cars stand up to their owners' neglect, but boats operate in a much harsher environment. Deprive them of the TLC they need, and you can count on a breakdown.

You definitely need to understand how to maintain your boat. Not only will you keep your boat in better shape and help it last longer, but you'll save money. For detailed information on engine maintenance and routine service, see Chapter 13. Here's a sampling of common boat maintenance tasks:

- **Check engine fluids.** This is like taking your own body's pulse and blood pressure. Your boat engine always operates at a higher speed than your car engine because in water a boat doesn't coast far — the engine is almost always pushing it. In a car, you run it hard to pass a car or get up to freeway speed, and then you let it settle down to 1,500 revolutions per minute to hold it at 70 mph. In a boat, maintaining 45 mph is like running your car at 100 mph *uphill*. So checking fluids is important to make sure that the engine is operating properly and isn't on its way to malfunction or disaster.

- **Winterize your engine.** At the end of your boating season, you need to winterize the engine, or have your mechanic do it. Many boaters (including yours truly) do it themselves. The steps are easy; see Chapter 14.

- **Check hose fittings and through-hull fittings.** Hoses either bring water to the engine through the hull or take water from the bilge outward. Some hose fittings drain other parts of the boat. These fittings can become corroded or broken, or the clamps can work loose. You should look through the boat's bilge area — it's kind of like checking under the hood of your car — and check for leaks now and then.

Chapter 2

Choosing the Right Boat Type and Engine for Your Boating Needs

In This Chapter

▶ Boning up on the parts of a boat

▶ Breaking down your fishing boat options

▶ Relaxing in a runabout or pontoon boat

▶ Cruising the open water

▶ Powering up with the right type of engine

Knowing what you want to do with a boat says a lot about what *kind* of boat you want. Heck, you're reading this book, so you must have a pretty good idea that you want one with a motor. That narrows it down a bunch!

A power boat is basically any boat that relies on a motor for its *primary* form of propulsion.

Many sailboats have motors, and some kayaks and canoes have little electric motors or small outboards, but for the most part, those boats rely on wind or labor to get and keep them moving. Even under power, they're not technically power boats. Power boats come in all sizes, but most often when boaters think of power boats, they're thinking of something between 17 and 35 feet in length.

After answering the power or no power question, your decision when choosing a type of boat becomes more involved. Narrowing the choices requires some thoughtful consideration because the power boat category contains many, many kinds. Your choice will be determined by whether you want to primarily spend a quiet day on the water, do some serious fishing, or go long distances and stay on your boat overnight. In this chapter I give you a rundown of your choices of boats and engines (as well as the power you need) for these and other activities.

Acquainting Yourself with the Parts of a Power Boat

Before you go shopping for a boat, you should be familiar with the parts that make up a boat — for your own understanding and in order to keep up with any boat salesmen (as well as impress your new boating friends). For more detailed tips on how to buy a boat, see Chapter 3.

Just like baseball has terms that are exclusive to the sport and not used in any other context, boating has terms like "inboard," "outboard," "port," and "starboard" that have no meaning outside of a boat. You don't necessarily have to use *all* these terms among your boating friends, but you still need to be familiar with them or you'll feel like you're living in a foreign country without knowing the language.

Some boating terms double as anatomical descriptions and directions, which may help you remember their meanings. For instance, on a boat, the *port* side is the left side, and turning "to port" means turning left. Other terms are strictly anatomical. The *stern,* for instance, is a boat's back side, or end. The *transom* is a specific part of the hull in the stern area.

Rather than just dump a bunch of text on you, check out Figure 2-1a and b to get a quick look at the terms and definitions that follow.

- ✔ **Aft:** The portion of the boat behind midships.
- ✔ **Anchor locker:** Usually in the bow under a hatch. It holds the anchor, chain, and rope.
- ✔ **Boarding ladder:** Built into the boat and must be accessible from the water in case someone falls overboard.
- ✔ **Bow:** The very front portion of the boat.
- ✔ **Bow navigation light:** A red light visible from the port (left) side of the boat and a green light visible from the starboard (right) side of the boat.
- ✔ **Chines:** The division between the bottom of the boat and the sides; some chines are molded with a downward angle turn at the edge to deflect spray.
- ✔ **Cockpit:** The seating area including the helm seat and aft seating.
- ✔ **Deadrise angle:** The angle at which the bottom of the boat rises from the keel to meet the chines.
- ✔ **Deck:** The top of the boat; the surface is removed to accommodate the cockpit and forward seating area.
- ✔ **Draft:** The distance between the lowest portion of the boat and the waterline when the boat is at rest in the water.

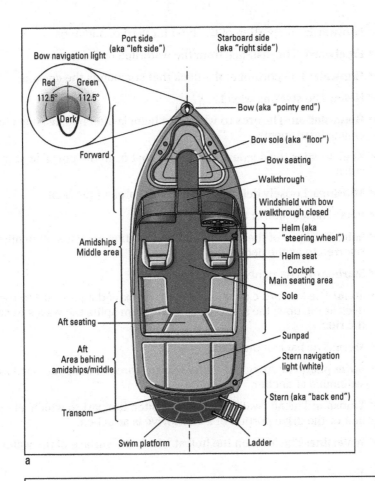

Port side (aka "left side")

Starboard side (aka "right side")

Bow navigation light

Red 112.5° Green 112.5°

Dark

Forward

Bow (aka "pointy end")

Bow sole (aka "floor")

Bow seating

Walkthrough

Windshield with bow walkthrough closed

Helm (aka "steering wheel")

Helm seat

Cockpit Main seating area

Sole

Amidships Middle area

Aft seating

Aft Area behind amidships/middle

Transom

Sunpad

Stern navigation light (white)

Stern (aka "back end")

Swim platform

Ladder

a

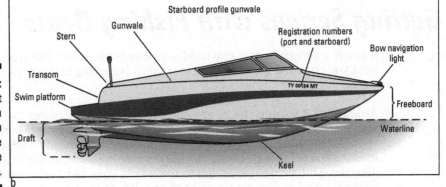

Starboard profile gunwale

Gunwale

Stern

Transom

Swim platform

Registration numbers (port and starboard)

Bow navigation light

TY 00134 MT

Freeboard

Waterline

Draft

Keel

Figure 2-1: Important parts of a boat from topside and profile views.

b

- **Foreward:** The portion of the boat forward of midships.
- **Freeboard:** The distance from the waterline to the gunwale.
- **Gunwale:** The portion of the deck that surrounds the cockpit.
- **Helm:** The steering wheel.
- **Helm station:** The area to which the helm is attached, usually including engine instruments.
- **Keel:** Divides the deepest part of the boat from the port and starboard sides.
- **Midships:** Loosely defined as the middle area of the boat.
- **Port:** The left side of the boat.
- **Sole:** The floor of the cockpit and bow seating area; it's often mistakenly referred to as the deck.
- **Starboard:** The right side of the boat.
- **Stem:** The forward extension of the keel, extending upward to the deck at the bow; the sharp peak of the stem splits the waves to smooth the ride.
- **Stern:** The back of the boat.
- **Swim platform:** Attached to the transom area of the boat; used for swimming at anchor.
- **Transom:** The aft "wall" of the stern; often the part to which an outboard unit or the drive portion of a sterndrive is attached.
- **Waterline:** The level on the hull at which the surface of the water rests.

Getting Serious with Fishing Boats

If you're a serious angler, you need a serious fishing boat. The type of fishing boat you choose depends on whether you'll be fishing in fresh water or salt water.

Around 200,000 fishing boats are sold every year, which makes the fishing boat class twice as big as the day boat class. (I cover day boats in the later section, "Kicking Back with Runabouts and Pontoon Boats.") Anglers are the most motivated group of boaters on the water. A runabout/day boat owner may shrug off the weekend jaunt to the lake in favor of hanging out by the backyard pool, but an angler won't miss a day on the water for anything — anglers think fishing is what weekends are for.

Some fishing boats are pretty general in nature — they're set up to go after fish, any fish. But most fishing boats are designed for anglers who, like Wile E. Coyote, have just one species in mind. In this section, you get to know the various kinds of fishing boats; I break down your options into freshwater and saltwater categories.

Freshwater fishing boats

Two primary categories of freshwater fishing boats make them particularly good for pursuing one particular species of fish and make them competitive in fishing tournaments: bass boats and walleye boats. Fish and ski boats have features that make them a compromise between competitive fishing boats and cruising and skiing boats. All these boats have three things in common: a large gasoline-powered outboard engine for getting to the fishing holes quickly, a small, quiet electric motor for sneaking around to cast easily from different angles, and at least one built-in freshwater tank to keep the catch (or bait) alive. When the fish aren't biting, anglers with fish and ski boats even hook up a tube and a rope to pull the kids for a fun ride.

Bass boats

Bass boats are sleek and sport more horsepower on the transom than you'll think you need — at first. Large horsepower engines give anglers plenty of speed to reach distant fishing spots quickly and return to port safely.

Bass hang out close to snags, logs, docks, and other cover much of the time, so accurate casting and a good view of the water is mandatory. An elevated casting deck on the front and back lets you step up high for a bird's-eye view to help you cast easily and accurately. Onboard electronics give you a clear view of the water below, and many bass boats have GPS units for keeping track of hot spots. (I talk more about electronics in Chapter 10.) The electric trolling motor is retractable and mounted on the bow to help you pull the boat around quietly to avoid spooking fish. And when you've hit the jackpot and brought in some bass, aerated tanks called *livewells* keep your catch alive and fresh.

Bass boats range in size from 16 to 23 feet long and sport engines from 50 to 250 horsepower. That speed is particularly necessary in competition angling, but it's also just lots of fun for cruising around to break the monotony of slow days with few bites!

For serious tournament fishing, you need a boat that's 20 to 23 feet long and powered with at least 200 horsepower. For general fishing or more casual buddy tournaments, smaller, lower-powered boats are just fine.

Bass boats are set up to make fishing comfortable for two or three passengers all day long. Although most claim to have passenger capacities of four or more, you'll have a hard time finding seating for more than three due to seating restrictions — most bass boats are designed and certified to carry three or four passengers only. Many walleye boats and most fish and ski boats are capable of carrying four to seven or even more passengers.

Walleye boats

Walleye are fish of a different feather . . . or fin. They often hang out in colder, rougher waters than other fish, and you have to approach them slowly and less aggressively than you would other fish. For these reasons, walleye boats tend to be deeper and not quite as sleek as bass boats, and they have higher hull sides to make them better able to fend off waves without having the waves slop over the side. (Flip to the color insert to see a walleye boat.)

Walleye boats usually don't have casting decks because you pull your lures behind the boat, called *trolling*. And you spend very little time casting baits or lures.

These boats range in size from 16 to 23 feet and sport 50 to 250 horsepower. Tournament anglers usually choose boats over 20 feet because competitions go on rain or shine and they need the size to combat rougher waters.

Walleye boats are often equipped for four or more passengers, and many offer windshields. By moving seats around, you can create a more cruising-friendly floor plan for sporty riding and even watersports. Tournament-ready walleye boats bristle with fishing gear and rod holders, and some aren't as sporty-looking as bass boats.

Fish and ski boats

It's often tough to tell if a fish and ski boat is more fish or more ski. Their clever design lets boaters do both, and these boats are popular among boaters who fish at least some of the time. (You can see a fish and ski boat in the color insert.)

Windshields cut the wind, and casting decks on the bow and stern can be equipped with cushions to turn them into sun pads. Tow pylons make fish and ski boats great for watersports, and an electric trolling motor (often removable) plus livewells equip anglers to fish seriously.

Most fish and ski boats range from 17 to 20 feet in length and sport 115 to 225 horsepower. If you plan to make your boat double as a watersports craft, I recommend 150 horsepower so you have plenty of pull to yank up a skier.

Fish and ski boats help accommodate the need of active families with mixed ambitions, which is what makes them so popular. Compromises between fishing ability and sports ability are made to accommodate both expectations, and most boaters go on to choose either a fishing boat or a sport boat the next time around.

Saltwater fishing boats

Saltwater fishing boats are designed for the adventure of pursuing the world's largest fish. They operate in the toughest boating conditions: Seas can be rough, and nothing is harder on a boat and motor than salt water. So the boats used to pursue saltwater fish are tougher, more corrosion-resistant, and easier to maintain in terms of cleaning and stowing than many other boat styles. Offshore boats have clean, fiberglass decks that drain overboard when hosed down. That and their simple seating make them easy to maintain.

Nearly all saltwater fishing boats have livewells and fish-finding and navigating electronics in common. This section presents the most popular saltwater fishing boat styles and some of their distinctions.

Flats boats

Flats boats are for fishing shallow bays and estuaries, often less than 2 feet deep. (You can see an example of a flats boat in the color insert.)

Flats boats resemble bass boats with their fore and aft casting platforms and aerated livewells, but they usually have a fiberglass deck instead of carpet, which doesn't hold up well to salt water. The fiberglass deck is easy to clean. A poling platform over the motor lets you climb up on it to push the boat around on the shallow water flats quietly with a pole. Some even have electric trolling motors so you don't have to pole, if you prefer.

Usually from 16 to 20 feet long, flats boats are equipped with outboards to keep the boat light and sport from 25 to 175 horsepower.

Flats boats tend to ride just a little rougher in choppy waters than offshore boats because their shallower V-angle to keel doesn't cut the waves quite as well.

Bay boats

Bay boats are designed to be a good compromise between shallow flats fishing boats (refer to the previous section) and deeper, larger offshore fishing boats (see the next section). It's not unusual to see a bay boat 20 miles offshore on a calm day, but most anglers who buy them chase fish in more sheltered bays. (You can see an example of a bay boat in the color insert.)

Bay boats have the helm in the center of the boat for balance and greater stability and control. Their keels have a deeper V-angle to handle rougher waters, but the sharper V keel sits deeper in the water, so bay boats aren't as good at sneaking into the shallowest waters as flats boats. Livewells keep bait and catch alive and electronics for navigation are essential.

Bay boats can range from 16 to 24 feet in length, but they're usually under 24 feet and sport 70- to 350-horsepower outboards.

The fiberglass deck is easy to clean, and bay boats are often equipped with stowaway or convertible passenger seating to make them comfortable for day cruising as well as fishing.

Center console offshore boats

Center console offshore boats are designed to take on rough waters and open seas. They're named for the helm station that holds the helm (the wheel) and dashboard, positioned in the center of the boat. The center console allows anglers to follow the largest hooked fish all the way around a boat. (You can see an example of a center console boat in the color insert.)

These offshore boats have a sharp V-shaped keel that lets them split waves for a smoother ride. Underneath the helm station is a compartment often equipped with a head (bathroom). Some have convertible passenger seating that stows away, making them fun for day cruising.

Even 20-foot center consoles can handle more chop than you'd think, but if regular offshore angling is your intent, you should get a 23- to 30-foot boat. For boats 23 feet and under, 150 to 225 horsepower is ideal. For larger boats and jaunts far offshore, twin engines of 150 to 350 horsepower each are important so that you can limp in on one engine if the other one fails.

Center consoles are as popular as bay boats for day boating, and many are equipped with convertible seats for the comfort and fun of large crews.

Offshore boats are larger, which means they require more horsepower, more towing capacity to get them to the water, and more fuel for a day of boating.

Walkaround boats

Walkaround boats are like cuddies (see the later section, "Cuddy cabins"), but they're set up for serious fishing and open water. Walkarounds earned their name because of steps to the deck and a walkway all the way around the front to let you chase a hooked fish from the back to the front of the boat and back. The high deck accommodates a roomy cabin below for ducking out of the weather. (You can see an example of a walkaround boat in the color insert.)

Walkarounds range in size from 18 to 36 feet and require from 115 to 600 horsepower for propulsion. Most popular are walkarounds from 23 to 27 feet.

Walkarounds have more creature comforts than other boats, like sleeping areas, a galley with cooking facilities, and a bathroom often with a shower. Creature comforts and a cockpit enclosed behind a windshield make these boats popular, especially in colder climates. In warmer climates, the cockpit can become stuffy behind the windshield, and many boaters find that, like cuddy cabins, the cabin area just collects unused gear.

Kicking Back with Runabouts and Pontoon Boats

Runabouts (also called *day boats,* usually among boaters in the northeastern United States) are designed for cruising, touring, skiing, and hanging out for the day. They're perfect for spending all or some of the day on the water but not for overnighting, as a general rule.

Both "day boat" and "runabout" are terms that originated from what people are apt to do with these boats, but rules — at least the unwritten ones — were made to be broken. Some boaters sleep in day boats and camp out on the water in runabouts.

Pontoon boats are a wildly popular category of day boat, but they don't quite fall into the runabout category because their original intent was to be a large lounging platform that cruises along the water at a stately pace. Lately pontoon makers have been adding big horsepower motors, though, and the added performance often makes these boats run about quite nicely.

Running around in runabouts

Runabouts are sleek, sporty, and, depending on their size and horsepower, can reach speeds of 65 miles per hour (although 45 to 50 mph is typical). Runabouts have a towing hook for connecting a ski rope, and many boaters use them to ski or pull kids (or adults, of course) on inflatable tubes.

This section helps you get a clear picture of the different kinds of runabouts, or day boats, whichever term you prefer, so that you can make an informed choice.

Bowriders

Bowriders are the most popular day boat. Ideal for day cruising and touring your favorite waters, most bowriders also have a tow hook so you can connect a ski or tube rope to add watersports fun to your day. (You can see a bowrider in the color insert.)

Bowriders range in size from 17 to 35 feet and are powered with 130 to 850 horsepower. An 18- to 20-footer is the most popular size. Most bowriders over 21 feet have a changing compartment with a toilet, making them very convenient for all-day play. Depending on the size of your boat, you can handle from 6 to 16 passengers. They come with open seating in the bow, which adds seating for two to six additional passengers, depending on the boat's size.

When you have riders in the bow, make sure to position them so they don't obstruct your forward view.

Bowriders are stable and easy to maneuver at higher speeds and are the best choice for covering lots of water quickly. Their quick acceleration makes them great for casual skiing and tube riding. However, all that speed takes horsepower, and all those horses are thirsty for gasoline.

Cuddy cabins

Cuddy cabins are runabouts without the open seating in the bow. (You can see a cuddy cabin in the color insert.) The bow space usually contains a sleeping berth, often a toilet, and sometimes cooking equipment.

Cuddies are great for tucking away overnight in a cove, but they have the sporty abilities of bowriders, so you can ski or tube behind them.

Like bowriders, cuddies range in size from 17 to 35 feet, although 35-footers more often are considered express cruisers (see the later section, "Express cruisers," for an explanation). Horsepower needs grow with hull size, so cuddy cabins usually range from 130 to 850 horsepower.

If you buy a cuddy with a toilet and galley, you may be able to deduct the interest on it as a second home. Ask your tax preparer to check the rules.

If you're like most boaters who have cuddies under 25 feet, you may find you hardly ever use the sleeping berth except to stow gear. You may wish you had seating upfront instead.

Deck boats

Deck boats are runabouts built for comfort and spacious seating rather than for sporty performance. Still, they manage to pull off pretty snappy acceleration and look and behave much like bowriders even though they tend to be somewhat heavier and wider in the bow for seating. (Turn to the color insert to see an example of a deck boat.)

Deck boats let you carry two or three more passengers than comparably sized pontoons while still pulling tube riders. Many over 20 feet also have changing compartments with a toilet for convenience.

You might find a few 28-foot deck boats, but most range in size from 18 to 24 feet. Because they're heavier than bowriders of similar size, you may find that you need a little extra horsepower to achieve the same performance.

The extra weight and horsepower will require more fuel, so make sure you really need the extra hauling power.

Watersports boats

Watersports boats are runabouts for serious skiers or wakeboard riders. (Wakeboards are sort of like snowboards designed to be pulled behind boats.) Wakeboard riders want their boats to form large, ramplike wakes (waves behind the boat) to jump over, and some watersports boats are designed to do specifically that. On the other hand, serious skiers want no wake at all, so tournament ski boats are designed to throw as small a wake as possible. (You can see a watersports boat in the color insert.)

Watersports boats range in size from 20 to 24 feet and are powered by large, inboard, V-8 automotive engines sporting 300 to 325 horsepower. They're known for their fast acceleration and rock-steady, straight-line tracking at riding speeds of 20 to 30 mph.

A ski boat usually has the engine in the center of the boat to balance its weight for a minimal wake. A wakeboard boat has the engine in the back to create a larger wake. If you go in for skiing or wakeboarding in a big way, you care about only three things: a great wake, fast acceleration to get quickly on top of the water, and plenty of space for your riding friends. Both boat types feature plush carpet, ample seating, and almost always the most rockin' stereo possible.

You may be surprised at the wakeboard tower made of sturdy, gracefully curving tubing with a tow point on top for connecting a wakeboard rope. Ski boats have a pylon for the rope that's usually set about waist high.

The fixed propeller and shaft don't allow you to adjust the propeller up or down to trim the engine for load or speed (see Chapter 7 for more on trimming), and watersports boats usually have a rougher ride in choppy water than comparable sterndrives or outboards.

Inflatable boats

Inflatable boats are growing in popularity due to their light weight and great performance on low-horsepower, fuel-sipping engines. Often thought of as cheap and frail, they're both expensive for their length and so rugged and tough as tanks that search and rescue personnel often use them.

Runabout-sized inflatables called *rigid inflatable boats* (RIBs) have a rigid fiberglass bottom and a large, tough-as-shoe-leather inflatable tube around them for added flotation. Many separate inflatable chambers make these boats safe, although seating is often limited. (You can see an example of a RIB in the color insert.)

RIBs range in size from 10 to 35 feet, and their light weight makes them very sporty on smaller, gas-saving motors from 50 to 225 horsepower. They pull skiers with as little as 50 horsepower. No boats safely carry more passengers per foot than these compact runabouts, and you can tow them with smaller, lighter vehicles, eliminating the need for a big truck or SUV.

RIBs cost more per foot than other boats, even considering their reduced need for horsepower.

Living large on pontoon boats

Sometimes called a floating living room, the pontoon boat is the most popular single category of power boat on the water today. It has a reputation of being a boxy-looking geek, but on average, nearly 45,000 new pontoons are sold per year, equaling about half of the total runabout category — and that's just new boats! (See the color insert for an example of a pontoon boat.)

Pontoons have a beamy (that's boat-speak for a wide body) rectangular deck fastened to hollow, log-shaped aluminum pontoons. Berber carpet and upholstered couches and lounges enhance the appeal. These boats are ideal for easy-paced cruises, picnicking on the water, and just hanging out swimming and socializing.

The broad, flat deck makes pontoons extremely easy to board and amble about on. Their popularity is growing among the young and active, but they also provide easy access to the water for the elderly or physically challenged.

Sized from 18 to as large as 30 feet and designed to carry from 12 to sometimes over 20 passengers, the Average Joe pontoon is equipped with 50 to 115 horsepower, but many pontoon boats now are sporting powerful engines of 200 or more horsepower, making them fun for skiing, tubing, and running about.

So, pontoon boats may not look like floating Ferraris, and at fast speeds they don't handle like 'em either, but at 15-mph cruising speeds, few boats are easier to handle. If hair-raising speed and cornering ability are on your must-have list, you probably already know that a pontoon isn't the boat for you.

Going the Distance with Cruisers

Cruisers are for extended boating trips with distant destinations in mind. They have many of the comforts of home, sporty horsepower, and the ability to handle rough waters if ocean cruising is on your agenda. Cruisers are most often used in the ocean and Great Lakes for long-range boating, but they're also popular for river cruises from town to town and are often the second home of choice among boaters who like weekends at the lake. Like the classes of boats covered earlier in this chapter, the cruiser class contains a number of different kinds of boat. This section introduces you to the three main types: express, sedan, and houseboat.

Express cruisers

Express cruisers look like large cuddy cabins (refer to the earlier section, "Cuddy cabins," for a description), but they have more comfortable living accommodations. Cruisers have one or two private, double sleeping berths, usually at least one convertible berth, a bathroom with a toilet and shower, and a galley with a stove, fridge, microwave, and sink. The cockpit of an express cruiser looks much like a runabout's cockpit but with more space.

The line between a cuddy runabout and an express cruiser begins to blur at about 25 feet in length. When the length exceeds 25 feet, generally boaters refer to these boats as *cruisers* or *express cruisers. Pocket cruiser* is the nickname for cruisers small enough to trailer. As you'd imagine, the horsepower needs are impressive, ranging between 425 horsepower and 850 horsepower.

The obvious advantage of an express cruiser is size, which pays off in cruising range for long trips and comfort for passengers sleeping onboard. However, their size is also a disadvantage because they aren't easily towed on trailers and usually require expensive storage in a marina.

Sedan cruisers

Sedan cruisers usually have two helm stations so that they can be driven from inside the main cabin or from a *bridge* on top of it. The option of piloting from an inside helm makes sedans especially nice in cooler, rainy climates.

Like sedan cars, sedan cruisers have more interior space than other cruisers, making them more comfortable for more people over longer cruises. A few sedan cruisers fall in the under 35-foot category.

Like large express cruisers, size and expense are the main drawbacks of sedan cruisers.

Houseboats

Houseboats are kind of like the pontoon boat of the live-aboard category. They really aren't cruisers, but they don't quite fit into any other category either.

These boats are somewhat boxy in style and have shallower freeboards than cruisers, making them best for protected inland waters. Compared to cruisers, they sleep more passengers per foot and usually sport more homey comforts in the galley and living area.

Houseboats can be as small as 25 feet, and these are often built on pontoon boat platforms. Larger houseboats have fiberglass or aluminum hulls and can reach 100 feet in length. Houseboats aren't expected to perform, so horsepower is generally just enough to safely move the boat from place to place at a stately pace. Houseboats tend to have a deck or floor plan that allows convenient access and easy mobility on board.

Like cruisers, most houseboats need to be kept in a marina, usually at considerable cost.

Understanding Different Boat Engines

When you combine the number of boat styles with the number of engine styles and toss in the fact that nearly every style of boat is available with nearly every engine configuration, the options become astronomical. But I narrow them down for you in this section based on my experience operating them and on what I've learned boat builders are doing to meet customer demands.

If you're an engine nut, you may be delirious with the following descriptions of boat engines. If you're not, you still need to wade through them so you can make an informed choice of the boat and engine that will work best for you.

Getting sporty with inboard power

An *inboard* engine is an engine inside the boat that's connected to a propeller outside the boat by a long, thin, steel shaft (see Figure 2-2). Inboard power is used most in watersports boats and cruisers.

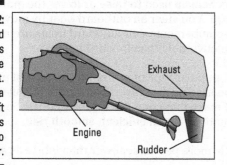

Figure 2-2:
An inboard engine is totally inside the boat. Only a thin shaft connects the prop to the power.

With the exception of the propeller, inboard engines are actually made by truck or car manufacturers. The whole combination — engine, shaft, and propeller — is fixed in place, and the propeller isn't adjustable, so you can't trim it up or down for the most efficient speed. (I talk more about trim in Chapter 7.) You steer a boat that has an inboard engine with a rudder that deflects the force of the motor from side to side, causing the boat to turn.

Ski boats and wakeboard boats are always equipped with inboard engines. Some cruisers and larger saltwater fishing boats are also often equipped with them. Low engine gear ratios and shorter pitch props give watersports boats snappy acceleration, and the shaft, prop, and rudder usually offer easier straight-line tracking, which skiers and wakeboarders like. (We talk about prop pitch in chapter 15.)

Inboard arrangements are slower at top speed and less efficient due to the downward angle of the prop. This also makes them ride rougher than outboards or sterndrives of comparable size.

Tooling around with outboard power

Outboard power combines the engine, drive shaft, and propeller in one unit that bolts to the transom at the back of the boat (see Figure 2-3). Outboard power is most popular on small boats.

Figure 2-3:
Outboard units hang on the transom outside of the boat.

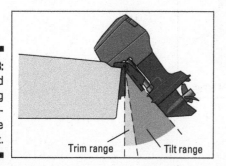

Trim range   Tilt range

An outboard has a tilting mechanism used to raise or lower the motor, changing the angle of the prop. You steer an outboard boat by moving the entire motor, which sounds cumbersome, but outboard boats are really much more efficient and maneuverable than inboard boats.

Outboard power is the most popular type of power on fishing and pontoon boats and some other day boats. The maneuverability, easy installation, and high horsepower per pound make them popular engine options. So does the ease with which you can trim them for an efficient, smooth ride.

Outboards tend to cost a little more per horsepower than inboards and some sterndrive engines.

Spending the day with sterndrive power

Sterndrive power combines an inboard engine with an outboard's propeller and shaft arrangement (see Figure 2-4). Sterndrive power is most popular on day boats and some cruisers. You steer the boat by turning the prop and shaft, making it very maneuverable, and you can raise and lower the propeller to trim it up or down for a smoother, more efficient ride. (Turn to Chapter 7 to get a better idea of how to trim a propeller.)

Sterndrives give you a choice of a single propeller drive or a dual propeller drive. Dual propellers are two aligned together but turning in opposite directions. They offer better control than a single prop drive but also slow the boat down, so don't accept dual propellers as a substitute for horsepower. An engine that's too small for the boat is slower still with a dual prop drive. But on cruisers or big day boats, when speed isn't the objective, dual prop drives make the boat turn better and give slightly better power at mid-range running speeds.

Figure 2-4: A sterndrive engine has the motor inside and the propeller and gears outside.

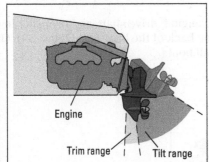

Engine

Trim range   Tilt range

Sterndrive power is most popular on bowriders, cuddys, and smaller cruisers. Unlike outboards, sterndrives don't interfere with a full-width swimming platform on the transom. In the northwestern and northeastern U.S., sterndrive power is also popular for saltwater fishing boats because cooler temperatures retard marine growth, making the engines less susceptible to fouling problems found in southern waters.

Sterndrive power is heavier than outboard power and harder and more expensive to maintain.

Maneuvering with pod drive power

Pod drives have been around for more than 75 years, but they've only been practical in pleasure boats (namely cruisers and small yachts) since 2003. That's thanks to computer wizardry in boat engines that makes them easy to control. They're actually a variation of sterndrive engines, but they have advantages so unique that they deserve a separate discussion.

With this kind of engine, the propeller mechanism, called the *pod,* comes straight out of the bottom of the boat, instead of out of the back of the boat. The propeller turns from side to side to steer the boat, making the pod drive perhaps the most maneuverable of all prop boats. And because the prop is situated perfectly parallel to the boat's direction of travel, there's no need to trim it up or down. Unlike an inboard with a prop tilted down, the pod drive loses no power to that inefficient angle.

As of this writing, pod drives are only practical in twin applications on boats longer than 35 feet, and they're expensive.

Zipping about with jet propulsion power

Jet propulsion uses an inboard engine to drive a propeller called an *impeller* that's concealed inside a jet pump, as shown in Figure 2-5. Jets (boats that use this kind of power) accelerate quickly and are the most maneuverable power boat on the water. Most jets range from 15 to 23 feet and 100 to 450 horsepower.

Jets are so maneuverable that it's easy to spin the boat all the way around. Some people do it for fun, but it can be dangerous because you may throw passengers from their seats.

Figure 2-5:
Jet-drive
engines
have a
concealed
propeller
that forces
water out
the back,
propelling
the boat.

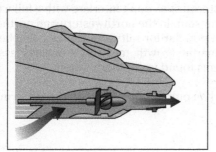

Jets work by sucking water in a large inlet using an impeller. The impeller expels the water from a much smaller nozzle that shoots straight out of the transom. The opposite reaction (remember your Newtonian laws from eighth grade science) makes the boat go forward — pretty fast, too! A jet boat is steered by directing the flow of the jet from side to side.

A jet boat has a very shallow *draft*, meaning there's very little boat below the water's surface. That's because the entire drive mechanism (except the nozzle) is inside the hull. With no propeller or shaft below the surface to create drag, the boat is more maneuverable than any other power boat.

Sometimes jet boats are too maneuverable. Due to the lack of a rudder or propeller under the water, they're harder to control at slow speeds and when docking. They're also harder to control when a skier is swinging back and forth on the tow rope.

Chapter 3

Finding and Buying the Right Boat for You

. . . .

In This Chapter

▶ Zeroing in on how you'll use your boat

▶ Counting the costs and setting a comfortable boating budget

▶ Considering the pros and cons of new and pre-owned options

▶ Shopping around

▶ Getting legal with registrations, licenses, and certifications

. . . .

*F*inding and buying the boat that fits you best can be daunting and may take some time, but it's doable. However, if you take too many shortcuts and make an emotional decision, as with any such purchase, buyer's remorse may weigh so heavily that your dreams of happiness on the water feel more like a nightmare.

Choosing a boat isn't exactly a straightforward process. Often the first boat purchase is something of a practice run, and boaters only get that "just right" boat for them on their second boat purchase. Sometimes it's because they didn't read a book like this to help them sort through the many options, and sometimes it's just because the first boat helps them find specific things about boating they like doing most, so they need a different boat to do it better. (It's sort of like learning to golf and then wanting to trade clubs to improve your game!)

When you buy a boat, I can't assure you that you won't want a different boat until you've used it for a season or two. But I can help you minimize the chances of buying the wrong boat the first time around. This chapter helps you figure out which boat will help you do what you want to do where you want to do it. I explain which kind of boat is best for which kind of environment.

To get you started on the hunt, the first thing I help you do is narrow down your choice from a few thousand boat types to a more manageable number. As you start looking for your boat, keep coming back to this chapter for a review to make sure you don't miss a step.

Narrowing Down Your Boat-Buying Choices

It has been simmering in the back of your mind for years — that secret desire to own a boat. Now, you feel like the time is right, especially since all your friends are talking about their boating experiences. Or maybe you and your family have just spent a day with some of those friends on the water. Now you, your spouse, and your kids are all talking about getting a boat.

You go online, visit a boat show, or stop in at the local marine dealer to see what kind of options are available. And the options seem endless! Don't despair. I walk you through some essential considerations in this section that will knock your mountain of choices down to size. The easiest way to do this is to zero in on where you plan to do most of your boating and what kinds of boating activities you want to pursue.

If you're still in the dark after reading this section, you can find a cool Web tool to help narrow down your choices at www.discoverboating.com/buying/boatselector.aspx.

Considering location and type of water

Most boaters boat within 100 miles of home and only occasionally venture outside of that radius. Your home waters are the waters you need to choose your boat to fit because that's where you'll most likely do most of your boating. Your dealer can help you select a boat, but the best way to start your shopping research is to hang around nearby marinas and boat ramps for a day or so to see what people are launching and loading up. It's an unusual boater who isn't open to conversation about his or her boat and what he or she likes about it.

Location has a powerful influence on boat selection. Big, rough, salty waters demand a lot from a boat, and smaller, smoother, fresh waters place their limitations on one. Deeper water gives more freedom in choosing hull and propulsion styles than shallow water, which restricts the draft of depth of your boat. Salt water offers different maintenance challenges to your boat than fresh water, too.

Here are some different types of waters you may face and considerations for selecting a boat to navigate each:

✔ **Offshore coastal waters:** The bigger the waters, the bigger the boat you'll need. You can sneak offshore on a calm day in a 20-foot boat, but you'd better have a reliable engine (or pair of them) so you can race back in if afternoon thundershowers and stormy waves surprise you.

Regardless of how capable your boat is, don't go offshore without a reliable radio to communicate with fellow boaters and the United States Coast Guard.

✔ **Inshore coastal waters:** Most inshore coastal waters are somewhat like inland lakes and rivers — except they're salty. Often inshore coastal waters are shallow, which makes outboards popular in them. Outboards often have shallower draft, which means you need less water depth to float and maneuver. Outboards also are easier to clean up than inboards after saltwater immersion. (You can find out all about salt and boats in the next section.)

✔ **The Great Lakes:** You may be surprised to find out that these waters are often the most treacherous in the United States. Storms crop up fast, and the waters turn to violent chop in minutes. Follow the offshore rules earlier in this list (and throughout this book) if you plan to head for the Great Lakes.

✔ **Large lakes:** I consider large lakes those over 5 miles across. These waters aren't likely to get violent in storms, but the larger the lake, the larger the boats. The larger the boats, the heavier the chop you'll experience from other boats' wakes. An 18-foot boat is big enough to be safe under such conditions, but it may not be large enough to comfortably stretch over the choppy waters without shaking the boat and crew roughly. For boating on large lakes, buy as much boat as you can afford, and slow down and take the waves easily if they get too rough.

✔ **Small lakes:** Lakes under 5 miles across are a real treat on a quiet afternoon, but even they can get choppy thanks to crowded waters on a nice, sunny weekend. For this reason, many small lakes surrounded by homes have local laws or bylaws limiting boat size and horsepower. Check for those laws and abide by them. In absence of such laws, an 18-foot runabout is ideal. A 25-footer may be overkill — unless you're thinking of a pontoon boat, which fits any waters with a launch ramp (Chapter 2 has more on pontoons).

✔ **Rivers and other shallow waters:** Rivers and other shallow waters have many obstacles in them, some of which are just 1 or 2 feet below the surface! That's deep enough that you won't see them but close enough to the surface that they could damage your boat if you strike them. Outboards are popular in these waters, and jet boats are growing in popularity.

Selecting a boat for saltwater (and freshwater) usage

Some boaters go strictly in salt water, and some go mainly in fresh water. But in a survey of my readers at *Boating Life* magazine, I found that 75 percent of readers took their boats back and forth between fresh and salt water, depending on how they felt on a particular day. There's no such thing as a saltwater boat (though you'll hear the term used among boaters to refer to boats used primarily in salt water), and there's no such thing as a freshwater boat. With proper care, any boat can be used in salt water and fresh water. But some boats have features that stand up better to salt's corrosive effects.

Salt water is hard on boats and engines because it's corrosive. For a boat that will hold up to the effects of salt water, follow these guidelines:

- ✔ **Avoid a boat with carpet in the cockpit.** Carpet quickly shows salt stains and even smells fishy from plankton, which runs rampant in salt water.

- ✔ **Choose a boat with fiberglass floors that drain overboard, making them easy to clean with a hose.**

- ✔ **Avoid a small boat under 20 feet for offshore boating unless you plan to keep a sharp eye out for weather and dodge into port at the slightest sign of storms.**

- ✔ **Choose an outboard motor for a smaller boat or fishing boat.** These engines have the best corrosion protection and are easier to resell in most coastal boating areas.

- ✔ **Avoid a standard sterndrive engine package unless you plan to trailer your boat or have a marina keep it in dry storage.** Unlike outboards, sterndrives can't be trimmed out of the water, so the propeller drive mechanism is subject to the corrosive effects of salt and marine growth when kept in the water for weeks.

  If you do go with a sterndrive engine, choose a corrosion-protected sterndrive and budget for more expensive closed cooling systems that keep salt water out of the engine-cooling system. Your dealer can help you make these choices.

- ✔ **Choose a boat with all stainless steel hardware and fasteners for saltwater protection.** Your dealer can guide you on that choice.

An aluminum boat is perfectly fine for use in salt water as long as you keep the bottom painted with protective paint. If you trailer it, make sure your trailer has nylon covered bunks or roller bunks instead of carpet. Carpet traps salt water between the boat and carpet, letting the salt continue its nasty corrosive destruction. I talk more about trailers in Chapter 5.

Before putting your boat in storage, it's essential that you follow the directions in your engine's owner's manual for flushing salt water out of the engine (see Chapter 6). You also should hose down the entire boat and trailer with fresh water to remove salt.

Selecting a boat for only freshwater usage

Fresh water isn't as corrosive as salt water. If your plan is to stick to rivers and lakes, corrosion problems will take longer to develop, and you can afford to be more flexible in saving money by selecting a standard sterndrive engine and hardware that isn't stainless steel. Even though all the preferences for salt water are allowable and even beneficial in fresh water, some less expensive and some more luxurious items are options for freshwater boating.

- Carpet is more common on freshwater boats thanks to a lack of crusty salt and the presence of fewer smelly organisms in the water.

- Some aluminum hinges and latches may appear on boats used primarily in fresh water.

- You don't need to flush the engine after use in fresh water unless it's extremely silty or you've run your boat aground. If that happens, it's a good idea to flush the engine thoroughly following the directions in your engine's owner's manual (see Chapter 6).

- Fresh water tends to be more sheltered than coastal waters, making smaller boats generally more acceptable because weather isn't as big a concern. However, keep in mind that big, open freshwater bodies like the Great Lakes still require larger boats or a very careful weather eye to stay out of trouble.

Matching boating activities to the right boat type

What you want to do with your boat has a lot of influence on where you'll want to do it, and both factors are key to your choice of boat. For instance, it's unlikely that you want to water-ski in shark-infested waters (although a lot of surfer dudes don't seem to mind surfing with them), and you can't catch marlin in Green Bay, Wisconsin.

Chapter 2 has a complete discussion of which boats do what best. Table 3-1 gives you another way to look at things by summarizing the detail presented in Chapter 2. I list several types of boats and grade them on their abilities in several popular boating pastimes. I grade each style of boat on an A to D scale (just like in school, A is very good). You can do almost anything you want (but not necessarily well) with any boat, so none get an F. But there are better choices for specific games and activities.

Table 3-1   **Types of Boats and What They Do Best**

Type of Boat	Boating Activities				
	Touring and Hanging Out: Seating Capacity and Stability on the Water	Tubing: Adequate Horse-power	Water-skiing and Wake-boarding: Ideal Tracking, Horse-power, and Wake	Cruising Overnight: Living Facilities	Enter-taining Large Crews: Most Seating Capacity for Foot of Hull
Bass boat	D	D	D	D	D
Bay boat	C	D	D	D	D
Bowrider	A	A	B	D	B
Center con-sole	B	D	D	D	B
Cruiser	A	C	D	A	A
Cuddy	A	A	B	B	B
Deck boat	A	A	B	D	A
Fish and ski boat	A	A	B	D	C
Flats boat	D	D	D	D	D
Multi-species fish-ing boat	C	D	D	D	D
Pontoon boat	A	A	B	D	A
Walka-round	A	C	D	B	B
Walleye boat	C	D	D	D	D
Water-sports boat	A	A	A	D	B

Choosing the right horsepower for your boat

"How much power do you need?" is an important question to answer before buying a boat. Surveys of boat owner satisfaction show that "too little power" is the top reason boat buyers dislike their new boats. Some boat salespeople try to sell low-powered boats to lure buyers into a purchase with a lower price. That usually turns out to be an expensive mistake. Underpowered boats aren't much fun and are much harder to resell.

Boat builders offer boats with several power options priced from the lowest horsepower to the highest. The best boat builders won't offer a boat with too little power, but others do. I wish there was a formula for determining exactly how much horsepower you need, but over the years, I still haven't found that magic formula that works absolutely. I *can* tell you that after testing hundreds of power boats, the lowest power engine on the option list is often the last one you should consider.

In the process of writing this chapter, I analyzed test data from 17 different boats with an average speed of 50 miles per hour. The results point to a formula that gives a realistic average of how much horsepower per pound of boat you need to make your boat go between 45 and 50 mph. My calculations show it takes 1 horsepower per 13.5 pounds of boat to attain speeds of 45 to 50 mph. Keep in mind the tests were conducted with only one or two passengers onboard, and you're more likely to have six or seven. You'll want to factor in your intended passenger load weight, too. After many boat tests, I've found that I can subtract about 1 mph from the top speed for every passenger onboard.

Popular boating magazines (such as *Boating Life* and others) test boats for top speed and acceleration, and based on my experience, they render reasonable judgments about the adequacy of the power onboard. As a rule, do some research and go with the power that gets glowing approval.

You may be encouraged by some salespeople to choose a smaller engine to save fuel. Forget that. A larger engine running slower almost always pushes a boat at the same speed on less fuel than a small engine running harder. Put another way, in hundreds of boats tested and reviewed, I've found many with too little horsepower and only a very few with too much. Here are some horsepower guidelines to keep in mind:

- **Fishing boats** give you a lot of horsepower options, and how much power you want in your fishing boat depends on how you want to fish. Different fishing boats and styles require different horsepower.
  - Aluminum bass boats and walleye boats up to 18 feet are powered well at 75 to 150 horsepower.
  - Fiberglass bass boats, bay boats, and small offshore boats need between 150 and 225 horsepower.

- For regular offshore fishing, start thinking about two outboards totaling 300 horsepower for 23- to 25-foot boats and 400 to 600 horsepower for boats from 25 to 30 feet.

✔ **Runabouts and cruisers** almost always need more power than the lowest option. You may test the boat with your spouse and kids and a salesperson, but without typical gear — a cooler full of drinks and ice, among other things — it will run faster and accelerate quicker than in everyday use. That leads to disappointment on delivery day. To avoid the surprise, skip the lowest power choice unless you've tested it with a full load and are satisfied with the engine's performance.

✔ **Pontoons** provide a lot of boating fun even with small motors. Most boaters want pontoon boats for their comfort and size at a relatively low price, but horsepower options have been climbing steadily because boaters have found these boats to be even more fun with more speed. Here's a rundown of which horsepower works best with which pontoon activity:

- For easy cruising, consider engines between 50 and 115 horsepower. For example, a 22-foot pontoon will go about 22 to 25 mph with a 90 horsepower motor.

- For tubing and wakeboarding, choose 150 or more horsepower.

- To break the 35-mph barrier, you usually need a pontoon boat that has three pontoons and that's built tough enough to handle the stress that 200 or more horsepower can put on your rig.

Setting Your Boat Budget

Deciding what you can spend on a boat isn't much different than setting a budget for buying a new refrigerator — except the ticket price is likely to be higher for the boat. There are three basic categories of expenses in boating, and I address them separately in this section. I also touch on how to pay for your boat. You'll be "on the hook" for the costs of buying your boat, owning it, and using it. This section helps you plan for these costs so you can set a budget you're comfortable with.

Budgeting for boat storage costs

Storing a boat is more involved and more costly than parking a new car in your driveway or garage — unless your boat fits in your garage or driveway. Depending on where you live and the size of your boat, storing it can cost from between $75 per month for a self-storage lot and $1,000 or more per month for a marina slip (in-water storage spot). Most boat storage rates are based on the length of your boat in feet.

Some communities or subdivisions have laws or bylaws prohibiting storing a boat in the open, say in a driveway or an unfenced backyard. Check for similar laws with your local city hall, the county courthouse, or your homeowner's association to avoid unexpected costs or even fines.

Here are some storage options to check out by calling around to marinas and boat storage yards in your area. Chapter 16 covers the ins and outs of storage options in detail.

- ✔ If you buy a boat and a trailer that fits in your garage or backyard, you pay nothing extra for storage and save significant cash. (But your spouse may complain about the car sitting in the driveway because there's no room in the garage.)

- ✔ Dry stack storage marinas use a forklift to put your boat on a rack. Some racks are five stories high and hold boats up to 50 feet long. When you want your boat, it's forklifted into the water — usually for no additional charge. This type of storage is economical and safe for your boat, too, because the boat doesn't gather marine growth or stains or risk sinking at the dock, which is where a surprising number of sinkings occur.

- ✔ Wet slips are attractive because they're so convenient. Just run down to the dock, untie the boat, jump in, and you're off. However, wet slips are more expensive per foot of boat length, and your boat is exposed to damage from corrosion and marine growth 24/7.

Figuring in trailer, fuel, and maintenance costs

The annual costs to operate, maintain, and store your boat are often estimated at 10 percent of the purchase price of a new boat. The proportion goes up on pre-owned boats because of expired warranties and the need for maintenance as things wear out. Ten percent may be a good rule of thumb, but I recommend that you get your pencil and paper ready and jot down some estimations as you read through this section, which breaks down general operation costs into trailer, fuel, and maintenance categories. You shouldn't ignore these budget estimates as you start to narrow down your boat selection.

Accounting for a trailer purchase

Ever hear of an undertow on a highway? A trailer goes under your boat so you can tow it on the road! You will need to buy a trailer to get your boat to and from the various waters you choose to boat in (see Chapter 5 for tips on proper trailering and towing techniques). Here are a few simple considerations to keep in mind as you look at trailer options:

- ✔ **Trailers can be standard equipment.** Sometimes your boat will come standard with a trailer as part of the package. Sometimes it's an extra fee. At the outset, ask the seller if the trailer is part of the package.

✔ **Boat manufacturers often recommend certain trailers.** Even if trailers are optional equipment, often the best trailer choice is the one offered by the manufacturer. It will fit perfectly the first time, and unless you choose a galvanized trailer for saltwater use, it will likely be painted to accent your boat.

✔ **Your vehicle's towing capacity is important.** There's a limit to how much boat your vehicle can safely tow. Talk to your boat dealer about the weight of your boat and trailer, and talk to your car dealer about the towing capacity of your vehicle.

Factoring in fuel

Fuel costs are higher for higher horsepower motors. Chat with your boat dealer about a boat's fuel efficiency, and do some quick calculations to plan for fuel costs. If your dealer can't give you fuel flow information, nearly every engine manufacturer posts fuel flow tests on its Web site. Here are some things to think about with regard to fuel:

✔ Big V-8 engines can burn 20 to 30 gallons of fuel per hour at wide open throttle (WOT).

✔ V-6 outboards burn 18 to 24 gallons of fuel per hour at WOT.

✔ V-4 outboards burn 10 to 16 gallons of fuel at WOT.

As a rule, you'll burn an average of half of the WOT fuel burn per every hour of boating — unless you spend a lot time swimming and hanging out at anchor, which many people actually do, or unless you're just crazy about speed and run wide open all the time (yikes!). And keep in mind that skiing burns more fuel than touring and hanging out because of the fuel required to accelerate and yank a skier from the water.

Don't choose a lower horsepower engine to save fuel. Typically, you'll burn less fuel running a big engine at a lower RPM to achieve the same speed as a smaller engine running harder.

Managing maintenance

Like your car, your boat won't run like you want it to indefinitely without regular maintenance. And when figuring out how much you can spend on a boat, you need to factor in the costs of things like a new battery, repairing a propeller, and cleaning and waxing the boat. You should also consult your dealer about scheduled service costs not included in warranties. Chapter 13 contains the specifics of general preventative boat maintenance, and you also can find more information in your boat's operating manual.

On a typical runabout, budget $500 per year for oil changes and regular seasonal service per engine. (Take some time to really think about that cost before you buy a twin engine powerhouse!)

If you don't plan for regular service intervals and then skip them when the time comes, you'd better budget in an extra $2,000 to $10,000 or more for major repairs because failing to follow the manufacturer's maintenance instructions can result in catastrophic (to your budget, anyway) engine failures.

If you buy a pre-owned boat that doesn't come with an owner's manual (and this is pretty commonplace), you may be able to find it online. Some manufacturers post manuals online in PDF format for downloading, often for free. Or check with a local marine dealer; they usually sell engine service manuals for every marine engine made in about the last 30 years. The manual will walk you through all maintenance and repair steps, helping you do some of the work yourself. And that's a bargain and a must for new owners of pre-owned boats.

Insuring your boat (immediately)

The minute you sign on the dotted line, you have an insurable interest in your boat, so shop your insurance options first and then bind or confirm your insurance purchase when you pen the boat deal.

The cost of insuring a boat can be surprisingly high and will vary depending on how much your boat is worth and where you plan to use and keep it. For example, after the hurricanes of 2004–2006, boaters in all coastal areas of the U.S. were shocked at their insurance rates. Inland boaters paid a pittance in comparison. As of this writing, coastal rates have stabilized but are still high. If you don't consider how insurance costs impact your monthly expenses, you could find yourself over-reaching when you make your first payment.

Here are some boat-specific insurance considerations:

- ✔ **When you shop insurance for budgeting purposes, tell your insurance agent what you expect to buy and how much you plan to spend, and then have him or her offer some estimates.**

- ✔ **You may find that by insuring your house, cars, and boat together at one agency, you'll get better overall rates.**

- ✔ **One way to save insurance cash is to set your car and boat liability limits lower and buy an umbrella policy that adds a higher liability amount to *all* your policies.** Umbrella policies are cheaper than basic liability policies because they don't kick in for the little dents and dings or stitches in your neighbor's head when he falls down in your boat.

- ✔ **Many insurance policies offered by auto insurers won't cover you and your boat when you leave the mouth of any harbor and enter the ocean. If your auto insurer can't handle that risk, you'll have to go to a marine insurer.**

> ✔ **Check online insurers for the best deal on coverage.** BoatU.S. is one of the largest insurers and specializes in boats and boat-towing insurance. Progressive, Allstate, and State Farm are three insurance companies usually associated with auto insurance that are aggressively pursuing marine customers. You can check out these insurers online:
>
> • www.boatus-insurance.com
>
> • watercraft.progressive.com
>
> • www.allstate.com/boat-insurance.aspx
>
> • www.statefarm.com/insurance/boat/boat.asp

Choosing how to pay for your boat

Buying your boat with cash is simplest, but most buyers prefer not to lay down that big stack of greenbacks upfront and instead finance the purchase. When buying a boat, you ask much the same budgeting questions as when buying a car. The advantages and disadvantages are much the same, too.

Paying cash

If you're a cash buyer, your budget is what you're willing to part with and still be able to meet all your operating expenses, plus your investment and savings goals.

The cheapest way to buy a boat is to pay cash and avoid interest and monthly payments. With no monthly payments, periodic career life changes aren't as likely to throw your boating and future into a panic — Wind Drifter can just wait in the garage until you feel like buying gas again.

The obvious disadvantage of paying cash is that you have to come up with the cash.

Financing

Financing a boat purchase is pretty popular, even among people who are able to pay cash. Like paying cash upfront, going the route of financing has its positives and negatives. On the upside, borrowing lets you boat now and pay for your purchase in manageable, monthly increments. However, failing to plan for both monthly payments and maintenance costs is a key cause of boatus interruptus.

Prequalify for a boat loan before you boat shop, just like you would for a car or a house. Prequalification helps you set a ceiling price and stick to it. It also gives you the best interest rate and makes you as attractive as a cash buyer to a seller, which helps in negotiating the terms of your purchase.

A better deal awaits

What I experienced recently in financing a tow vehicle also applies to buying a boat. It gave me food for thought on future purchases. Here's what happened:

I planned to finance a new truck, so before I shopped, I called my bank to see what loan terms they could offer me. They don't make vehicle loans, it turns out. Quite a few banks don't. They suggested a credit union, but none were convenient or served any groups to which I belonged. So, next I went on the great old World Wide Web. I searched "auto loans" and came up with a half dozen groups with recognizable brands and names, and I filled out their application forms. In less than 48 hours, I had a blank check to be made out to the dealership of my choosing. Signing the check would seal the loan at an interest rate I thought was pretty darned good. I selected my truck, and when I whipped out the check, the dealership said they'd beat the terms — which they did nicely. Had I gone into the dealership unarmed, I think I would have been offered a much higher rate, and not knowing any better, I would have thought it was a great deal.

The face of financing is changing, and so is the complexity of it. In poor economic times, it takes a higher credit rating to buy a boat than to buy a house. In good economic times, boat loans are almost easier to get than home loans. If you've financed a car, the climate for a boat is much the same, but often manufacturers underwrite the loans to make the sale. Boat manufacturers also do that occasionally. Your boat dealer will have some financing hookups that may or may not be better deals than you can get on the street from banks, so it's important to shop around for financing and not agree to the first offer you get.

Head to the following four places to make sure you get the best financing deal:

- ✔ **Online:** Search "boat loans" and you'll find several loan organizations that can confirm an amount for which you'll be qualified to borrow on a boat. Web sites such as www.boatinglife.com, usedboats.com, and newboats.com also post links to marine lenders.

- ✔ **Your bank or credit union:** Your existing relationship with your bank may bring you the best loan terms possible on a boat. In the same vein, if you work for a company or belong to a group that sponsors a credit union, it may offer you the best loan.

- ✔ **Home equity line of credit:** Although the terms of this kind of loan can fluctuate with economic times, a low interest rate may make it the most cost effective way to buy your boat.

- ✔ **Your dealer:** As I mention earlier, boat dealers work with financing companies to finance their inventory. Often, their relationships with these lenders give them access to favorable loan terms for their customers. But you won't know if your dealer offers you the best deal unless you investigate the previously listed resources beforehand.

If you choose a boat with a sleeping area, a bathroom compartment, and cooking facilities, your tax preparer may recommend that you deduct the interest on the boat purchase under the same rules that apply to deducting interest on second homes.

Deciding Whether to Buy a Pre-owned or New Boat

If you've narrowed down your boat-buying decision to the type of boat that fits your needs, determined how you'll make your purchase, and tallied the ongoing costs, one other major consideration is whether to go with a pre-owned boat or a new boat. Obviously, each choice has advantages and disadvantages, which I help you wade through in this section along with some buying basics.

Buying basics for pre-owned or new boats

Whether you choose to buy a new boat or a pre-owned boat, there are a few basic considerations to keep in mind. You need to know what to look for to ensure the quality of any boat, and it always helps to have a negotiating strategy in mind. No matter what, you should insist on a sea trial and make sure the boat comes with an appropriate, well-maintained trailer.

Checking for quality construction

A good "fit and finish" is boat-speak for a well-made boat. In pre-owned boats, you have to make some allowances for age. For example, the vinyl may be worn or the hull scratched, but those sorts of problems have to do with the boat's condition, not the quality of its construction.

Good fit and finish is present if

- A boat's ergonomics (the way it fits the passengers and skipper) are comfortable and secure. For example, the steering wheel, actually called the *helm* by boaters, and throttle should fall comfortably within reach, and the helm seat should offer a clear view all around the boat.

- Caulk is evenly applied around hatches and other areas that should be watertight. The caulk bead should be smooth, and the caulk should be in good condition and not peeling, moldy, or cracked.

- Every switch and lever and the items they control function properly.

- Every through-hull fitting is tightly clamped and caulked to the hull, and all hose clamps are tight. The best boats are double clamped.

- ✔ It feels solid in sea trials and takes reasonable waves without heavy rattling or flexing.

- ✔ The hull is dry in the bilge or engine compartment. At the very least, any water in these areas should be slight and not increasing in quantity!

- ✔ It reaches its WOT (wide open throttle) revolutions per minute without missing or sputtering. You can find this specification on your engine manufacturer's Web site. An RPM range that's too low or too high at WOT indicates a poorly matched propeller or a poorly running engine.

- ✔ Ladders, rails, and grab handles are firmly fastened.

- ✔ Storage compartments are ample, easy to access, and allow water to drain away from their contents.

- ✔ The boat has a logical floor plan that lets people move around it as easily as possible in a boat its size.

- ✔ The engine idles smoothly without stalling, accelerates smoothly, and accepts some acceleration and deceleration of the throttle without stalling.

- ✔ The hatches and doors fit and latch and stay latched even if you hit waves.

- ✔ The screws are tight and the heads are snug and even in their holes.

- ✔ The stereo and every speaker produce normal sound.

  Bring a CD to test and a CD or MP3 player to plug into the system.

- ✔ The upholstery is firm, the stitching tight, and the vinyl snug with no wrinkles.

- ✔ The windshield is on straight and firm, and any panels that open and close function and latch properly.

- ✔ The wiring is logical, easy to trace, and labeled with respect to what each wire powers, and the connections are tight.

- ✔ The engine compartment hatch fits tightly and latches and doesn't pop up while underway. You'd be surprised at how many boats fail this test! At WOT, the wind can rip a hatch all the way off if it pops open.

Never buy a boat without first taking it out on a sea trial. You'll have to be firm in demanding one. You may even have to sign a contract and post a deposit. The deposit should be guaranteed refundable, in writing, should you elect to reject the boat for any reason. When you sea-trial any boat, pre-owned or new, keep the preceding list in mind.

Determining a fair price

There are no clear rules for pricing a boat, and even published pricing guides are sort of like Captain Jack Sparrow's Pirate's Code — they're just guidelines. Like real estate, boats tend to have "hot markets" and cost more in some places than others. Certain regions have favored styles of boats, too, and boats that don't meet the local preferences are at a pricing disadvantage.

Here are some tips for determining value:

- Shop comparable boats, comparing brand, horsepower, length, and condition.

- Compare the cost of a brand-new model to a pre-owned model. Expect a boat to depreciate at about the same rate as a car — 25 to 35 percent the first year and 10 to 20 percent every year after that.

If the asking price lines up with comparable boats, you can agree on a price with the seller. For a pre-owned boat, the price is contingent on a clean bill of health from your surveyor (see the section, "Hiring a marine surveyor," later in this chapter). A satisfactory sea trial (test drive) should also be part of the bargain. (The previous section lists what to check both out of the water and during a test drive.)

Just like buying a new car, boat buying is part science, part shopping, and part horse-trading. Most boat builders offer their dealers exclusive regional territories, so to shop two dealers of the same brand against each other, you'll have to go the extra mile to visit one that may not be in a convenient location for you.

After you've done enough research to make you confident in your estimate of the boat's worth, and if you think the dealer's price is excessive, you can try making a lower offer based on repairs your surveyor found (see the later section, "Hiring a marine surveyor") and any insight you've gained from comparison shopping. Follow these deduction guidelines:

- **Deduct the retail cost of any repairs your surveyor or mechanic has identified.** I also would add 20 percent to the anticipated cost of repairs, because in my experience, few boat repairs are accomplished for the expected price.

- **Deduct from the price of a boat that's sort of a fish out of water.** Some boats are more popular in certain regions, so don't be afraid to ask for a price concession if you're considering a boat that's not so popular in your region.

- **Deduct from a price in tough economic times.** You may feel bad about it, and it may break a boat dealer's heart to let a great boat go for a song, but it may also be better for the dealer to make the deal than to sit on the boat for another season, paying interest. Be fair, but be firm in your shopping.

If the dealer has a sound reputation for excellent repair service, it may be worth it to buy the dealership's boat even at a price higher than your offer.

Making sure the paperwork is in order

Before your boat is legal to hit the water, you have to register it, usually with your county clerk.

If your boat's over a certain weight, you can choose to document it with the federal government; the government can commandeer documented vessels in a time of war or other emergency, such as if the U.S. Coast Guard needed your boat for rescuing Hurricane Katrina victims. It's likely the government would reimburse you for damages and use, but still . . . some people understandably don't want to do that. If you don't want to document your vessel for use by the U.S. government, just register it in your home state.

Your county clerk needs the following to register your boat:

- ✔ A title notarized and signed over to you. If it's a new boat, a *manufacturer's statement of origin* (MSO) is required in place of a title, and the state issues your title after registration.

- ✔ A bill of sale, required by some states. This is just a letter from the seller, dated with the boat's serial number and, if it's an outboard, the serial number of the outboard engine as well.

Exercising your right to have a marine surveyor inspect a pre-owned boat and your right to take any boat on a sea trial are mandatory to concluding a purchase. Make sure the seller is aware that you'll buy the boat only after the satisfactory conclusion of an inspection and sea trial and after you're sure the paperwork is in order.

If you buy from a dealer, the sales staff will handle the paperwork for you, simplifying the process. That's one way the dealer earns its money. If you buy a boat in a driveway, don't release the check until

- ✔ The seller signs the title over to you in front of a notary so the signature is verified for the registration authorities in your state.

- ✔ The title identifies the lien holder (the person who loaned money for the seller's purchase) if there's a loan against the boat. You'll need a letter of satisfaction from the lien holder that releases his or her lien on the boat.

- ✔ You have copies of the current registration and previous registration information. This documentation may be helpful in transferring registration to you, and having the previous registration information may also allow you to keep the current registration numbers, saving the cost of changing them.

If the seller can't provide the title and bill of sale to you before you buy the boat, you'd better look at another boat or give the seller a couple of weeks to acquire the legal documents. Hold onto your money until you get the documents.

Considering a pre-owned boat

Pre-owned boats comprise about 75 percent of the total number of boats that change hands every year, according to National Marine Manufacturers Association (NMMA) statistics. You probably already have a preference for buying new or pre-owned based on your experiences buying cars or homes. If you're choosing to go the pre-owned route, I give you some advice in this section to help you find the right boat and eliminate at least some of the lemons.

Inspecting pre-owned boats for wear and damage

An up close and personal inspection of pre-owned boats is mandatory. You don't need an expert yet — just look at these boats as you would a pre-owned car, and eliminate candidates that show the following obvious defects (unless you're a do-it-yourselfer on the hunt for a project):

- Notice the overall appearance of the boat. Does it show obvious signs of neglect like dirt and leaves or broken or badly torn upholstery? If so, it's probably neglected on the inside, too.

- Open doors and hatches. Are all the hinges and latches in place and functioning?

- Turn all the switches on one at a time. Does everything work?

- Check the fuse panel and wiring connections in the bilge by the engine and under the dash. Do you see greenish tarnish and residue? These are signs of corrosion that indicate the boat may have been underwater.

- Look for waterline scum in the bilge that looks sort of like a bathtub ring. If that line is higher than the height of the bottom of the engine, chances are good the boat was flooded or sunk.

- Check the oil. Is it fresh, clear, and at the appropriate level? If it's dirty and low, the boat may not have undergone routine maintenance and you may have a ticking time bomb on your hands.

If a boat passes this cursory inspection, you like it, and you think the price is in your ballpark, hire a surveyor to check it out thoroughly.

Hiring a marine surveyor

Unless you're a mechanic and know boats well, you'll have a difficult time determining a boat's worth without professional help. A marine surveyor's job is to spot defects and repairs needed to make the boat seaworthy *before* you buy it. Survey rates vary, depending on the size and complexity of your prospect, but a surveyor will often save you more than the cost of his or her services by telling you what the seller needs to repair before you buy a boat — or by steering you clear of hopeless lemons.

Here are two great resources to find a marine surveyor near your prospective boat:

- The Society of Accredited Marine Surveyors, Inc.: `www.marine survey.org`

- The National Association of Marine Surveyors: `namsglobal.org`

Take your marine surveyor's advice and adjust the price you're willing to pay based on his or her findings.

Looking at a new boat

Nothing beats the feeling of buying a brand-new boat. The new boat smell, the crisp clean upholstery, and the gleaming finish are intoxicating. But just because a boat is new doesn't mean it's in perfect operating condition. It's very possible that you'll have to take your new boat to your dealer more frequently in the first year than you'd wish to work out the kinks.

Loose fittings, latches that don't latch, pumps that don't run, and even leaks aren't uncommon in new boats. A sea trial can help expose problems right away, but some only show up after you've used your boat for a while. The manufacturer supplies your boat with a warranty to cover these sorts of repairs, but if the list gets too long, the frustration of boat ownership far exceeds the relaxation. To minimize the problems you'll face with a new boat, keep in mind the pre-delivery precautions covered in this section.

Getting stuck with a lemon

If you buy a new car in many states and it then spends more than a certain amount of time in the shop for warranty service, it's considered a *lemon,* and lemon laws give you some extensive rights for faster satisfaction. Some laws require the dealer to take back the car and replace it with a comparable one. The climate for boat buyers is much different.

Though some states, such as California, do have a lemon law covering boats, most states don't. Some boat dealers and some manufacturers will step up and replace a new boat that has chronic problems, but in most states, no laws exist requiring them to do it. That's why I recommend you insist on a sea trial before you buy the boat. It lets you quickly identify many manufacturing flaws, and when the sale is contingent on the repairs, they often happen on a much tighter schedule.

Understanding widely varying pricing

There are no laws requiring boat builders to put a sticker price on a boat, and that creates some interesting challenges in shopping.

The dealer can charge whatever price he or she thinks the traffic will bear. It isn't unusual to find two dealers offering the same boat at substantially different prices.

You can shop an out-of-town dealer to get a better price, but for many boat brands, only the selling dealer has the obligation to handle warranty repairs for your boat. For that reason, if you don't think a boat price is fair, it's better to switch to a comparable brand in your area than to buy from an out-of-town dealer and forfeit your warranty repairs or be forced to travel to the dealer anytime your boat needs work under warranty.

Going Shopping for Your Boat

Some people search high and low for their boats, and for others, their boats just find them. The latter get sucked into the romance of buying a boat by the enticing availability of one. The former get the bug and do their research. Guess who has a better boating experience?

This chapter shares my favorite strategies for selecting boats. This section points you to the various places where you can actually look for a boat.

- ✔ **Buying new:** If you're looking to buy a new boat, check out area dealers, Web sites, and boat shows.
- ✔ **Buying pre-owned:** If you're planning to buy a pre-owned boat, check out area dealers, Web sites, and individuals with boats to sell.

Whether you're shopping new or pre-owned boats, coming up with a short list of the specific boat types, models, and accessories that you're interested in is a good idea. Developing the list forces you to narrow your choices within reason. Referring to the list as you shop helps keep you focused on getting the right boat for your needs.

Buying through a Web site

Many Web sites specialize in posting new and pre-owned boat listings, and now most newspapers post their boat classifieds online as well. The Web allows you to search the nation for your perfect boat.

Web sites where you can find dealers and individual sellers include:

- ✔ www.boattraderonline.com
- ✔ Newboats.com
- ✔ Usedboats.com

Advantages

Web sites let you browse thousands of boats in their databases one at a time, or you can narrow it down to a short list by factors such as length, style, brand, horsepower, model year, price, and even proximity to your home. You can set parameters for all these criteria to really drill down deep, or you can narrow your options by just one or two points to get a longer research list.

If you're interested in a particular brand, type the name into your favorite search engine and you'll find plenty of information on it, including an online dealer locator. Thanks to the Web (and insightful books like this one), most dealers report that their customers come to them with a pretty strong idea and understanding of what they want.

On Web sites, you'll find boat listings from both dealers and individuals. Some people prefer to buy from individuals to try to strike a more favorable price, and sometimes that approach works. But dealers have to compete with individuals, so dealer prices are usually competitive — and they sometimes offer warranties to boot.

A nationwide Web search helps you get a handle on appropriate pricing and inventory availability. Heck, if you found 2,012 different Death Raptor 25s for sale across the country, the relative glut of them could give you some good buying leverage.

Disadvantages

Online boat-buying isn't without some bumps in the road. A major one is the length of the road to your new boat. You have to arrange all the inspections long distance and either tow the boat home yourself or have it shipped.

Buying from an individual

You've driven through your town and seen boats with "For Sale" signs on them. Drive through a lake community and it seems like every third driveway and strip mall parking lot sports such an opportunity. Scanning the local classifieds yields even more boats being sold by owners.

Advantages

Some people prefer to buy from individuals because they hope individuals are more motivated sellers and therefore will give them a better price. Individual sellers may have less at stake in the sale, no "overhead" to cover as a dealer might, and no manager to speak with about your offer.

Disadvantages

Keep in mind that both dealers and individuals post classifieds in the paper, and only some newspapers require dealers to identify themselves as such in the ads. Also, you can't check the references of an individual seller, so you don't know what you're getting without careful inspection. Without a motivation for future sales and the desire to maintain the respectability of a dealership's good business name, you may find it difficult to eliminate hidden faults in a boat offered by an individual. It pays to be wary in these cases, so follow the buying tips I discuss earlier in the chapter.

Buying from a dealer

Marine dealers usually have scads of pre-owned boats and a pretty good selection of new ones, too. A good, friendly dealer can help you sort out your boating priorities and aim you at a boat that may best fill those needs. You want a dealer with an impeccable service department because you'll need it for routine maintenance and sometimes not-so-routine maintenance.

Readers often write to me asking, "What's the best boat?" That's a loaded question that no one can answer quickly, but one pat answer that I've found to be universally true is this: The best boat from the worst dealer is the worst boat.

Advantages

One of the biggest advantages of buying your boat from a dealer is that you can check a dealer's references. Ask to be referred to some customers, and then ask them about both their purchase and service experiences. How long did they have to wait for service at their last visit? Did the shop get things fixed right the first time?

Spend an afternoon at the local launch ramp and chat up the people bringing their boats in to find out where they bought them. Ask if they'd recommend their dealers. If they don't recommend them, find out why not.

The National Marine Manufacturers Association (NMMA) has established a dealer certification program in partnership with its member boat builders and dealers. The program sets benchmarks for dealer training programs designed to give the customer a better experience. Find an NMMA-certified dealer that has the seal shown in Figure 3-1 on the door, and chances are you have a dealer you can trust.

Disadvantages

Some boat buyers prefer buying from individuals because the individual seller is the one who operated the boat last. If you follow the tips I've suggested for investigating pre-owned boats, you can learn a lot about a boat from an individual, and that same information won't be available to a dealer who traded for the boat. In addition, dealers may have markups in the boats they need to receive to cover their expenses in carrying and storing the rig.

Figure 3-1:
This NMMA
seal
indicates
the dealer
has met
high marine
industry
standards
for customer
service and
satisfaction.

Buying at a boat show

Most boat shows are held in the winter before boating season starts, and if you find the right boat there, it will be ready to launch on the first sunny spring day.

Advantages

Boat shows are a terrific place to learn about boats and comparison shop because virtually every boat model in every brand in the industry is represented. Boat manufacturers depend on shows for an enormous proportion of their annual volume, so they offer very attractive prices during boat shows that they may never offer again.

Disadvantages

The only disadvantage to buying at a boat show is that you can't test drive your favorites. But you can insist on a satisfactory sea trial before you seal the deal. One way is to establish a contract to buy the boat at a price set at the winter boat show but to close on it after a satisfactory test in April.

Getting Licensed and Educated

At one time, anyone could get behind the wheel . . . ahem . . . *helm* of a boat and take off. Now many states require first-time boaters to pass a test or take a safety course. The laws vary state by state, and you have to check with law enforcement agents or your local dealer to find out what the requirements are. In any case, the test and the body of information you need to know is really minimal, but occasionally somebody underestimates them and fails. This section discusses a little bit of what you can expect.

Getting a captain's license

Some boaters get really enthused about the game and want to learn more than the basics of navigating channels and how to safely cross paths or pass boats. For recreational boating with friends and relatives, nothing more than the study and licensing covered in the section, "Getting Licensed and Educated," is necessary. But if you want to carry paying customers or just want the challenge and prestige of earning your captain's license, I say go for it. The most popular captain's license is nicknamed the "six-pack license" because it allows you to carry six or fewer paying customers.

The body of knowledge required for a captain's license is extensive and the test mind-numbing. Here are the requirements:

✔ **Know the Rules of the Road inside and out.** This is the U.S. Coast Guard's book of exhaustive rules that deal with both inland navigation laws and navigation on international waters offshore. You can download a copy of the book free at www.navcen. uscg.gov/mwv/navrules/navrules.htm.

✔ **Undergo extensive first-aid and CPR training.** As captain, you're responsible for the safety and welfare of everyone onboard your boat.

✔ **Pass a physical exam and a drug-screening test.**

✔ **Pass the captain's test.** Taking the test is inconvenient at best, unless you're lucky enough to live close to where one is administered or take a course online (the Mariner's School offers one at www. marinersschool.com). It's exhaustive, and be warned that the wording is designed to trick you. (The Coasties say it's designed to make you *think,* but some questions are real sucker punches!) The good news is that if you prepare yourself properly and know the laws, you can pass the test.

Passing the state boating exam

All but a handful of states require new boaters to take an exam to show they've familiarized themselves with boating laws. Boaters must score 70 to 80 percent on these exams to pass, depending on the state. Exam fees vary, but most fall within a range of $15 to $30.

Taking a boater safety course

Some states require new boaters and young boaters born after a specified date to take a safety course and then pass a safety exam. Some states offer these courses online and others offer only classes with instructors.

The Web site of the National Association of State Boating Laws Administrators (NASBLA), at www.nasbla.org, lists boating laws by state and has links to individual regulatory and enforcement agencies in boating. You can find your state's boater safety requirements there.

Chapter 4

Accessorizing Your Boat
for Safety and Fun

In This Chapter

▶ Choosing quality safety gear

▶ Protecting your boat with good mooring lines and fenders

▶ Enhancing your boating experience with electronics

▶ Preparing your boat for watersports

*L*oading up with the right safety gear and water toys is mandatory to obtain the full measure of fun from your boat. The moment you sign the purchase contract for your boat, you *need* safety gear. And although you may be tempted to put off buying water toys until later, you'll *want* skis or a wakeboard or a tube to ride very soon. So, including them with your boat purchase is really a good idea.

Why get everything all at once? The best time to build a pile of safety gear and water toys is when you're in the negotiation stage of buying your boat. You never know what a salesperson will throw in to sweeten the deal. Plus, some safety gear needs installation, so you may as well get it taken care of upfront.

I describe these goodies in order of mandatory to optional in this chapter. Rather than read this chapter as a primer on safety laws and skiing techniques, look at it as a primer on must-haves such as life jackets, boat fenders, and tow ropes.

Getting Quality and Approved Safety Gear

Choose your safety gear thoughtfully because even though you may think you'll use it only in case of an emergency, you'll use some gear, like life jackets, on an everyday basis, and daily use can wear out gear even if you never have an emergency. If you buy really cheap, uncomfortable life jackets, you and your crew may resist wearing them, putting you at further risk. Things like fire extinguishers are easy to forget about, so buying them when you purchase your boat eliminates the likelihood of operating unprotected later (and being in violation of local laws). The idea is to start boating right after you buy your rig, not to spend your weekends in the marine store!

The safety gear I discuss in this section is required by law in most states and on all federal waters (that is, out to the 12-mile international limit offshore). Boating safety and safety equipment requirements vary state by state. You can check your local state laws with the National Association of State Boating Law Administrators (www.nasbla.org).

Staying afloat with life jackets

Life jackets are the epicenter of boating safety. They're vests filled with buoyant material to keep you afloat, and they're designed to automatically turn an unconscious person face up in the water when worn according to the directions. Standard life jackets may differ from watersports jackets, which I explain later in this chapter in the section, "Jacketing up for safety and looking cool."

In every state and territory of the United States, every boat is required to have one properly fitting, U.S. Coast Guard–approved life jacket for every passenger onboard. Annual boating fatalities range from 500 to more than 700 boaters, according the U.S. Coast Guard. Most of the fatalities are drownings, and authorities believe most drowning victims would have lived if they were wearing life jackets.

Five types of life jackets are available, and they fall into two general categories:

- ✔ **Type I, Type II, Type III, and Type IV jackets are inherently buoyant and float without inflation.** These vests satisfy the requirements of the U.S. Coast Guard and state law enforcement agencies when there's one life jacket for each person onboard.

- ✔ **A Type V jacket is inflatable, but it doesn't float if it's not inflated.** It can be deployed by pulling a rip cord, or some jackets automatically inflate when they get wet or are forced underwater. Type V life jackets cost three to six times more than the other types, but they enhance the wearer's freedom of movement.

You must *wear* Type V life jackets in order for them to satisfy the law. By contrast, all other life jackets must merely be onboard and accessible.

Being prepared with throwable life preservers

Throwable life preservers aid rescues when someone falls overboard. Many times, one boater wants to jump in to rescue another boater, and that almost always results in two people needing rescue. It's better to throw a life preserver to a person rather than jump in after them. Attaching a rope to the throwable life preserver is an even better idea because you can pull the person in — and the rope gives you a second chance if your first throw is off the mark.

When retrieving a passenger from the water, turn off the engine and leave it in gear. In neutral, propellers can still spin in the current, making sharp props still a danger. The engine won't restart until you put it in neutral, giving you an extra step and a second or two to be sure passengers and ropes are clear of the props before you restart your boat.

Throwable life preservers come in various shapes:

- ✔ **Horseshoe-shaped** ones are easy for victims to pull around themselves but are large and cumbersome to stow in small boats.

- ✔ **Ring-shaped** life preservers are practically a cliché image of boating and have a rope around them for throwing. Like the horseshoe, rings are bulky and difficult to store on small boats.

- ✔ **Square** seat cushions are the throwable life preserver of choice for small boats. Their buoyant material makes for good padding on hard benches and even boosts a smaller captain for a better view over the bow. Sitting on these life preservers doesn't hurt them and keeps them handy and easy to store.

The only important criterion is that you have a throwable life preserver that bears the U.S. Coast Guard seal of approval (see Figure 4-1) and is in usable condition. For example, a broken horseshoe or ring is verboten. So is a throwable cushion if the straps are broken, leaving the victim nothing to grip.

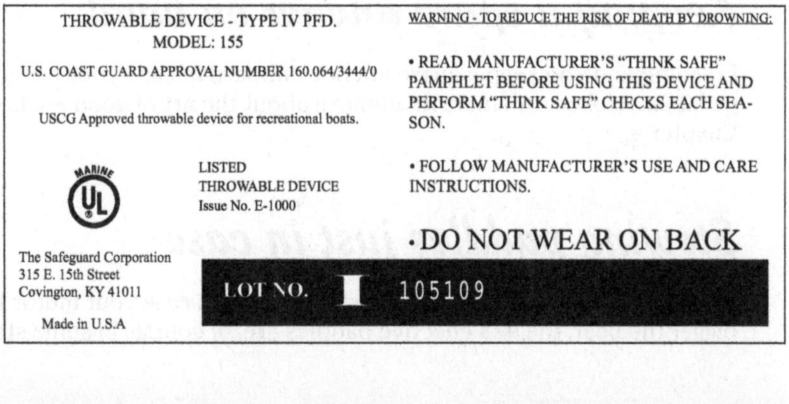

Figure 4-1:
The U.S. Coast Guard seal of approval on a throwable life preserver.

THROWABLE DEVICE - TYPE IV PFD.
MODEL: 155

U.S. COAST GUARD APPROVAL NUMBER 160.064/3444/0

USCG Approved throwable device for recreational boats.

MARINE
(UL)

LISTED
THROWABLE DEVICE
Issue No. E-1000

The Safeguard Corporation
315 E. 15th Street
Covington, KY 41011

Made in U.S.A

WARNING - TO REDUCE THE RISK OF DEATH BY DROWNING:

• READ MANUFACTURER'S "THINK SAFE" PAMPHLET BEFORE USING THIS DEVICE AND PERFORM "THINK SAFE" CHECKS EACH SEASON.

• FOLLOW MANUFACTURER'S USE AND CARE INSTRUCTIONS.

•DO NOT WEAR ON BACK

LOT NO. I 105109

Having the right fire extinguisher onboard

Fire extinguishers are required on most boats. Different-sized boats have different requirements in terms of how many and how big the fire extinguishers need to be. The National Marine Manufacturers Association (NMMA) works in conjunction with the U.S. Coast Guard and member boat manufacturers to make sure they meet stringent safety standards. If you buy an NMMA-certified boat, appropriate fire suppression equipment is considered part of the purchase, eliminating a decision and the risk of getting it wrong. Many boat builders include the appropriate extinguishers as standard equipment with their boats, anyway. If your boat doesn't come with fire extinguishers, consult your dealer.

Two classes of extinguishers are most commonly used in recreational boats: B-I and B-II. The classifications relate mainly to capacity; all you need to know is which one you're required to carry. Three categories of requirements for fire extinguishers apply based on the size and type of boat:

✔ **Outboard boats under 26 feet:** Not required to carry fire extinguishers unless they have permanent fuel tanks. Despite the lack of requirement, carrying a fire extinguisher is still a good idea.

✔ **Inboard and sterndrive boats under 26 feet:** Required to carry one B-1 class carbon dioxide extinguisher. This fire extinguisher is ideal for fighting gasoline fires, which is your main fire risk on a boat.

✔ **Inboard and sterndrive boats between 26 and 40 feet:** Required to carry two B-I class extinguishers or one BII class extinguisher.

Most fire extinguishers need annual maintenance, or annual replacement if they're disposable. Some have gauges on the side that indicate if they're serviceable. It's a good idea to get into the habit of looking at the gauge every time you boat to make sure the needle indicates the unit is charged and capable of fighting a fire.

For a discussion about dealing with boat fires, turn to Chapter 12.

Keeping a spare anchor on hand

I recommend you keep a spare anchor onboard in case your primary anchor gets lost, broken, or stuck. Read more about the art of good anchoring in Chapter 8.

Stowing paddles just in case

In some states, paddles are required as backup in case your motor fails. The bigger the boat, the less effective paddles are, of course. In some states, boats with two motors aren't required to have paddles as part of their safety equipment. So you really need to check your local laws when you equip your boat.

If state law requires you to keep paddles on your boat, here are your options:

- ✔ **Stowable paddles:** They're about 2 feet long and satisfy the requirements of the law, but they'd be a pretty big handicap if you ever had to use them — unless your boat is only about 8 feet long!

- ✔ **Aluminum paddles with plastic blades:** These are the best choice. They're made tough for canoeing rocky rivers, and if you throw one in the bottom of your boat and forget about it until you need it, it won't be rotten or brittle with age when you take it out.

- ✔ **Wooden paddles:** These were once the standard type of paddle, and if you keep them varnished and protected against the effects of moisture, they'll last for years. (But who wants to go to that kind of work?)

Securing and Protecting Your Boat with Mooring Lines and Fenders

You need mooring or docklines to secure your boat to a dock, and fenders are important for protecting your boat from *dock rash,* the scratches and dings that come from a boat rubbing on the dock.

Choosing the right mooring lines

Selecting the proper mooring lines (also known as *docklines*) for your boat requires a little science — and it must require a little voodoo too, because it seems like every marine retail Web site you visit offers slightly different advice on dockline length and diameter. I've seen many boats (and some docks) that have been damaged when docklines broke from being too thin and weak. The suggestions in this section are based on my experience. Weigh it against your local expert's advice . . . and voodoo.

Selecting the right line material

Mooring lines are available in nylon, polyester, or polypropylene. But in my experience, you should only invest in nylon lines.

Avoid polypropylene because it doesn't hold up well under chafing and breaks down quickly from ultraviolet (UV) sunlight. Polyester braided line is tough and has similarities to nylon. But it has very little stretch and can transfer the shock of the boat straining against the dock to the mooring points on your boat, which can result in damage to your boat.

Nylon resists UV breakdown, holds up well to chafing, and absorbs some of the shock of tugging against the dock. Here are two types to consider:

- ✔ **Three-strand braided nylon line:** This line is easy to handle because it's supple and has no memory or tendency to return to the coils you stored it in. It's the least expensive of braided nylon lines and is one of the sturdiest. To prevent it from fraying, the ends need to be *whipped* by wrapping tape or finer nylon line around them, or by melting them over a flame. This kind of line seldom comes in colors other than white.

- ✔ **Braided and cored nylon line:** Some braided line is made from eight or more strands and has a strong nylon core inside as well. These lines are more expensive, but you can buy them in colors to match your boat; some people feel that's an even trade.

Buy braided and cored nylon line in the length you need; the ends are already whipped to avoid fraying.

Selecting the right line diameter and length

All line comes in a variety of diameters. Line diameter speaks directly to its strength and, as you may already suspect, lines should be thicker for heavier boats or boats moored in rougher waters, where wave action works the boat against its lines. If constant wave action may fray your lines, you may want to choose thicker ones than I recommend. Just don't get lines so thick that they're difficult to hitch around your cleats.

As far as length goes, see Table 4-1 for my suggestions on selecting the right diameter and length of lines to go with your boat's size.

Table 4-1	Mooring Line Specs		
Boat Length	*Line Thickness*	*Line Length*	*Number of Lines*
Under 23 feet	3/8 inch	Length of boat	4 to 6
23 to 27 feet	1/2 inch	2/3 length of boat	6
28 to 45 feet	5/8 inch	2/3 length of boat	6
46 to 55 feet	7/8 inch	2/3 length of boat	6

You can make your own lines of appropriate length and diameter from a length of anchor rope by cutting lines and braiding or knotting loops. But buying lines already set up for docking doesn't cost much more and saves a lot of time — time you should be spending out on the water!

Boat hooks help you handle lines and more

While not a required safety item, a boat hook is handy around a boat. It's a long pole with a hook on the end, and you use it to loop lines over pilings or remove them when they're out of reach. A boat hook is also handy for snagging a cap that takes a dive overboard.

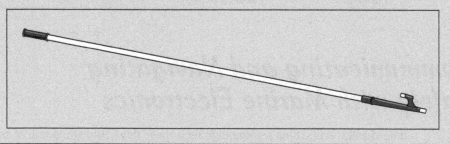

Fending off scrapes with fenders

Fenders serve as bumpers for your boat, absorbing the damage of chafing and bumps between the boat and dock or between boats moored together. Fenders are made of several materials, such as vinyl, foam, and harder plastic not as resilient as vinyl.

My favorite fenders are inflatable and made from flexible vinyl. As temperatures fluctuate, air inside them expands or contracts causing the fenders to get too stiff or too soft. So fenders with needle valves such as you'd find on a basketball let you add or release air when temperature changes make them harder or softer. Some also have little pumps built in that actually let you add air to stiffen them without a basketball pump.

Fenders made from polyethylene foam don't need air at all, but in rougher waters they tend to wear out quickly and are more apt to get embedded grit or splinters that will scratch the boat, which is what you buy them to avoid. Foam fenders usually cost less than vinyl, though, and if you use care in storing them, they work well enough.

Beyond durability, the material isn't as important as choosing the right size of fenders for your boat. Bigger fenders offer more protection than smaller ones, but storage becomes an issue. The optimum size both protects your boat and stows away in the compartments onboard.

I keep six fenders on my 25-foot boat. That's a pretty good number for boats up to 40 feet. Smaller boats can get by with two to four fenders. Table 4-2 helps you choose the right size and number of fenders to fit your boat.

Table 4-2	Fender Specs	
Boat Length	*Fender Diameter*	*Number of Fenders*
17 to 19 feet	4 inches	4
20 to 26 feet	6 to 8 inches	4 to 6
27 to 45 feet	10 to 14 inches	6

Communicating and Navigating Safely with Marine Electronics

It seems like everything's going high tech these days, and when you're considering a boat purchase, marine electronics should be part of your thought process. I get more in-depth about boating electronics and their use in Chapter 10, but this section gets you started with an understanding of what's available and how it can make for a safer, more comfortable experience on the water.

The bottom line is that marine electronics make boating safer. And lucky for you, devices are small and easy to use. For example, a navigation system that once required a bathroom-sized compartment now fits in a package the size of a paperback copy of Hemingway's *The Old Man and the Sea.* You have quite a selection of brands and models to choose from, and the applications include radar, navigation assistance, and communications.

Avoiding the bottom thanks to a depth finder

There's a saying among boaters that goes like this: "There are boaters who have run aground and those who lie and say they haven't." You'll likely run aground, too, unfortunately. I admit to having done it more than once.

Depth finders help you avoid hitting what's below the surface of the water. Also called a *sonar unit* or *bottom finder,* a depth finder helps you avoid hitting rocks and sandbars if you navigate cautiously and keep one eye on the screen. Many sonar devices are sold to anglers who use them to spot fish and the things on the bottom that fish may call home. (I discuss sonar depth finders in more detail in Chapter 10.)

If you're traveling fast in unfamiliar water, the depth finder can't report depth changes fast enough to keep you off the rocks.

If you plan to use your boat for cruising and skiing, the simplest depth finder will be very helpful. You can buy a good monochrome LCD-screen depth finder that will be useful to depths of a couple hundred feet for around $100. If you're an angler, you may want to invest in a unit that gives more detailed information. You can spend as much as $2,000 for color units with greater detail and better ability to distinguish fish.

Verifying your location with a GPS

Global Positioning Systems (GPS) have become so easy to use in cars and even on cellphones that they're a natural tool to have even on small boats. (I'm not letting you give up on a compass, though; it may be low tech, but when my GPS went out 20 miles offshore on a sunless day, my trusty compass led me home.)

For around $100, you can buy a new GPS unit that could get you around the world if you wanted to try. I suspect your aspirations in boating are less extreme, but even if you just stick to small lakes, I recommend you get one. Avoiding damage to your boat can make a GPS unit a pretty economical buy. Just think: A new propeller for your engine can cost as much as $500, but with a $500 GPS chart-plotter that includes built-in charts, you can easily avoid the rocky obstructions that could destroy your propeller. And in the event you lose a propeller and don't have a spare onboard, being able to pinpoint your exact location when you call for help can be very handy! (See Chapter 12 for details on how to deal with boating emergencies and make emergency calls.)

In treacherous waters, depth finders work hand in hand with GPS, but neither is a substitute for the other.

The cost of GPS units increases with additional features such as a larger screen, improved screen visibility in sunlight, and more detailed charts. For $100 you can get a handheld unit that tracks your course and allows you to enter waypoints, which are sort of like the addresses of spots you've visited and would like to revisit later. You record waypoints in latitude and longitude terms, and GPS units let you enter a convenient name to remember them by. Bump the ticket price to $200 to get basic mapping capability in order to avoid the rocks; some built-in units can even run several thousand dollars — and for the right guy or gal, they're worth it. See Chapter 10 for more information on GPS and other navigation tools.

Staying in touch with a VHF radio

A VHF radio is useful on big waters. It's not required by law, but I wouldn't venture offshore or into the Great Lakes without one. The U.S. Coast Guard can often determine your position in an emergency by tracking your VHF signal. You should get one of these radios for its ability to aid in rescues alone.

Handheld VHF radios are ideal for small boats. If you follow VHF radio protocol, you can even have some fun keeping in touch with fellow boaters. You can usually have a good one, including an antenna, installed on your boat for about $400. Chapter 10 has more information on selecting a VHF radio, and Chapter 12 tells you how to make emergency calls.

Choosing Safe, Fun Watersports Accessories

The right water toys can broaden your boating fun. Board sports like skiing and wakeboarding can be fun, and serious riders can go all out and enter competitions. Tubing is just like a wet roller coaster ride. This section is a rundown of the toys and their games to get you thinking about what you want to buy to ensure that everyone on your boat has a great time.

Inflating the fun with tubes

The most popular towed water toy is an inflatable tube. Originally, boaters just towed an inner tube from a tractor or truck tire. Now, an entire industry supports the fun of towable inflatables. They seldom look like tubes anymore (see Figure 4-2), but boaters still call the sport *tubing*.

These toys come in a variety of shapes and sizes and can be intended for one passenger or several. A two-passenger deck tube is most popular and sells for about $100 to $150. Tubes take no skill to ride, just the guts to hang onto the padded handles as the boat driver yanks you through S turns and crack-the-whip maneuvers. For any type of tube, you need an inflator as well. I like 12-volt pumps because you can blow up the tube in a few minutes right on the water, and then deflate it and stow it and the pump in a compartment when you're done.

For safety and a better tube ride, blow up the tube drum-tight. Soft tubes are apt to tear or puncture. You should be able to stand on a properly inflated tube without it compressing more than 1 or 2 inches.

Figure 4-2:
Inflatable
tubes come
in many
shapes and
sizes.

Photo courtesy of Ted Lund

Washing away boredom with wakeboards

Wakeboard riding evolved from snowboarding, and the riders who do it have
developed a culture all their own, much like surfers. Figure 4-3 shows a wakeboard rider suiting up.

The wakeboard is about 4 feet long and 15 inches wide with bootlike bindings that securely hold the feet. The size can vary somewhat, meaning larger
boards for larger people and smaller boards for smaller folks. You can even
get kid-sized wakeboards. When the bindings are tight enough to do their job,
it takes a special lubricant to help slip your feet in them. The later section,
"Selecting the correct tow rope to match your watersport," tells you what
kind of tow rope to buy for wakeboarding. Wakeboard riders love to jump the
wake, performing spins and flips as they go. An ideal speed for wakeboarding
is 20 to 25 mph.

If you plan to get one wakeboard for your family and guests to share, choose
one around 4 feet by 15 inches. Some boards are available with universally
adjustable bindings to fit nearly any size foot. As riders get more skilled and
more enthusiastic about the sport, they'll certainly want to get custom boards
with fitted bindings — just like snowboarders or skiers.

Cracking the whip with tubes

One of the most fun (and mildly terrifying, if you overdo it) tubing maneuvers is crack the whip. The idea is to swing the tube far outside the wake and then bounce it and its riders over waves. To do it, you turn the boat in one direction until the tube slides over your outside wake, and then turn the helm hard in the other direction to make the tube jump back across your wake and zoom way out to the side on the end of the rope. Hold the turn until you cross your wake to give the riders a really bumpy ride. Just don't go too fast: The ideal speed for tubing is about 20 miles per hour. Remember, when the boat is turning a small circle, the tube is making a large one and going much faster as a result.

Figure 4-3:
A wake-board rider properly equipped with a life jacket and board.

Photo courtesy of Tracker Marine

Getting started on two skis

A pair of skis, or *combo set,* is the most popular starting place for watersports enthusiasts. Two skis give riders more lift and can make the job of getting up out of the water easier. Few people who get up on two skis and like it ever stick to two skis for long, though; usually they want to progress quickly to one ski (whether one standard ski or a slalom ski, which I address in the next section).

Most combo skis have one ski with two foot bindings so the rider can quickly transition to skiing slalom on that one ski. Combo skis come in child, youth, and adult sizes, and it's best to match the combo to the rider. Trying to learn on skis that are too large or small is frustrating, so if you plan to entertain people of all ages on your boat, you may want to consider buying a pair in each size so that everyone can join in the fun and give skiing a try. Expect to spend $150 to $300 for a pair of combo skis, depending on the size.

The trick to getting a skier up is giving the boat just the right amount of acceleration to get the skier out of the water, and then pulling back on the throttle to settle into a speed of about 20 mph.

Slipping through the water on a slalom ski

In recent years, slalom skiing seems to have lost favor to wakeboarding, just as snow skiing has lost ground to snowboarding. But for skiers who get into it, nothing beats the feeling of gliding back and forth on glassy smooth water on a single slalom ski.

Most slalom skis are made of fiberglass and other composite materials with fixed or adjustable bindings for your feet. A *tunnel,* or large groove on the bottom, gives better control when turning or "cutting" from side to side, and a deep fin on the back adds stability in turns. You can easily spend $300 to $500 on a good slalom ski. Slalom skis are sized differently for skiers of different sizes, and a ski shop can help you choose the one best for you. For children, you can often use combo skis because one ski will have bindings for each foot. The next section tells you what kind of tow rope to buy.

It takes plenty of power to get a slalom skier up out of the water — usually full throttle acceleration for an adult. Then, quickly back off and adjust the speed to 25 to 30 mph.

Selecting the correct tow rope to match your watersport

Selecting the correct tow rope for watersports isn't hard as long as you remember that each game needs a different kind of rope.

All tow ropes have a loop on one end to attach to the boat's tow point. The *tow point* is a sturdy ring on the *transom,* or back of the boat. Some boats have towers or pylons for towing, in which case there's a knob on the top that holds the rope's loop.

Here's the breakdown of tow ropes by watersport:

- **Tubing:** You need a much thicker and sturdier rope than for other watersports. Tubing ropes are labeled for the passenger load, so buy one to match the size of tube you buy. A tube rope has a loop on one end and a nylon connector or a loop for attaching to the tube on the other.

- **Wakeboarding:** You need a rope with as little stretch as possible because stretch makes it harder to control your ride. The best wakeboard ropes are made of Spectra fibers that have virtually no stretch. They're costly, but riding without them isn't as much fun. The handle should be about 15 inches long to make it easy to switch hands, and it should be padded to help prevent blisters.

- **Water-skiing:** You need a nylon rope with a little bit of stretch in it. The stretch absorbs shock when you cut back and forth. The handle should be about 12 inches long and padded to cushion your hands and prevent blisters.

Jacketing up for safety and looking cool

Any time you mention safety to a bunch of eager kids ready to hit the water, you're apt to get groans and bored looks. But *watersports jackets* — life jackets for tubing, wakeboarding, and skiing — are anything but boring. Cool brands and hip, surf-looking styles are blended into watersports jackets that fit snugly and trim, keep you afloat if you fall, and protect your ribs from the effects of hard falls.

Competitive skiers and wakeboarders once rode without life jackets, feeling that their experience and familiarity with the water was enough to protect them in falls. But serious accidents and fatalities eventually changed that outlook, and flotation devices have become a must. Here are some tips on what to look for to protect your riders:

- **Durability is key.** Life jackets can double as watersports jackets, but they must meet a higher standard of durability to do their job for skiers. Labels on watersports jackets indicate a jacket's suitability for both regular boat safety and watersports. (Some watersports jackets are suitable only for riding.) For more on standard life jackets, refer to the earlier section, "Staying afloat with life jackets."

- **One size can fit many users.** Most watersports jackets are highly adjustable, which lets you fit the jacket snugly and safely to a rider as well as use it for other riders of similar size.

- **Comfort comes from a good fit but also from new uses of old materials.** For example, neoprene was once used mostly in diving wetsuits, but now thicker neoprene pads sewn into neoprene jackets with durable web straps and tough buckles make watersports life jackets more comfortable than standard flotation materials in regular life jackets.

Part II
Safely Operating Your Boat

The 5th Wave   By Rich Tennant

PREPARE TO LAUNCH!

YOU'RE KIDDING! I JUST HAD BREAKFAST!

In this part . . .

Piloting a boat is fairly easy to master — in fact, some
people say the hardest part of boating is getting the
boat into the water. Trailering a boat isn't nearly as much
fun as boating, but to make it even easier, in this part I
explain step-by-step tactics for getting your boat around
on dry land and launching it like a pro. I explain how to
handle your boat in open water like you've been boating
all your life, and I give easy-to-follow tips on docking a
boat without dinging it on the dock.

Chapter 5

Towing Your Boat and Maintaining Your Trailer

- -

In This Chapter

▶ Hitching up your trailer

▶ Moving your trailer forward and backward

▶ Keeping your trailer in tiptop shape

▶ Adding helpful gadgets to your boat trailer

- -

For many people considering buying a boat, the most daunting challenge may be getting comfortable with the idea of maneuvering a boat on a trailer on the highway and into the lake. Although a boat and vehicle sinking beneath the waves or crashing through the side of a garage, or an unhitched boat zipping down the wrong side of the road may make for funny videos, you don't want these things to happen to you! (However, you may want to keep a video camera handy, just in case.)

Sometimes, towing difficulties can be attributed to a bad match between boat and trailer — a problem simply solved with a different trailer. Most often, though, the explanation is merely lack of comfort with what can seem like a juggling act between hitching the boat and getting it to the water. Relax! Towing techniques are easy to pick up and will come naturally after some practice.

Understand the principles (which I share in this chapter) and practice maneuvering your trailer in the right environment, and you'll master it in no time. Then you'll want to make sure you keep your trailer roadworthy and consider purchasing some inexpensive trailer accessories to make trailering and towing even easier.

In this chapter, I lay out how to hitch, pull, and back-up your trailer safely. I also cover essential trailer maintenance and recommend some handy trailer add-ons.

Getting Properly and Safely Hitched

The first step in safe towing is getting your boat-loaded trailer properly and securely connected (or *hitched*) to your towing vehicle.

I like to keep things upbeat and optimistic, but a couple of worst-case scenarios can convince you not to skip this chapter.

- ✔ If you forget to latch the hitch but remember to hook up the chains, your hitch could come uncoupled, letting your trailer sway around behind you. As you try to stop it — which you should attempt to do quickly — it will bang against your vehicle, breaking windows, bending fenders, and ruining an otherwise perfectly good time.

- ✔ When improperly hitched, some trailers come loose and can cross into another lane at worst or roll into a ditch and flip at best. Few such incidents end well for anyone.

To get your boat hitched up right, you need to know the parts of the equipment and what to do with them. To back your vehicle up to the trailer, you need a spotter (any boating buddy can help here) to keep an eye on the hitch ball and the trailer tongue and to guide you as you back the vehicle to the trailer. Finally, you should employ a standard routine for ensuring everything is secure.

Defining the parts of the vehicle-trailer connection

To ensure a good connection between your towing vehicle and trailer, it's important to know the parts you're dealing with and how they work together. Following is a list of the parts and explanations of what they do; they're illustrated in Figure 5-1:

- ✔ **Ball (also called ball hitch):** This looks like its name and is a steel ball on the ball mount. It fits into the socket on the tongue of the trailer.

- ✔ **Ball mount:** The ball mount is the steel bar with a hole in it into which you screw the ball. On some hitches, the ball mount is permanently attached to the vehicle. On others, it slides into a socket and is held there by a thick steel pin.

- ✔ **Bow strap:** At the bow (that's the pointy end), you hook the winch strap to the bow eye and turn the crank on the winch to reel in the bow strap, thus dragging the boat into place on the trailer.

✔ **Brake cable:** This is a thin wire with an S-shaped hook at the end. For safety, it must be hooked to one of the safety chain loops on the vehicle hitch.

✔ **Eye bolts:** These bolts have a ring in the end that accepts the strap hooks. Sometimes you knot lines onto them.

✔ **Hitch locking lever:** This lever is on the tongue of the trailer near the ball socket. To lower the ball socket onto the ball, the lever must be up in the unlocked position. After the socket is fully seated on the ball, you must press the lever down into the latched position.

✔ **Locking pin:** Many trailers come with a locking pin attached to the trailer tongue by a small chain or cable. You insert this pin into a hole on the hitch-locking lever to prevent the lever from working itself to the unlatched position.

If your trailer doesn't come with a locking pin, which may be the case with a pre-owned trailer, use a small padlock to secure the connection.

✔ **Safety chain loops:** Heavy steel loops on either side of the ball mount on the vehicle receive the safety chain hooks from the trailer.

✔ **Safety chains:** These are heavy chains fastened permanently to the trailer. They have hooks on the other end that you hook to the heavy steel safety chain loops on the vehicle hitch.

✔ **Tongue jack:** The tongue jack is mounted on the tongue of the trailer and has a hand crank that, when twisted, lowers or raises the trailer tongue to allow you to hitch or unhitch the trailer.

✔ **Trailer coupler:** This is the term for the entire mechanism on the tongue of your trailer.

✔ **Trailer running light plug:** This plug may be round or flat on your trailer. You insert it into a similar socket or plug on the tow vehicle. It powers your trailer's running lights, turn signals, and brake lights.

✔ **Trailer tongue jack:** The heavier your trailer, the more likely it is to have a tongue jack near the ball socket. A crank on the jack raises and lowers it. Some jacks can be swiveled parallel with the tongue so they're fully out of the way when towing.

✔ **Transom straps:** These two heavy nylon web straps are designed to keep the trailer and the boat tightly connected during towing. They're not permanently attached to the trailer but rather are hooked to eye-bolts on the trailer and stern. You remove the straps before launching and fasten them into place after loading.

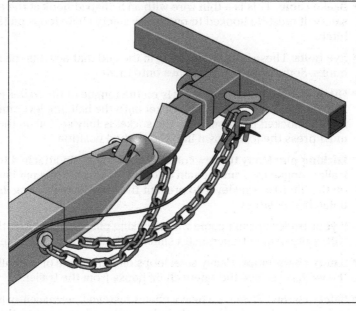

Figure 5-1:
The parts connecting the towing vehicle to the trailer.

Getting help aligning your vehicle and trailer

Never try pulling a trailer to your towing vehicle by hand, especially with the boat on it. It's safer and smarter to move the vehicle to the trailer. Although you may be able pick up some trailers by hand and pull them to the vehicle, it's a risky move because you may not be able to stop the trailer from rolling after it starts going, and it could damage your vehicle. Or you may pull a muscle lifting it.

When trying to get your vehicle in place, it helps to have a spotter to guide you while you back up to the trailer as slowly as you reasonably can (that lake or river isn't going anywhere!). Most any boating partner should be able to stand by the trailer and guide you with the following simple, intuitive hand signals:

 ✔ Moving his or her hands progressively closer together to indicate the progress of the hitch moving toward the trailer tongue

 ✔ Pointing to the right or left and spreading his or her hands apart or moving them closer together as needed to show you how much to move to the right or the left

✔ Clenching one hand into a fist to indicate immediate stopping when the ball is under the trailer tongue

If your spotter isn't experienced at hooking up the trailer, tell him or her to leave things alone and let you make the necessary connections.

The same old routine: Coupling the trailer securely to the vehicle

It pays to establish a routine (or even create a checklist) when hitching the trailer to your towing vehicle and to make it a strong habit through repetition. If you play it by ear each time and miss a step, you may see your boat and trailer pass you by on the highway. After your vehicle and trailer are aligned and in position (see the previous section), follow these steps:

1. **Lower the trailer onto the ball by lowering the trailer jack.**

2. **Raise the tongue jack as high as possible so that the jack won't hit bumps or train tracks while you're driving.**

3. **Latch the ball socket by pulling down the hitch locking lever.**

4. **Put a padlock or the locking pin (if your trailer comes with a pin) through the hole on the latch.**

   Either one will ensure that it doesn't bounce open.

5. **Hook up the safety chains.**

   They should cross over each other under the tongue and connect to the safety chain loops near the hitch.

6. **Hook up the brake cable, if your trailer has brakes.**

   This thin cable is designed to jam on the trailer brakes if the hitch coupling comes loose from the trailer.

7. **Connect the trailer light plug on the trailer to the matching plug on the vehicle.**

8. **Have your spotter watch the trailer lights as you test the brakes, turn signals, and nighttime running lights.**

9. **Before driving away, make sure your vehicle mirrors are adjusted for optimum viewing. Without moving your head from side to side, you should be able to see the lanes next to you and your trailer tires in the side-view mirrors.**

When all these steps are done, you're ready to pull the trailer down the road.

Pulling Your Trailer Safely and Efficiently

Most people don't have much trouble *pulling* a boat-loaded trailer — the trick is backing it up (which I discuss in the next section). Just the same, pulling a trailer requires planning and caution. Pulling a trailer is a riskier activity than simply driving a vehicle; here are a few of the risks and how to account for them when towing your trailer and boat:

- ✔ **Stopping a towing vehicle requires much longer distances.** In fact, it takes at least twice as much distance as usual to stop a vehicle with a trailer in tow.

- ✔ **Turning corners safely requires wide turns because the trailer follows a smaller arc than the vehicle.** Turn as widely as you safely can to avoid scrubbing tires on curbs.

  One of the leading causes of trailer tire failure is scuffing tires on curbs — usually when turning corners too closely. So watch those turns!

- ✔ **Acceleration is much slower due to the added weight.** This means you'll need to allow much more time for passing on a two-lane road (if the law and your nerves allow it) or for merging onto a highway.

Adding any weight or drag to your vehicle (and a trailer with a boat is a lot of weight and a big drag) also increases your fuel consumption. You can minimize your fuel use by following these smooth trailer-towing tips:

- ✔ **Map your route before you hit the road.** This is more important than ever when you're pulling a boat trailer. The last thing you want is to have to back out of a tight spot or travel a couple of extra cloverleaf highway interchanges to get back on track.

- ✔ **Find a comfortable, easy highway pace, and hold it.** Putting your vehicle into cruise control is feasible with lighter loads. With heavy trailer loads, you should manage acceleration yourself, letting the rig slow down some while you accelerate just a little. Cruise control wants to maintain a steady speed and will really rev the engine on a hill or even gentle incline to make it happen.

- ✔ **On dual-lane roads, stick to the right-hand lane — in fact, that's the law for towing in some states.** It's easier and less stressful to let the traffic pass you by, anyway.

✔ **If the trailer starts to wag because of wind, take your foot off the gas until it settles down.** Trailers add a significant amount of wind drag. You'll feel it when driving in a crosswind or when an 18-wheeler passes you by.

✔ **Stop frequently for fuel and to kick the tires.** Touch the wheel hubs gingerly to make sure they aren't overheating — that's a sign of bearing problems from lack of grease. Make sure all chains and straps are tight.

Bring 'Er Back: Mastering Techniques for Backing Up a Trailer

Backing up your trailer is counterintuitive. In fact, trailers just seem downright contrary when all you want to do is launch the boat. You know what to do when backing up the vehicle alone, but do the same thing with a trailer and it goes in the opposite direction you expect. So I encourage you to forget everything you ever learned about backing up and follow the strategies I talk you through in this section.

You have a couple of methods to choose from when you're backing up your trailer: You can either look over your shoulder or use the side mirrors. With both, there are some simple tricks to turning the steering wheel to make the trailer move where you want it to; here's a hint: The key is where you place your hands on the steering wheel. If you follow the tricks exactly, they'll work like a charm.

Whichever strategy you choose, have a spotter stand by to warn you if you approach an obstruction or if someone strays into your path. Also back up very slowly. In the long run, you'll get the job done faster if you go slowly. At slow backing speeds, it's easier to catch mistakes and steer to correct them. It's also a lot easier to stop quickly if you're moving slowly.

Practice backing up your trailer in an empty parking lot — maybe at the mall, but so far away from buildings that even Christmas shoppers wouldn't park there.

When you can proficiently back your boat between the lines of two parking spots, you're ready for the boat ramp. You're aiming for success here, not perfection, and the ramp is often much wider than a parking slot, so don't feel intimidated if you cross the lines slightly. In Chapter 6, I give you detailed tips for backing your boat and trailer down a ramp and into the water.

Backing up while looking over your shoulder

Most drivers look over their shoulders when backing up in a vehicle, even without a trailer and boat attached. Follow these steps to accommodate the trailer and get it where you want it:

1. Put your *left* hand on *top* of the steering wheel, and look over your *right* shoulder toward the trailer tongue.

2. As you back up slowly, move your left hand in the direction you want your *trailer* to go.

Backing up while looking in the side mirrors

Some large trailers and boats obscure your view so much that it's better to back up using the side mirrors. Follow these steps to back up your trailer using your vehicle's side mirrors as a guide:

1. Put either hand on the *bottom* of the steering wheel, and watch the trailer wheels in either side-view mirror.

2. Move your hand in the direction you want your *trailer* to go.

Keeping Your Trailer Roadworthy

Anytime something gets wet repeatedly, you can expect to run into trouble with it. It's one thing to drive your vehicle in the rain, but it's another to back your trailer into the water until you submerge the lights, wheels, and brakes. As a result, things tend to rust, corrode, leak, and break. Boats are built to resist the effects of repeated soakings, but trailers aren't. This section covers maintenance essentials to keep your trailer operating safely and extend its life.

Lighting and wiring are the first things to fail

Repeated flooding and drying will cause your trailer's lighting wires to corrode and light sockets to rust. Sometimes a hot light bulb even breaks due to a splash of cold water. This section includes suggestions for preventive maintenance and some tips on fixing lighting wires.

Before you try to work on lighting wires, it helps to know which wire goes to what! It took me a long time to realize that all trailer wiring follows a specific color code — that is, if your trailer was wired by the factory or an expert. Table 5-1 translates the different colors of wires.

Table 5-1	Trailer Wire Color Coding
Wire Color	*What It Is or Connects To*
White	Ground wire (completes the circuit for all the other connections)
Yellow	Right turn signal and brake light
Green	Left turn signal and brake light
Brown	Running lights (come on when your headlights are on)
Blue	Deactivates surge brakes (if you have them) when you put the vehicle in reverse. Because surge brakes work on pressure between the vehicle and trailer, this is an important connection when you're backing up.

Lubricating your wiring connections

To help delay the onset of wiring problems in your trailer lights, follow these steps to do some preventative lubrication on the parts shown in Figure 5-2:

1. **Locate the wire connections on the lights.**

   They're easy to spot: Look for wires leading to a screw head or wires joined with a plastic wire nut connection.

2. **Lubricate the wiring connections on the lights with spray grease.**

   Silicone spray grease does the best job of repelling water on these connections.

3. **While you're at it, you may as well remove the light bulbs and spray some lubrication into the light bulb sockets, too.**

What to do when a single light doesn't work

If a single light on your trailer doesn't operate, most of the time the problem is in the light itself. Start by doing the easy thing: Replace the light bulb.

If the light still doesn't work with a fresh bulb, the connections may be loose. You can often identify loose wiring connections by wiggling them while the lights are turned on. If the lights flicker on and off while they're being wiggled, you've spotted the problem. Secure the wiring connections by twisting the screws on the terminal to which they're attached.

If changing the light bulb and tightening wiring connections doesn't solve your single light problem, you may need to take the trailer to the shop for additional service.

Tracking down the problem when all the lights go out

If *all* the trailer lights don't work, the problem is most likely the white wire — the ground wire that connects the system to the battery (see Table 5-1 for an explanation of each color wire). Here's what you do:

1. **Find the white (ground) wire at the trailer light plug at the end of the trailer wiring harness by the trailer tongue.**

2. **Trace the wire to its connection on the trailer, and make sure it's secure and undamaged. If it's not secure, tighten it by following the instructions in the previous section.**

3. **If the wire is in good shape at its connection to the trailer, trace it from the vehicle plug to its connection with the vehicle wiring system, usually found under the bumper. Make sure it's secure and undamaged at that location. If it's not secure, tighten it by following the instructions in the previous section.**

4. **If the white wire is okay but the lights still don't work, take your trailer to the shop for diagnosis and repair.**

A test light from an automotive store is the handiest gadget to help find bad lighting wire connections. It looks like an ice pick with a clear light bulb in the handle and a black wire attached. You hook the black wire's alligator clip to the vehicle or trailer, and then poke the ice pick into the connection you want to test (see Figure 5-2). If the problem is with the turn signal, the test light will blink in rhythm with your turn signal. If the problem is with the brake light, the test light will illuminate when you press the brake.

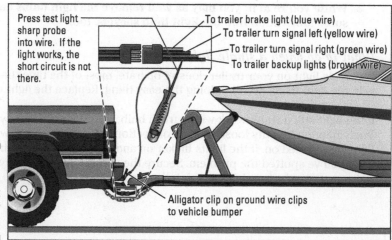

Press test light sharp probe into wire. If the light works, the short circuit is not there.

To trailer brake light (blue wire)
To trailer turn signal left (yellow wire)
To trailer turn signal right (green wire)
To trailer backup lights (brown wire)

Figure 5-2: Using a test light on trailer wiring.

Alligator clip on ground wire clips to vehicle bumper

Keeping those trailer wheels rolling

Trailer wheel bearings need grease periodically or they could start overheating and cause the wheel hub to actually fall off. And of course just like the tires on your vehicle, you need to keep a close eye on your trailer's tire pressure and tread wear.

Monitoring your wheel bearings

It's a good idea to stop periodically when you tow and quickly touch the center of the trailer wheels to make sure they aren't overheating. These center grease hubs get hot when they're low on grease. When properly greased, they may feel very warm but not too hot to touch. When checking your wheel bearings, touch them quickly at first in case they really are hot.

If one or more of your hubs feels too hot to touch without burning your hand, call for service and stay put. If you drive any farther, you'll have a breakdown.

To keep your wheel bearings maintained, stop by a service station annually and again before any long haul over 200 miles. Have the technicians inspect your wheel bearings and grease them.

If you prefer, you can do the work yourself and check the grease level in your trailer's bearings. With a $20 grease gun, you can easily grease them by following these steps (see Figure 5-3):

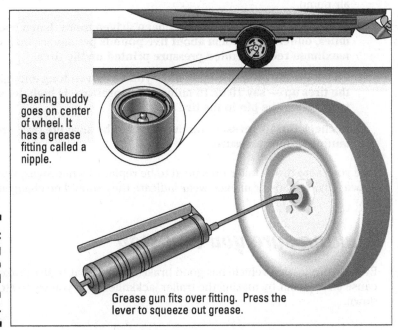

Bearing buddy goes on center of wheel. It has a grease fitting called a nipple.

Grease gun fits over fitting. Press the lever to squeeze out grease.

Figure 5-3:
Applying grease to a wheel hub with a grease gun.

1. **Find the bearing grease fitting at the center of the wheel hub.**

2. **Press your finger against the fitting and try to rock it. If it doesn't rock, it needs grease.**

3. **Snap the grease gun onto the fitting.**

4. **Squeeze grease into the fitting by pressing the grease gun lever. Be careful not to overfill it.**

   You'll actually see the grease fitting move toward you slightly as grease fills the bearing. You'll know you're done when it becomes slightly harder to squeeze the grease gun lever and you can rock the fitting.

Checking your tires

Of all the tasks in boat trailer maintenance, checking the tire pressure is the easiest and one of the most important. The loads on each trailer tire are extreme. Underinflated tires create unnecessary drag and can cause tire failure. You don't want to see your boat worth thousands of dollars destroyed on the highway because of a blown trailer tire that could be replaced for less than $100! Here's how to stay safe:

1. **Find your tires' maximum inflation pressure in the fine print around the rim of the tire.**

2. **Remove the stem cap — it's just like the one on your car tires — and press the nozzle of a tire gauge onto the tire.**

   You can either buy your own gauge or use the gauge on the gas station air pump.

3. **If the tires are cool and haven't been driven more than a couple of miles, underinflate them about five pounds per square inch below the maximum recommended pressure printed on the tires.**

4. **Check the air pressure again after you've driven long enough to warm the tires up — say 10 or 15 miles. If the pressure is high, let a little out by pressing the pin in the tire stem.**

5. **Recheck the air pressure on every trip to be sure the tires are maintaining proper pressure.**

Like your auto tires, trailer tires need to be replaced when signs of wear appear. Bald treads or uneven wear indicate they should be changed.

Making sure you can stop

Even if your towing vehicle has good brakes, failed boat trailer brakes could cause an accident by making the trailer jackknife when you try to stop or slow down.

Your trailer brakes need an annual trip to the boat dealer or mechanic, who will make sure the calipers work freely, grease the moving parts, and check the pads. Technicians also will bleed any air out of the hydraulic lines and generally just make sure everything is up to standards.

Between annual servicing, refer to your trailer maintenance guide to keep the brakes in great shape. Here are two things you should consider doing regularly:

- **Rinse salt off your brakes.** After every time you use the trailer in salt water, make sure you rinse off your brakes with fresh water — a simple garden hose works great. Nothing destroys brakes faster than letting salt water evaporate in them, corroding and eroding them.

- **Top off your brake fluid.** It's easy to check your brake fluid, and you should do so every few months to give yourself a heads up on impending brake failure. Here's how to check and top off brake fluid:

    1. **Find the black cap on the fluid reservoir near the front end of the trailer.**

    2. **Pry off the cap and look inside. The brake fluid should be near the top of the hole.**

    3. **If the level is low, add brake fluid until the reservoir is full.**

If your brake fluid reservoir seems low, you should check it before every use to insure that the fluid isn't leaking. If you find that you have to add fluid frequently, that's a good indicator that professional service is in order.

Checking all the hardware regularly

Call me crazy, but I'm guessing you want your boat trailer to stay connected to your vehicle and your boat to stay *on* the trailer. Here's some advice on checking your trailer hardware to keep your towing rig moving down the road safely (even if you do sometimes cross potholes and railroad tracks a little too roughly):

- **Make sure the bow and transom straps are strong, not frayed, and drum-tight (not sagging even a little bit).**

- **Some trailers have both a bow strap and a safety chain on the bow. Use them both, and make sure they're secure and not frayed.**

- **Inspect the eye bolts that hold the straps to make certain they're strong.**

- **Inspect nuts and bolts all over the trailer, and tighten them with a socket wrench or an adjustable wrench if needed.**

- **Step on the ball hitch periodically and bounce up and down on it to make sure all connections are tight and secure.** If you notice that it wobbles or seems loose in any way, take it to a hitch shop for inspection.

Getting Some Handy Trailer Gadgets

You can purchase several accessories to help ensure a soft landing when you return the boat to the trailer. (I discuss that whole process in Chapter 6.) These gadgets are generally not expensive and can make you look like a better boater than you actually are — kind of like oversized golf clubs do for golfers.

✔ **Guide-ons** are like goal posts on the end of your trailer (see Figure 5-4). They're made of sturdy galvanized steel and covered with PVC pipe that won't damage your boat when it rubs on them. With guide-ons installed and adjusted to the exact width of the boat, you can push the nose between them and they help you guide the boat right onto the center of the trailer.

✔ **Keel rollers** protect the hull (see Figure 5-5). You attach them to the trailer to protect the boat's keel and help guide it onto the trailer. I found some handy self-centering rollers manufactured by SeaSense (available at www.seasense.com) that feature a spiral groove to make the keel roll to the center as it passes over the rollers.

✔ **Retractable transom straps** are handy (see Figure 5-6) because they fasten to the back of the trailer and roll up when not in use. That keeps them handy and solves the security problem of where to store them.

Most of these gadgets are easy to install — each takes about 30 minutes with an adjustable wrench. And you don't have to be particularly handy; just follow the directions that come with the accessories.

You can find many of these gadgets and more at several top online retailers of marine accessories. Some of the following Web sites also provide tips and instructions for installing and using gadgets:

✔ www.basspro.com

✔ www.boatersworld.com

✔ www.cabelas.com

✔ www.campersworld.com

✔ www.marinemax.com

✔ www.overtons.com

✔ www.westmarine.com

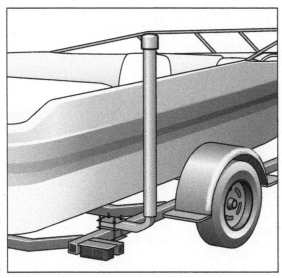

Figure 5-4:
Guide-ons.

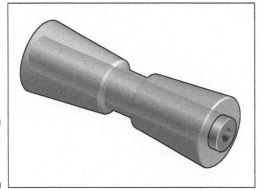

Figure 5-5:
Keel
rollers.

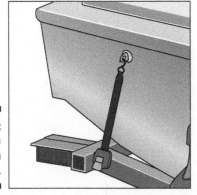

Figure 5-6:
Retractable
transom
straps.

Chapter 6

Launching and Loading Your Trailered Boat

. . . .

In This Chapter

▶ Brushing up on ramp etiquette and what to do before you hit the ramp

▶ Launching your boat with help or on your own

▶ Approaching the ramp to load up at the end of the day

▶ Loading your boat on the trailer and hitting the road

. . . .

For some boaters, the music from the movie *Jaws* plays in their heads as they approach a boat ramp. Many have ended their enchantment with boating here, and more than a few have ended marriages or friendships at the ramp as well — and that's only a slight exaggeration.

I won't lie: The work of launching a boat from a trailer into the water and then loading it back up again is stressful, and it definitely doesn't help when experienced boaters are around to watch — and sometimes critique — every move you make. However, you can greatly minimize this stress by being prepared and knowing what to expect.

In this chapter, I walk you through the entire launching and loading process. I explain preparations you need make before you ever leave the house, and then give you the tactics to properly use the ramp without getting in the way of other boaters — and without ever doing anything that gets you featured on *America's Funniest Home Videos*.

Getting your boat safely onto the ramp and into the water (and then back on the trailer later on) isn't all that hard. You just have to understand the steps and tactics and follow them to a T. Much of the process is really common sense, there's some courtesy involved, and the rest is a new skill you get to show off when you've given the process a little practice. But if you skip a step, things can go wrong. So, promise me you won't skip a step.

Being a Prepared and Polite Boater at the Ramp

When you arrive at a boat-launching ramp, often there are many other boaters at the ramp eager to get underway, too. Preparing your rig and crew for launching and finding your place in the launch ramp lineup isn't hard, but you also need to be aware of some unwritten rules that, well, I've written down in this section. When followed, these rules for preparation and politeness will draw goodwill and helpful assistance from other boaters when you need it.

A smooth launching experience comes from planning and preparation, and a major part of that preparation is practicing backing up your trailer, which I explain in Chapter 5.

Get it together at home

You can (and should) prepare for your launch even before you leave home. Being organized for the launch ramp takes some forethought about what you'll need in the boat and what you'll want your crew to do. Here are a few basic tips to keep in mind:

- ✔ **Well before you leave for the ramp (preferably the day before), chat with your crew about the departure time and the return time.** This information will help them determine what personal gear they'll need. Remind them to collect things like sunscreen, towels, and a dry change of clothes in a bag before you meet.

- ✔ **Pack your cooler of drinks and snacks at home, and load it onto the boat in the driveway, while there's no pressure to move out of the way — like there is on the boat ramp.** In Chapter 17 I give you some tips for packing a cooler for your crew.

  If you don't have a cover on your boat, be sure to secure the cooler and anything in the boat that could blow away while you're high-tailing it down the highway.

- ✔ **Decide in advance who will back the boat down the ramp and into the water and who will manage the boat while the driver parks the vehicle and trailer.** Ideally, you'll have a skipper who can back the boat off the trailer while you handle the vehicle and trailer, or you can captain the boat while someone else drives the vehicle. But if there's no one to take the helm while you park, you can appoint someone to fasten a rope to the boat and hold onto it so the boat doesn't float away while you park the vehicle.

Don't be a ramp hog

One goal or benefit of preparation is minimizing the number of tasks you need to perform at the ramp before launching the boat, so you can maximize your fun. Another is to help you be quick about it so you don't inconvenience the other boaters who are also trying to begin their boating quests. Inconsiderate people do things, such as pouring ice in the cooler or loading the tube or skis into the ski locker, on the ramp that they could have accomplished at home or in the boat-staging area that's usually located near the ramp.

Follow these simple steps to launch without breaching the etiquette of the boat ramp:

1. **Direct your crew where to wait for boarding.**

2. **Back the boat into the water.**

3. **Unleash the boat so your skipper or line-holder can take it from there. Most ramps have a courtesy dock to which your helper should secure the boat.**

4. **Park your vehicle.**

5. **Rejoin your crew, load everyone in the boat, and take off.**

Staging for Launch

Imagine you're just about to loosen the bow strap that holds your boat to the trailer winch so that you can launch, when you realize you left the bilge plug out and your boat is filling with water. That mistake is frustrating for everybody, but for you it's both embarrassing and time-consuming, especially if you have to leave your place on the ramp, find the plug, and take a new place at the back of the line.

You can avoid scenarios like this one by following a preparation routine in the staging area near the ramp. Most ramps have a staging area where boaters temporarily park with their trailered boats to make final preparations for launch. This is where you do the things you couldn't do at home, like load beach towels or other items that may have blown out on the road if you'd loaded them earlier. It's also where you do things you shouldn't do until you're ready to float the boat, like put in the bilge plug. You may want to jot down the following steps as a checklist and keep it handy when heading out for some time on the water.

Whenever you approach a new boat-launching area for the first time, it pays to take a look around before you dive right in. Park your rig out of the way and walk over to the ramp. Watch how the other boaters take their place in line or pull up to the staging area and prep their boats. After you have the full picture and a feel for the local customs, ease into the process, beginning at the staging area with the following steps:

1. Put the bilge plug in!

Very few boaters can claim that they haven't forgotten this at least once in their boating careers. If you forget to put in the bilge plug, your first sign of a problem will be a jet of water streaming from the bilge pump outlet on the side of your boat as you back your trailer down the ramp. You either have to load the leaking boat back onto the trailer to drain it and plug it, or swim to the back of the boat to install the plug and let the bilge pump remove the water.

I've heard of a number of unique ways to remember to install the bilge plug. Some boaters keep the plug with the boat keys, and others tape the plug to the winch handle so they automatically spot it as they prepare to launch. You may want to try these or come up with a trick of your own.

2. Disconnect and remove the transom straps, and lock them in your tow vehicle. (You'll find a full discussion of straps in Chapter 5.)

Launching lore is full of funny but probably phony stories of green boaters who called mechanics and complained they couldn't get their boats up to speed. The mechanics' cursory examinations revealed the boaters had left the trailers attached to the boats and disconnected the trailers from the vehicles. The staging area is the only safe place to remove these straps. Your first sign of forgetting this step is that the boat doesn't float off the trailer when you release the bow strap.

3. Loosen the bow winch (see Figure 6-1) just enough so that the strap has a few inches of slack.

Forgetting this step usually isn't the end of the world, but sometimes the boat is held so tightly to the front of the trailer that it becomes difficult to loosen the bow winch after you back the boat into the water.

The bow winch is the device on your trailer with a hand crank and a spool of nylon strapping. The strap hooks to the boat, and when you turn the crank, it pulls the boat snug onto the trailer. A small lever on or near the strap spool reverses the cranking direction so you can let the strapping out to launch.

4. Attach fenders and docklines.

If the boat-launching ramp has more than one courtesy dock and you're not sure which one you'll use, it's best to keep your options open by putting at least two fenders on each side of the boat (I discuss fenders in

Chapter 4). Courtesy docks are often located at ramps to provide tempo- rary mooring while parking the trailer. They ease loading and unloading passengers.

Attach a line to the bow cleat and one to each cleat near the transom at the back of the boat, too. With those in place, you won't have to scramble to put them in place later, and you can safely moor the boat to the courtesy dock while you park the vehicle and trailer. (Find out more about mooring lines in Chapter 4.)

5. Load any last-minute gear.

This gear may include the beach towels, the chart, or everyone's per- sonal gear bags. Stow everything safely, and have the crew wait by the courtesy dock near the ramp or somewhere else safe and handy while the boat is launched.

6. Turn on the battery switch, if you have one.

Figure 6-1:
A bow winch crank to unwind (when launching) or wind (when loading).

7. Double-check the battery charge level by turning on the key just long enough to hear the engine fire, and then quickly turn it off.

Don't let the engine run more than a second or two out of the water; doing so could damage the engine's water pump impeller and eventually the engine if it runs long enough to overheat.

- **If your boat is an outboard,** tilt the engine up and disengage the engine trailering support bracket by swinging it toward the boat. The bracket should be right near the pivot point on which your engine tilts, and disengaging it allows you or your skipper to easily trim the motor down into the water when your boat is on the ramp.

- **If your boat is a sterndrive,** the drive mechanism won't have a supporting bracket. The trim mechanism holds it up in the traile-ring position. Be certain to tilt it up in the staging area so you don't damage it on the ramp.

After you follow these steps, you're ready to get in line to launch your boat. If you haven't already, it pays to take a good look around to get a feel for how things flow and how the lines form. It's also a good time to have everyone visit the restroom facilities, if some are available at the ramp.

On the downward slope of the ramp, many boaters use *wheel chocks,* which are simply blocks of wood they put behind their vehicle tires to prevent it from rolling backwards should the brakes fail. If you have wheel chocks to use when launching, get them out and ready to go while you're in the staging area. I have a pair tied together with a rope; I put one under the left wheel, stretch the rope over the bumper hitch and put the other under the right wheel. When I drive away after launching, the chocks drag harmlessly under the center of the trailer until I get to flat ground and stow them.

You may be tempted to let your crew climb into the boat while it's still in the staging area, but don't load your crew until *after* you launch. No matter how convenient it may seem, it's just not safe to put everyone in the boat before the boat is safely away from the trailer and in the water. There's still a small danger of the boat coming disconnected from the trailer or the trailer coming disconnected from the vehicle. And you may be surprised to hear that more than one flustered boater has backed the entire truck and trailer fully under-water by confusing reverse and forward or forgetting to set the vehicle's emer-gency brake.

Sizing Up the Boat Ramp to Tailor Your Technique

I wish I could tell you that I back my trailer to the perfect depth every time I launch or load up my boat on the trailer. If I were to use the same ramp every time, maybe I could do that. But one weekend I'll use a steep ramp at a favor-ite fishing hole, another weekend I'll use a shallow ramp at my favorite lake, and still another I'll find myself at a ramp on a river with a 5-mile per hour current sweeping past. Each one takes a different approach and presents different challenges. In truth, you have to go through some trial and error to find the sweet spot for launching or loading your boat, and it may vary from place to place.

In this section, I give you some tips to minimize your learning curve and make backing your trailer down a ramp for launching or loading an easy challenge to conquer.

No matter what kind of ramp you're using, the trailer driver should always follow these steps after the trailer is backed into the water:

1. **If the vehicle has an automatic transmission, put it in Park. If it's a manual, put it in Reverse.**

2. **Turn off the vehicle.**

3. **Set the emergency brake.**

4. **Put chocks behind the rear wheels as insurance in case the emergency brake fails or the vehicle pops out of gear. If your rear wheels are in the water, as is sometimes the case, put chocks under the front wheels as an alternative.**

5. **Double-check everything!**

6. **If you're launching alone, park quickly and trot back to the boat. If you're loading alone, get back to your boat as soon as you can after the vehicle is secure on the ramp.**

Mastering a shallow ramp

The easiest ramps are the shallow ones with a gentle slope. They make it easy to launch and load the boat from and to the trailer. A shallow ramp that's just right is a treat. You know you've got a beauty if, when the rear bumper of your vehicle is stopped at the waterline, the tops of the trailer tires are just about even with the surface of the water. However, sometimes a shallow ramp can be *too* shallow.

When launching and loading on a shallow ramp that's at the proper shallow depth, the trailer bunks or rollers on which your boat rests should be mostly underwater, which makes it easy for the boat to slide off the trailer, or in the case of loading, to nudge the bow of your boat right up on the trailer. When the ramp's too shallow, you need to back your vehicle's back wheels into the water to get the trailer bunks and wheels underwater. Getting your vehicle's wheels wet isn't a problem, but traction may be an issue; if you get a chance, watch others pull out their boats on such a ramp to see if they have trouble getting traction. Usually a shallow ramp poses no such risk, but anytime you get your vehicle's wheels in the water, they can sometimes slip on marine growth on the ramp. (For details on what to do in this case, see the section, "Getting Up a Slippery Ramp," later in this chapter.)

Meeting the challenge of a deep ramp

Deep ramps are usually a welcome sight to boaters because the depth often allows you to get your boat fully into the water without wetting your vehicle's rear wheels — something I try to avoid when I can. Deep ramps also minimize the risk of striking the bottom with the prop as you push the boat up on the trailer or back it off.

For the purposes of launching or loading your boat onto the trailer, a deep and steep ramp is great as long as it isn't so steep that your vehicle struggles to pull itself and the boat up the incline to level ground. Your first concern at a ramp like this isn't getting the trailer wet enough for an easy load but rather getting the loaded trailer and vehicle to go up the ramp. I talk about that in the section, "Getting Up a Slippery Ramp," later in this chapter.

Immersing your trailer to a workable depth on a steep ramp is pretty easy. Back it in until just the tops of the trailer wheels are out of the water. This puts the bunks or rollers under the water at a steeper loading angle that requires the boat to take a pretty gingerly approach to the trailer, because your boat's stem — the peak of the bow — will nose into the bunks instead of having more of the bottom engage the bunks. (I discuss how a boat approaches the ramp and trailer in more detail later in this chapter in the section, "Approaching the trailer.") When launching, take care to keep the bow strap attached to the bow eye. If you don't the boat could slide off the trailer onto the concrete before it reaches the water.

Combating a crosscurrent on the ramp

A ramp with a crosscurrent is the toughest of all ramps to negotiate, mainly when loading your boat. Launching isn't impacted much because the boat stays firm on the trailer until you take it off and away from the trailer. In loading, though, the current makes landing the boat like an aircraft carrier landing — almost like aiming at a moving target. A strong crosswind with no current can offer a similar challenge.

Aim the trailer with the current at as sharp an angle as the ramp and the depth of the water allow. Scan the water for obstacles, because the angle of the trailer requires the boat to come in at an angle when launching, and you don't want that path to cross rocks or stumps if you can avoid it. When the trailer driver aims the trailer downstream, the boat handler can approach the trailer by driving the boat more directly into the current, giving him or her more control of the boat than with a following current or a perpendicular crosscurrent.

Stop backing the trailer down the ramp when it's a little shallower than you would be on ramps with no current. By leaving the trailer bunks a little higher, they engage the boat sooner, giving added control when the boat handler nudges the boat into them. If you find the trailer is too shallow to finish loading, you can quickly back in a couple of more feet while the boat handler holds the boat in the trailer with a little throttle.

Launching Your Boat with a Crew

Chances are you didn't buy your boat to boat alone, so you'll have friends or family with you when facing the tasks of launching from and loading onto a trailer. It's the social nature of boating that actually makes it fun, and you can enhance that by engaging your crew in the tasks of boating — starting with launching the boat. But engaging them safely and without seeming to be a Captain Bligh may make this the trickiest part of launching — even more than skillfully backing the trailer into the water.

Loading safely and engaging the crew is mostly about good communication and teamwork in executing the tasks I outline for you in this section. I lay down some guidelines with the assumption that you have at least one other boater who can help you by handling the boat as it's launched.

You may be boating with guests or family, all with varying degrees of familiarity with the launching process. In short, you have three categories of crew: a person who handles the boat, a person who handles the vehicle and trailer, and guests or children who wait while the boat is launched. I assume you'll fall into one of the first two categories, especially after reading this book.

The boat handler

Whether it's you or a skipper you appoint, this person is responsible for getting the boat safely off the ramp and into the water — or if he or she isn't comfortable driving the boat, holding a rope attached to the boat so that it doesn't float away while you park the vehicle and trailer.

Here's how to proceed with a boat handler who can drive the boat:

1. **Before you get started, the boat handler and the vehicle driver need to agree in advance when the boat handler will start the boat engine.**

   The best time is usually just before the driver disconnects the bow strap, releasing the boat from the trailer.

2. **The boat handler boards the boat only as it's about to be backed into the water. The vehicle driver stops at the water's edge and lets the boat handler climb in.**

3. **The boat handler guides the driver, signaling him or her when the boat is in the water far enough to submerge the propeller.**

4. **The boat handler tilts the propeller down far enough to get it fully into the water.**

   In addition to enabling the propeller to make the boat move, this task also ensures that cool water flows through the propeller drive shaft housing, so the water pump impeller doesn't burn up.

5. **The handler starts the boat engine and signals the driver when it's running smoothly.**

   At this point, the driver is standing at the bow winch, ready to release the boat. This signal is important because the driver may not be able to hear the boat's motor, especially if the vehicle's engine is idling.

6. **The boat handler waits for the driver's signal that it's safe to put the engine in reverse and back the boat off the trailer.**

   The driver gives this signal after disconnecting the bow strap.

7. **If it takes much more than idle speed propeller force in reverse to move the boat off the trailer, the boat handler should hold the idle speed steady while the driver backs the trailer down a little farther to let the boat float off.**

8. **The boat handler loads the crew, not forgetting the driver, who may have had to park waaaaaayyyy back in the lot.**

If you need to drive the vehicle and you don't have a skipper who can actually drive the boat, here's how one of your passengers can help launch the boat by serving as a makeshift boat handler:

1. **Attach a long line to one of the bow or front cleats on the boat.**

2. **Give the rope to the stand-in handler to hold tightly onshore as you back the trailer into the water.**

3. **Stop the vehicle, and disconnect the bow strap to float the boat free.**

   Be sure the stand-in handler is stout enough to arrest the boat's drift while standing on the shore. You don't want him or her accidentally pulled into the water by the boat's momentum!

4. **The handler uses the rope to control the boat while you park the vehicle and trailer.**

The vehicle driver

Whether it's you or someone else, the vehicle driver has the most difficult job in the launch process until the boat is fully in the water. Nothing in boating is more eventful than backing the trailer down the ramp (I discuss backing-up techniques in Chapter 5). Here's how the driver's job should stack up:

1. **The driver and boat handler decide on a pickup point so the driver can meet the boat after parking the trailer.**

2. **While the passengers wait safely on the sidelines, the driver should have the boat handler ride in the vehicle as they approach the ramp.**

3. **The driver lines up the rig in the launch lane and backs down the ramp until the boat is about to enter the water.**

4. **The driver stops and lets the boat handler climb into the boat (or, if the boat handler isn't going to drive the boat, the driver ties a rope onto it for the handler to hold while onshore).**

5. **The driver checks that the boat handler is settled behind the boat's wheel and backs the boat farther into the water until the trailer wheels are nearly covered by water, as seen using the side rearview mirrors.**

   Nearly submerging the trailer wheels is usually the best depth for unloading the boat, but some ramps have different angles and often require the wheels to be deeper or shallower. Figure 6-2 shows the most common proper trailer depth.

Figure 6-2: Usually the best trailer depth for launching or loading is when the wheels are nearly covered by water.

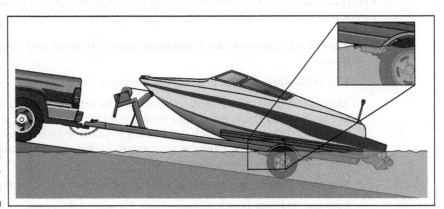

6. **The driver stops the vehicle, puts it in Park, and sets the emergency brake as firmly as possible.**

   To prevent a mishap, the driver should double-check these settings before leaving the driver's seat.

7. **The driver puts wheel chocks behind the vehicle wheel(s) (if chocks are being used).**

8. **The driver signals the boat handler that everything's ready for launch, and the boat handler signals back when the boat's engine is running.**

9. **The driver disconnects the boat from the trailer by unhooking the bow strap.**

10. **If the boat doesn't come off the trailer easily, the driver removes the chocks and backs a little farther down the ramp until the boat floats free.**

11. **The driver parks the vehicle and trailer, checks for any items left in the vehicle that may be needed on the boat, locks the vehicle, and then boards the boat at the predetermined meeting spot.**

Guests and kids who board after launch

Those in your crew who don't have an active role in launching still need to know where to wait and what to do while the process is taking place. Coach them along the following steps to board from a courtesy dock, and do it with your best manners on display. Launching is often stressful for everyone, and what you think may be gentle suggestions can come across as grumpy commands.

1. **The crew gathers up any last-minute personal items and hangs onto them.**

2. **The crew waits for the boat on the courtesy dock.**

   Although it may seem handy to have crew members help moor the boat at the courtesy dock, make sure they know that docking will go more smoothly if they don't reach out and try to push or pull the boat as it approaches the dock. Doing so may result in their injury or make the boat land harder than it would have without their help.

3. **The crew boards the boat only after it's secured to the courtesy dock.**

   Ever watch those boating bloopers on TV where everyone falls into the water? Nearly all those boats weren't secured to the dock while the crew boarded.

The launching process is the same even if there's no courtesy dock — it just isn't as convenient to handle the boat while parking or loading passengers. Here are a few suggestions to handle this occasional situation:

✔ If you can, move and secure the boat away from the launching ramp before you park your vehicle.

✔ Beach the boat if the nearby shoreline isn't too rocky. Sandy shores and even fine pea gravel or grassy shores are usually safe for beaching a boat. To beach the boat, trim up the engine as far as possible while keeping the prop in the water, and nudge the boat onto the beach with little "bumps" of the gearshift in and out of forward gear.

✔ Hold the boat off the shore if it's so rocky that beaching could damage your boat.

✔ If you suspect you'll be launching at a ramp without a courtesy dock and you know the spot has a rocky, unbeachable beach, let your crew know that they should be prepared to wade into the water in order to board the boat.

Launching Your Boat Alone

Sometimes boaters go it alone. Fishermen in particular tend to head out alone and often find themselves having to fill the roles of driver and boat handler. Getting past the hurdle of launching alone isn't hard if you plan your approach after scanning the ramp area to see what you have to work with.

Swimmer's solo launch

On a calm summer morning, I watched a guy prep his boat for launching. I was ready to offer my assistance, but he charged down to the ramp, circled his rig, and backed in smartly, plunging the boat in the water. It left the trailer with such momentum that it drifted out 50 yards while the boater parked his rig. Moments later, he raced down the ramp, executed a flat racer's dive, and swam to the boat in seconds.

This guy had the stamina and training for the swim, but many boaters think they can swim to a drifting boat and find it's farther away than they thought. Every year, boaters drown when they underestimate the swimming distance to their boats. Or they may undertake the swim and then find that the boat moves in the force of current or wind, carrying it farther out of reach and the swimmer farther from the safety of shore.

Follow these steps to launch your boat alone:

1. **Prep your boat in the staging area just like you would with a crew, as I describe earlier in this chapter. Install the bilge plug, remove the transom straps, tilt your propeller up to avoid dinging it on the ramp, and load any final gear into the boat.**

2. **Put fenders on both sides of your boat near the front and back to protect the boat from the dock.**

3. **Select a rope from your gear that's long enough to reach from the bow of your boat to the courtesy dock after you back the boat down the ramp but *before* you take it off the trailer. Fasten this rope, the bowline, to a deck cleat on the front or bow on the side nearest the courtesy dock.**

4. **Tie the other end of the bowline to your trailer winch, hitch, or some other convenient fastening point. Leave the coiled end in the boat. It will pay out as the boat drifts off the trailer.**

5. **Back your boat carefully down the ramp, keeping it near enough to the courtesy dock to reach it with the rope you just fastened on the bow.**

6. **Stop backing in before you wouldn't be able to reach the rope without getting your feet wet.**

7. **Put the vehicle in Park, set the emergency brake, untie the end of the bowline on the vehicle or trailer, and walk onto the courtesy dock. Attach the bowline to a dock cleat past the transom or back of the boat.**

8. **Return to the boat and trailer, and unhook the bow strap.**

9. **Get behind the wheel of the vehicle and back the boat farther into the water quickly enough to cause it to drift back until the bowline becomes taught and stops its drift.**

10. **Carefully snug your boat to the courtesy dock using the procedure I discuss in Chapter 8.**

11. **Park your vehicle and trailer, and return to your boat.**

If there's no courtesy dock and you're launching alone, you have two options:

- Beach the boat on a sandy or grassy shore by trimming up the engine as far as possible while keeping the prop in the water, and nudge the boat onto the beach with little "bumps" of the gearshift in and out of forward gear.

- Use your anchor line for the bowline, and set the anchor on the shore to let the boat drift back on the line until you return from parking. Then haul it in toward the shore and climb in.

Anchors aweigh

One morning at a photo shoot, long before the coffee kicked in, I watched a lone angler back down the ramp. He did it quickly and efficiently before my sluggish reflexes prompted me to offer assistance. He backed the boat in, put his vehicle in Park, and set the emergency brake. He disconnected the bow strap and then pulled an anchor from the bow and tossed it aside, leaving the rope coiled on the boat, tied to a cleat. He jumped back in the vehicle, backed the boat in sharply, giving it some backward inertia, and as it floated free he charged off to the parking lot. The boat drifted to the end of the anchor rope and stopped, waiting for his return. He reeled in the boat, climbed aboard, and went fishin'.

It wasn't a bad launching strategy and it had probably worked many times, but the boat could have had a little too much inertia and dragged the anchor down the ramp, forcing the angler to wade in to retrieve it.

Either way, you should come to the water prepared to wade, either barefoot or with water shoes or rubber boots if the water is cold.

Time to Go Home: Getting Your Turn in the Loading Line

After you've had a ball on the water all day, you're apt to feel like loading your boat back onto the trailer is no big deal. You'd be mostly right. Loading your boat is *different* from launching it but definitely not *harder*. On the other hand, you're probably a little fatigued by the wind and the sun and the fun. All that has taken a toll on your body and brain, making you a little sluggish and maybe a little irritable. When it comes to loading up at the end of the day, one of the most difficult things to master may not be the mechanics of backing your trailer into the water or loading your boat and hitting the road. Instead, it may be coordinating with the other boaters to courteously find your spot in the apparent chaos of the ramp line.

On weekends, unless you've found a hidden jewel of a ramp, there will be some traffic waiting to load up when you're ready to load your boat. Your goal is to find your place in the line, wait your turn, and get your boat out of the water as quickly as possible so the next guy can get his or hers out. Doing this safely without irritating the other boaters requires communication and astute observation. In this section, I tell you how to read the ramp so you know when it's your turn and how to approach things when it is.

Juggling act

Somebody suggested a lone angler tie a long rope to the front of the boat and stretch it forward to the driver's seat of the tow vehicle. Unhooking the bow strap was the next step. Then, holding the rope in one hand, the suggestion was that the boater back down the ramp until the boat floated free and he wrangled it while trying to put the vehicle in Park and set the emergency brake.

I can't recall seeing this solo-launching method in action, but for most people, backing a trailer is like patting your head and rubbing your tummy. Adding one more management problem to the mix seems impractical to me. What does work, though, is tying the long rope to the trailer and letting it uncoil as the boat drifts away. You have time to set the brake, put the transmission in Park, pull the boat to the beach or courtesy dock, secure it, and then park your vehicle.

Whenever boaters are waiting at a busy ramp, stay focused and be as quick about tasks as you can be. If you're stopping to rummage around for the keys you should have already had in hand, wash the sunscreen off your face, or dig the last soda out of the bottom of the cooler, you're discourteously holding up other boaters.

Figuring out what's going on around the loading line

As the boat handler — whether that's you or a crew member — guides the boat toward the ramp, you're likely to see boats idling around it, boats tied to the courtesy dock (if the ramp has one), vehicles with trailers queued up to back into the water and grab their boats, and some trailers already in the water with boats in the process of loading. You probably don't see much order to all this as you approach the ramp, and in fact, there are probably a few other boaters who don't see much order to it either. What's going on? Well, it's a bit of a mess and somewhat of a guess, but I'll try my best to explain:

- ✔ **Idling boaters:** Boaters circling their boats outside the ramp area are probably either waiting for a spot at the courtesy dock (if the ramp has one) or, having already dropped off passengers at the courtesy dock, are now waiting for their trailer drivers to get the trailers. When such a boater sees his or her trailer coming, expect him or her to make a beeline to the ramp. Stay out of the way; it's his or her turn.

✔ **Boats at the courtesy dock:** If your ramp has a courtesy dock, you're likely to see some boats there unloading passengers. Unoccupied boats tied to the courtesy docks should be left there only while a boater who doesn't have a partner to drive the trailer retrieves the trailer to load up. If a boat's occupants are onshore playing softball or volleyball while their boat takes up space at the courtesy dock and perhaps even blocks the ramp, they could — and should — get a ticket.

✔ **Boats loading up at the ramp:** Whether acting alone or with help from a partner, getting a boat onto the trailer and out of the water takes some maneuvering. As soon as one trailer is pulled out of the water and driven safely away, the next vehicle in the trailer line backs into its spot.

✔ **Boats in the staging area:** When a boat is secured to its trailer, the driver quickly whisks it away to the staging area away from the hustle and bustle of the ramp. As I explain in the section, "Staging for Launch," earlier in this chapter, the staging area is specifically designated for readying your boat to launch or for making final preparations to tow it on the highway. Activities done there include making sure the boat is secured to its trailer, rinsing down the boat if water is handy, and stowing loose gear so it doesn't blow away on the road.

Offloading passengers and getting into position

After the boat handler understands what's going on around the ramp, it's time to make a move. Handling this situation is an exercise in finesse, good manners, and mind-reading because there's no one directing traffic. Here's how you can seize the moment as the boat handler without forgetting your manners:

1. **Pull up to the courtesy dock and secure the boat to it, or beach the boat if there's no courtesy dock. If the shore is rocky, you may want to have someone hold the boat afloat in shallow water to avoid chipping the bottom on the rocks.**

   When a space at the courtesy dock opens and no boater in the area before you goes for it, you can ease that way. If you have to squeeze past another boat, make sure it's waiting for a trailer and not a place at the courtesy dock. Ask if the other boaters mind if you offload passengers and a driver. If they indicate that they too are waiting for the courtesy dock, back out and signal them ahead.

   Before you approach the courtesy dock, put out fenders on the side of the boat you intend to dock on to keep your boat from being scratched up, and tie at least two lines on your cleats for securing the boat to the dock. For further instructions on docking, turn to Chapter 8.

If there's no courtesy dock, wait your turn to gently beach the boat near the ramp. When you beach the boat, pick an area with the softest bottom; chunky rock bottoms will damage your boat. If it's a rocky bottom, you may want to have someone step in the water to hold the boat off the bottom. Do this only after the boat engine has been turned off, and trim your propeller up as much as you can without lifting it out of the water.

If you're going solo: If you're handling the boat and trailer alone, tie your boat to the dock as far away from the ramp as possible so other boaters can get through to the ramp while you retrieve the trailer. Remember, there are probably boats milling around waiting for their trailers to come to the water. If you block the ramp while you retrieve your own trailer, you may as well have cut in line. In some smaller ramp areas, blocking the ramp may be inevitable, so give the trailers in line a chance to load up before you dock in the loading lane.

 2. **Secure the crew.**

When the boat is safely docked or beached, the crew and trailer driver get off the boat. Have the crew settle down somewhere safely nearby to wait until the boat is on the trailer, and make sure someone's supervising any kids in the group.

 3. **Release the boat from the dock and take it back out.**

After passengers are offloaded, you take the boat back out into the water to await the trailer.

 4. **The driver retrieves the trailer.**

If the trailer driver takes anyone else with him or her up to the trailer, that's fine. But when the driver's turn at the ramp comes up, passengers should get out of the car and step to a safer place onshore until the loading is done.

 5. **The driver gets in line for the ramp.**

The driver drives the vehicle and trailer to the end of the line of vehicles waiting for their turn at the ramp. Meanwhile, the boat handler is idling the boat out in the water, waiting for the trailer.

If you're going solo: If blocking the ramp was inevitable when you docked at the courtesy dock in order to retrieve your trailer, the other boaters probably want you to skip ahead and load your boat. It doesn't hurt to communicate with the first couple of drivers in the lineup and get their go-ahead.

When the trailer driver's turn comes, the next step is backing the trailer down the ramp so you can load the boat. Backing the trailer down to load the boat is basically the same as backing it in to launch the boat, which I cover earlier in this chapter.

Loading Your Boat on the Trailer

It seems like there are more horror stories about boat loading gone crazy than boat launching gone crazy. Learning to apply just the right amount of throttle to ease the boat onto the trailer comes with a lot of room for error. In this section, I give the boat handler some tips on approaching the trailer, handling current and wind, and managing engine speed for a perfect landing. To make things easier, I assume the boat handler is you.

Approaching the trailer

In a perfect world, your trailer is submerged on a ramp that lets the boat coast onto the trailer bunks with no throttle, perfectly aligned with the center of the trailer and with nothing to push you off your course. The front of your boat meets the trailer's bow roller and winch with a gentle kiss.

Sounds too good to be true, and sometimes it is. But landing perfectly isn't as important as landing safely without damaging your boat. The following sections have some pointers to make your landings safe and snug and, more often than not, perfect as well.

Sizing up the wind and water conditions

To land your boat perfectly on the trailer, you need to know what you're up against with regard to the conditions of wind, water, and current. Accurately assessing them is crucial to managing them with throttle and steering adjustments. Here's what to watch for:

- ✔ **Drift:** Approach the trailer from a distance at an idle speed, and stop one or two boat lengths away from the trailer. Note how quickly or slowly the wind or current causes the boat to drift off the path that would center it on the trailer.

- ✔ **Current:** Look for swirling water on one side or the other of the trailer. This is a sign that current is moving past it, and you have to adjust your course upstream to compensate for it.

- ✔ **Chop:** If the ramp you're using is tucked in a quiet cove, you don't have to worry about chop. If the ramp is out in the open, exposed to boat traffic and wakes, you have to take chop into consideration when loading. If wakes from other boats meet your trailer at the same time your boat does, you're in for a bumpy landing. Let passing boats pass and wait for their wakes to dissipate before you aim for the trailer.

Determining the right speed

The right boat speed is critical when approaching your trailer to load up. Misjudging the speed of the approach and using too much or too little throttle is the key cause of bumpy landings. Here are your three options, Goldilocks:

- **Coming in too hot (quickly):** Driving your boat to the trailer with too much speed causes the boat to bounce around in the trailer bunks, which can sometimes damage the boat and even the trailer. Almost as bad, landing too quickly looks pretty embarrassing. It's better to approach too slowly than too quickly.

- **Coming in too cold (slowly):** Bringing your boat in without enough speed lets wind drift or current take over for you, and these two forces aren't usually on your team. They work to push the boat out of alignment with the trailer. However, coming in too slowly is absolutely easier to correct — and less likely to damage your boat — than coming in too quickly. You can always pop it in Reverse and back out again for another try. Pulling a mulligan — you golfers will know what I mean — is sometimes all you need to learn to adjust your speed for the conditions you face on any loading attempt.

- **Coming in just right:** The ideal loading speed is, unfortunately, a matter of trial and error. Coming onto the trailer even at idle is usually about 4 or 5 miles per hour, and that's too fast. You want to make only enough headway to steer the boat, which means you're shifting from Neutral to Forward and back to keep the speed just high enough to steer the boat.

If two people are working together to load the boat, as the boat approaches the trailer, the trailer driver can help the boat driver manage speed and direction by using a thumbs up or down and gestures right or left for more or less speed and course corrections. The driver can stand on the ramp with his or her hands overhead so the boat handler can see the signals.

Overcoming steering challenges

Steering the boat at the low speed required for loading presents some new challenges, and meeting them requires the experience that comes with time. Two common steering challenges are

- **Wandering course:** At slow speeds, your boat probably wanders to the left and right of your steered course, but over a distance it probably stays roughly on course (I talk more about wandering in Chapter 7). If the effect of wandering is great enough to risk missing the center of the trailer, you may need to correct for it by steering against the oscillations. It takes timing and a little intuition, but as you get to know your boat, you'll be able to anticipate it wandering to the left and steer to the right (and vice versa) before it happens.

✔ **Overcorrecting:** As a new boater, you aren't alone in expecting your boat to react to the steering wheel like your car does. When you see or feel the boat veer slightly off course, you want to correct, and when you correct slightly, nothing happens, so you correct some more. Boats take time to react to steering inputs. Give each steering correction a second or two to take effect before you add more.

With a two-man loading crew, as the boat approaches the trailer, the trailer driver can give the boat driver directional guidance by pointing to the right or left, whichever way the boat needs to go to meet the center of the trailer. It's often hard for the boat handler to judge when the boat is centered from the helm, so the guidance is usually appreciated.

Dealing with a strong current or wind

Landing your boat in a crosscurrent is daunting the first time you do it. Most public ramps seem to be well located to avoid that situation, but I find a nasty one out there often enough that I think a little special coaching on the subject is in order. Earlier in this chapter, I recommend that the trailer driver aim the trailer downstream on the ramp as much as practical to help minimize the angle of the crosscurrent and to allow the boat handler to steer into the current to minimize its sideways effect. Here are some things you need to do as the boat handler to compensate as well:

✔ **Handling drift:** To compensate for the downstream drift, press your throttle lever forward. Ideally you should be making very slow headway, and steering is easier because your boat's speed through the water is higher due to the speed of the current you're driving into. You've probably already realized that boats steer more easily as they increase in speed.

✔ **Swimming upstream:** Start your approach downstream from the trailer, and aim the boat about half its width upstream of the trailer's bunks. Proceed at just enough speed to maintain steering control.

✔ **Throttling down:** As you get close to the trailer, pulling back on the throttle a little and holding a steady course are often enough to allow the current to push the bow of the boat in line with the center of the trailer. If you need a little steering correction, be judicious about it and remember to wait for its effect so you don't overcorrect. After your boat begins to turn downstream, it will turn at an accelerated rate.

Making contact with the trailer

All your maneuvering as the boat handler is aimed at making the contact between boat and trailer soft but firm enough to get the boat up on the bunks far enough that friction holds it in place. This section covers the fine points of the loading.

Finessing the final approach

Approaching the trailer is the most stressful part of boating in my book. It's not really as hard as it seems, but driving straight at a fixed object with pipes and posts and cranks sticking out of it seems like nautical suicide. But truthfully, the approach is painless if you do it slowly and follow these steps:

1. **Keep your eye on the target, and aim the boat at the center of the trailer.**

   As I drive the boat, I like to lean over toward the boat's centerline so I can line up the peak of the bow with the bow roller and winch at the front and center of the trailer. That way, if the boat begins to drift off course even a little bit, I can spot it and correct for it while the correction required is slight. The closer to the trailer you get, the harder it is to make corrections that help.

2. **Drive the boat onto the trailer, starting out slowly.**

   A 28-foot cuddy weighing in at 7,000 pounds has much more force at 3 mph than a 1,200-pound bass boat. You will find there's a perfect speed for landing your boat, and it's almost always less than walking speed. You can judge it only with experience, though, so start out each landing slow. If you find that one speed barely gets you into the bunks, next time add a little more throttle. Or if no one is waiting to load behind you, back off the trailer and take another shot at it.

With a two-man loading crew, when the boat is centered on the trailer and far enough up to be reached with the winch, the trailer driver can give a clenched fist to signal the boat handler to stop. The boat handler should back off the throttle but leave the engine idling in gear, which prevents the boat from drifting back off the trailer.

Getting your boat situated on the trailer

If you follow the steps in the previous section, most of the time your boat ends up most of the way onto the trailer. Use the winch to pull it the rest of the way in place. Instead of using the winch, some boaters power load their boats, using the brawn of the engine to push the boat the rest of the way onto the trailer against the bow roller near the winch. I use both tactics — the winch and power loading — depending on circumstances I explain in this section.

In some places power loading is illegal. It's also a tricky maneuver that you shouldn't try until you're comfortable with every other tactic for loading your boat. But you'll see it done and eventually want to try it yourself, so in this section I discuss both ways of getting the boat in place on the trailer.

Using power loading

One of the times when power loading is most useful is when you're loading the boat by yourself and don't have a helper.

With power loading, you face some risks. The worst is the risk of misjudging the power needed to load the boat on the trailer and instead launching the boat into the truck or the back of your tow vehicle. Yes, it has been done. More likely is that, as you throttle up your boat, the propeller fans the bottom with an enormous rush of water, contributing to a deep hole near the end of the ramp and a problematic mound of sand beyond the hole. It soon becomes impossible to pass the mound of sand without grounding your boat. On rocky waters, power loading has little effect on erosion under the water and it's legal. On lakes with sandy or muddy bottoms that erode easily in current, power loading is almost always illegal. Watch for signs that indicate it is. Violate the signs, and you'll discover a third risk — you could get a ticket and a fine.

When you understand the risks, loading with power isn't hard if you have some experience loading your boat and are confident in how it handles on the ramp. Here are the steps — decide for yourself if you're ready to use them:

1. **Get the boat centered and nudged into place on the trailer (refer to the earlier section, "Approaching the trailer").**

2. **Center the helm — that is, make sure the steering wheel is set for straight travel and not turns.**

   Sometimes it pays to just walk back and look at the propeller over the transom (back of the boat) to make sure it's straight.

3. **Apply throttle to move your boat forward in the bunks until it meets the bow roller. This shouldn't require more than about half-throttle — midway between wide-open throttle and idle speed — and it may require less.**

   Add power progressively until you get the forward motion you want. If your boat moves forward, stops, and requires more than half-throttle to move again, opt for the winch to finish the job.

4. **When the boat is all the way on the trailer, lean over the bow and snap the winch strap in place on the bow eye.**

5. **Shut down the engine and trim up the propeller with the trim switch on the throttle lever.**

If you don't raise the propeller, it's very likely to drag on the ramp or pavement as you pull away. This could damage the prop, the drive mechanism, and even the hull when pressure on the drive mechanism is transferred to the transom where it's mounted. You don't want this to happen.

Using the bow winch with a partner

Using the winch to secure the boat is slower than power loading but safer — and there's no risk of it being illegal in certain areas. When you're loading the boat with a partner and you're acting as the boat handler, here's what the trailer driver does:

1. **Pull out enough of the bow strap to meet the bow eye.**

   The winch has a ratchet that lets you reverse the direction of cranking and a center position that lets you freely unwind the strap before resetting the ratchet to crank the strap in.

2. **Put the bow strap on the eyebolt on the bow of the boat, and reset the ratchet lever on the winch to allow the strap to be cranked in. Test the setting by turning the crank to make sure it's right.**

3. **When the boat is secured to the winch, call out to the boat handler to shut down the engine and tilt up the propeller with the trim switch on the throttle lever to prevent damage.**

4. **Crank the winch and pull in the strap until it pulls the boat up tightly against the bow roller.**

Using the bow winch alone

If you're loading your boat alone and the ramp doesn't allow power loading, here's what you do:

1. **Get the boat on the trailer far enough for the winch strap to reach it, put the engine in neutral, and see if the boat stays in position.**

   If the boat wants to slide back on the trailer, put the engine in gear, nudge it up the trailer a little farther, and then test it again by shifting to neutral.

2. **Shut off the engine, and trim up the prop so it doesn't get damaged.**

3. **Climb over the bow and walk the trailer like a tightrope until you get to the bow winch (this is the part I hate). Grab the strap and connect it to the bow eye, and then winch the boat snug against the bow roller.**

Getting Up a Slippery Ramp

In tidal waters, the area of the ramp between high and low tide is often very slippery with a slight slime on it. In rivers and impoundments, when water levels drop, areas of the ramp once underwater are covered in slippery algae. Even if this part of the ramp stays in the water, the algae are there for your sliding pleasure if you have to get your vehicle's wheels in the water.

Following are some ways to get you, your vehicle, and your boat trailer off a slippery ramp:

- ✔ **Rough up the ramp:** A bag of plain clay kitty litter, coarse sand, or fine gravel makes handy work of putting traction on slippery spots. I've used all these materials at times, sprinkling them onto the slimy or slippery part of the ramp so my wheels get better traction. It works, and the next boaters usually appreciate it!

- ✔ **Kick into four-wheel drive:** You don't usually need four-wheel drive to get up a slippery ramp, but when you do need it, you'll say that one time you used it was worth the extra price on your vehicle. All-wheel drive or four-wheel drive puts some of the drive load on the front wheels of your vehicle, so if the back wheels are slipping in slime, the front wheels make up for it and pull you out. If you have four-wheel drive on your tow vehicle, set it to the lowest gear ratio when hauling out your boat so it gets the most traction.

- ✔ **Engage an anti-slip transmission:** My vehicle, a two-wheel drive Nissan Titan, has an anti-slip transmission that senses when one rear wheel is slipping and transfers the drive power to the other rear wheel. On a boat ramp, depressing the emergency brake halfway to just begin putting pressure on the brakes seems to activate the anti-slip mechanism, which always gives my vehicle a cleaner getaway. Release the brake as soon as you get good traction again.

- ✔ **Get a boost from your trailered boat:** This is a tricky maneuver, so I don't recommend it. But I have done it and seen it done many times, so I know that it can work. With the vehicle driver in the vehicle and ready to go, the boat driver tilts up the prop high enough that it won't hit the ramp and starts the boat engine. I usually wrap the kill-switch device (discussed in Chapter 7) around my left hand and grasp the throttle with my right hand. On a mutual signal, accelerate the boat as the driver accelerates the car. Just as the prop clears the water — you can tell when that happens because the exhaust noise increases astronomically — yank out the kill switch to stop the engine. By that time, the vehicle has enough momentum to carry on.

Making Your Boat and Trailer Road-Ready

In a day of boating, you open the hatches a dozen times, move things around, and unfasten things that are ordinarily fastened. At 45 mph on the water, these loose ends usually aren't much trouble. But on the highway at 65 to 70 mph, things left loose or open are guaranteed to be lost or broken.

Getting your boat ready to tow home is a project of details, and if you forget one, the ramifications are usually expensive, if not dangerous. Here's what you need to do to secure your boat to the trailer, make sure the trailer is safe to tow, and make sure the boat is ready to stow when you get home:

1. **After the boat is loaded, pull away from the ramp to the staging area.**

   If there's a line for the staging area, take your place. You need to stop here to get things squared away for the road home.

2. **In the staging area, put away loose things, close and latch hatches, and make final boat position adjustments.**

   It's possible that pulling your boat up a steep ramp caused it to slide back a little. Put another turn on the bow winch to snug it up.

3. **Hook the safety chain through the bow eye — the same eye on the bow that the winch strap connects to.**

   Newer trailers come with these safety chains, and on more than one occasion I've been glad I kept this chain connected.

4. **Connect the transom tie-down straps, and buckle them in place.**

5. **Remove the bilge plug so any future rainwater can run out. Stow the plug in a place you'll remember, like the side door pocket of your vehicle or in a cup holder near the helm.**

6. **Double-check the trailer's brake lights, red running lights, and turn signals.**

   A bulb could've failed when it was subjected to the cooler water. Always keep some spare trailer light bulbs in your vehicle for this purpose.

7. **If you were boating in salt water, rinse the trailer with fresh water as soon as possible. It's as easy as the following three steps:**

   1. Use a garden nozzle on the hose to increase water pressure.

   2. Spray the entire trailer with fresh water, and pay special attention to the lights and rollers on the trailer, dousing them liberally with fresh water.

   3. Kneel down near the wheels and spray the back side of the wheels to get the brakes flushed of salt water in order to prevent corrosion.

8. **If you were boating in salt water, flush your engine with fresh water.**

   • Outboards have a special nozzle on the back of the motor cowling onto which you can screw a hose. Attach the hose and turn on the water. Let it run while you run the motor for about five minutes, until the water running out is not longer salty. Keep the engine in neutral, and steer clear of the prop until the job is done.

- Sterndrives often don't have a flushing fitting. (You need to ask your dealer to install a flushing fitting on your inboard engine.) Ask your marine accessories dealer for a set of *ear muffs* — he'll know what you mean — that fit over the water pickups on the gear case of your motor. The *water pickups* are a series of holes or slots or sometimes mesh grill over an opening into the gear case. Water enters there and is pumped up to the engine. Attach a hose to the ear muffs and put them over the water intake openings. Run the hose while you run the engine for five minutes until the salt water is flushed out. Keep the engine in neutral, and steer clear of the prop until the job is done.

9. **On your drive home, make regular safety stops.**

   Make the first stop after 10 miles or so. By then, the boat may have shifted a little on the trailer, and you can tighten the bow and transom straps. After that, I'd stop every 100 miles or so to check the hubs for overheating (see Chapter 5 for more on that) and to let the vehicle and trailer cool off while you get refreshments and stretch your legs.

The steps in this section are all simple enough, and elaborating on them may seem unnecessary. But I'm reminded of my last trip boating. I confess that I forgot one of the steps and left a hatch open on the hard top over the cockpit. At highway speed, it flapped open and closed repeatedly until it broke off and flew away. It was certainly inconvenient and an expense to me, and it could have been dangerous to a vehicle behind me. The hatch is somewhere along the Beach Line Expressway, east of Orlando, Florida. I'll never forget that step again.

Chapter 7

Hitting the Open Water: Driving Your Boat

· ·

In This Chapter

▶ Fueling your boat safely

▶ Engaging the motor like a pro

▶ Maintaining and changing course on the water

▶ Shutting down properly

· ·

Boats aren't cars. If they were, what would be the fun in owning one? Still, too many people like to draw comparisons between boats and cars on their first boating excursions. Instead of trying to apply your driving knowledge to boating, erase what you know about driving a car and look at the boat for what you want it to be: something entirely new, adventuresome, and *fun!*

In this chapter, I show you how to safely fuel up your boat, get the motor purring like a kitten, and then put the pedal to the metal. Soon enough you'll be holding your course and turning like a pro. You'll discover how to adjust the boat's trim and tabs for a great ride, plus some tricks you need to perform when you shut down so you can make a clean *get*away when next you get *under*way. I also include some nuances in this chapter that, in just a few trips, will make you look like you've been boating all your life.

Fueling Up Your Boat

Before you can enjoy your boat on the water, you need to put fuel in it. Gassing up seems so easy that you're probably growling something like, "Oh, for Pete's sake. I fuel a car, a lawn mower, and a weed eater. How hard can it be to fuel a boat?" I actually hope you *are* muttering that, because some of what you already know applies to what you do when fueling your boat.

But the truth is you also face some important and unique safety and critical mechanical considerations when fueling your boat. If you disregard them, a fire or engine failure could result.

In this section, I tell you how to fuel up on land at a gas station or at the dock at the marina. But first, you need to determine if your boat needs special oil in the fuel.

Taking care of your engine's special oil needs

All engines need oil (as well as gas) to operate. Your boat may need special oil, and where you put it may surprise you! Oil maintenance depends on the type of engine your boat has.

Two-stroke engines

If you have an older outboard engine, chances are it's a two-stroke engine. If you have a chainsaw or a gas-powered weed eater, you already know what I'm about to say. A two-stroke engine normally uses oil at the same time it uses fuel, and you either add oil directly to the gas or pour oil into a special reservoir on the motor. Here are some considerations to keep in mind when dealing with two-stroke outboard engines:

 ✔ Really old two-stroke outboards — say, those made before 1980 — usually need oil added to the gas. If you have one of these, it's a classic, and if it has lived this long, you can count on even more years of enjoyment if you take care of it. Add oil to the gas at a ratio of 50 parts gas to 1 part oil. That amounts to 1 pint of oil for 6 gallons of gas.

   Engines vary in fuel/oil mix, so give your marine mechanic a call and ask exactly what oil mixture and oil type you should add.

 ✔ Most outboards made since 1980 have an oil reservoir on top of the motor cowling, under a large black twist-off cap. Most motors over 115 horsepower have separate oil reservoirs, usually located under a hatch in the bilge or under the helm station (call that the *dashboard,* if you prefer). It's best to keep these reservoirs filled and not let them get low, *so check them every time you gas up and replenish the oil as needed.*

The two-stroke oil standard is TCW-3. That's the *minimum* standard of oil quality you should consider for your outboard. Make sure the oil you buy has the TCW-3 code on the label, and don't settle for the cheapest TCW-3 oil you can get. I've seen some things behind the scenes at oil formulators, and I think paying more — though not necessarily paying the most — gets better oil for your engine.

Other engine types

Your car is a four-stroke engine, and your dad probably told you all you need to know about that when you learned to drive: "Check the oil!" If your boat has a sterndrive, inboard, or one of the new four-stroke outboard engines, you have to add oil to the engine and check the level *frequently*. Find the yellow-handled dipstick on your engine and check the oil level every time you fill up and every time you start boating on any day. If it's low, add the oil recommended by your owner's manual. (I talk more about engine maintenance in Chapter 13.)

Fueling up on land

Fueling up on land at a regular gas station is often the easiest and least expensive method to begin your boating excursion with a full tank. Heck, you already stop there to fuel your car, so why not fuel your boat there, too?

Another plus to buying fuel on land is that gas station prices are almost always much cheaper than on-the-water prices.

Because most of your crew will either remain in the car or go inside to buy candy and soda while you fuel up, some of your safety considerations are already mitigated — you're crew is out of the boat and out of the way! You always want your crew out of the way whenever and wherever you fuel up.

When you pull into the gas station, approach the pumps slowly and, if you need to, stop far short of the pumps to scope them out. You need a pump that meets the following criteria:

✔ It allows you to make a wide turn so you can pull the vehicle past the pump, turning wide to let the boat come up to it without hitting the end of the pump island.

✔ It's on the same side as your boat's fuel point when the boat is stopped next to it.

Make sure you know on which side your boat's fuel point is located before heading to the station!

✔ It lets you drive your rig forward out of the station without backing up when you're done filling the tank. You *can* back up in a pinch, but backing around pumps and other cars in a fuel station is pretty difficult — even for an expert.

Start out by checking your engine oil and adding oil if the level is low. When fueling up, follow the same safety precautions as when filling your car: Don't smoke or use your cellphone, don't overfill the tank, and wipe any spilled fuel from the boat so it doesn't stain the finish.

When you leave the pump, turn wide around the end of the pumps and watch carefully that you don't clip another car or a pump with your trailer.

Boating lore is full of stories of boaters who unwittingly filled their bilge with gasoline by sticking the nozzle in a rod holder or other non-fuel opening on the boat. The result can be explosive! Your boat's fuel point will be marked "gas," "fuel," or "gasoline." Take the time to read it before you stick the gas nozzle into it.

Fueling up at the dock

Fueling up at the dock isn't as convenient as it may sound. The boat moves around on the water, making it difficult to keep up a steady fuel flow from the pump. Marina pumps also tend to be more primitive than gas station pumps and sometimes don't work as well. And at the dock, you need to follow some special safety precautions.

All the same, if you're out having a ball, you may need more go-juice to keep the dream alive, so chances are you'll need to know the ropes of gassing up at a marina sooner or later.

Fuel vapor is heavier than air, and your boat behaves like a bowl, trapping all those fumes inside. Get your crew out of the boat before you add fuel, and keep them out until you follow the safety precautions I outline in the following steps. Anyone left in the boat during fueling could be exposed to a terrifying fire hazard.

Here's your step-by-step guide to safely fueling your boat at the dock:

1. **Be courteous.**

   When you approach a fuel dock, it's possible that you aren't the first one there. If you see other boats drifting around nearby, they may well be in line before you. Find out "who's on first" before you just barge in and gas up.

2. **Secure the boat to the dock.**

   Tie docklines between the bow and stern of the boat and the dock to ensure it's secure.

3. **Offload the crew.**

   When your boat is secure at the fuel dock, ask all your passengers to step up onto the dock. The combination of settled fuel vapor and a spark or thoughtless smoker could cause a disaster, so get your passengers out of the boat.

4. Find out where the safety equipment is.

Marinas are required to keep equipment nearby to deal with fuel spills in the water. And many marinas prefer to fill your boat themselves to avoid just that. If you're left to your own devices, make sure you know where the cleanup equipment is so you can handle any spills before they spread and foul the water.

5. Close all hatches.

Fuel vapors are heavier than air and can drift and collect in low places, creating an explosive problem. Before fueling, close all hatches so fuel vapor can't collect in compartments or in the cabin, if your boat has one.

6. Fuel up, and be patient while pumping.

Boats are notorious for taking fuel slowly. So, if you're fueling your boat yourself, run the pump at the slowest speed until you're sure how fast the fuel tank can accept the fuel. You can increase the pump velocity a little at a time until you're sure it won't splash back from the nozzle.

Keep a rag around the filler nozzle to capture fuel that may splash back out around the nozzle. Some fuel stations have an absorbent collar on the nozzle to do that for you.

7. Let the fumes dissipate before boarding.

After you've fueled the boat, wait a few minutes before climbing aboard. Buy a soda or an ice cream bar and enjoy the marina action for a while before you settle back in, allowing time for lingering fuel fumes to start dissipating.

8. Run the engine blower before starting up.

You should get in before anyone else and run the engine compartment blower for five minutes before starting the boat. Marked with a picture of a fan, the blower switch is near the helm, also called the *steering wheel.* Running the blower clears out any fuel vapor that has settled in the boat and bilge area where the engine is located. Outboards don't have bilge blowers because the engine is outside the boat, but you should still let the fuel vapor drift away for several minutes before you board your refueled outboard.

9. Reboard the crew when you know it's safe.

Let your crew get in after a few more minutes. As the captain, the risky work is up to you! You know the lore: The captain goes down with the ship. (Frankly, I'd rather do things right and keep the ship from going down, wouldn't you?)

Getting Your Motor Running

Because you put a key into an ignition, starting your boat's motor may seem the same as starting a car at first. But you need to keep in mind some significant differences and safety precautions. You have no brakes and no clutch — and, well, it's a *boat!* In this section, I fill you in on the differences so you can safely get your boat's motor purring.

I start out with safety precautions and then tell you what you need to know about your motor before you can determine which tactic to use for starting it. And I get you prepared for what to expect from your first boat ride.

Putting safety first

Although starting a car involves a few safety steps (such as making sure nothing is behind your car), there's a little more to be aware of with a boat.

Checking around the boat and propeller

Before you start the motor, do a safety check around the boat. Make sure nothing, and certainly no one, is near the propeller or anywhere else nearby the outside of the boat. Get any overboard crew inboard right away, and don't start the boat if people are swimming nearby.

Pulling up the anchor

It may seem silly to mention it, but make sure you've pulled up the anchor before you start the motor to move away. Too many boating injuries occur when an anchor is forgotten and a boat takes off. In some cases, the anchor can skip along behind the boat, stretching the anchor line like a rubber band until it snaps the anchor into the boat, injuring passengers.

Making sure the propeller is in the water

If you have an outboard or sterndrive engine, both of which can be tilted up out of the water, make sure the propeller is in the water. If you have an inboard engine with a fixed propeller and shaft that comes out beneath the boat, you can ignore this step.

With an outboard or sterndrive motor, running the motor more than a few seconds with the propeller tilted up can damage the water pump and the engine.

The trim switch raises and lowers the propeller in outboards and sterndrive boats. It's located on the throttle lever at the helm (you know the helm; it looks like a steering wheel). (See the section, "Adjusting the boat for a great ride," later in this chapter for more on trim.)

Using the kill switch lanyard

All boats made in the past 20 years or so have a kill switch intended to stop the motor if the captain falls out of his seat or overboard. The lanyard is usually a red plastic cord that looks like a phone cord. For safety, attach it to you, the captain, and to its special button on the boat (see Figure 7-1). Follow these steps:

1. **Clip the lanyard's metal or plastic hook to your belt or to one of the D-ring loops on your life jacket.**

   Sometimes it's more convenient to loop it around your wrist or knee and clip the line to itself.

2. **Clip the other end of the lanyard to the plunger button on the boat.**

   Putting this clip in place lifts the spring-loaded button so the boat can run. When it's pulled off — for instance, if you momentarily forget your duties as captain and step away from the helm (I know, I know, you wouldn't do that, but just if . . .) — the motor stops running.

Sterndrives and inboards have a different kill switch connector. The connector is usually located near the gearshift and throttle levers. The lanyard fits over a small lever and is secured by switching the lever to the Run position. If you pull the lanyard away, it resets the switch to an Off or Stop position.

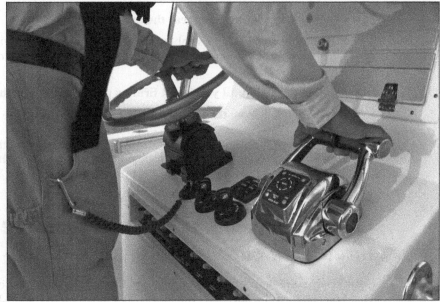

Figure 7-1:
The kill switch needs to be connected at the ignition and to the captain.

Courtesy of Marine Tracker

Even though you can run the boat without attaching the lanyard to yourself, it's not advisable. The engine can only run when the lanyard is attached to the button near the starting key or gearshift. When you're attached to the lanyard, should you hit an unexpected wave and be knocked from the captain's seat, the lanyard will pull out and automatically stop the boat. If the kill switch lanyard isn't attached to you and you're boating alone, you could be left stranded in the water, or worse, be hit by your own boat. Or the boat could travel until it strikes someone else, injuring that person. In some states, like Arkansas, making full use of the lanyard on both ends is mandatory.

I'm embarrassed to admit that more than once I thought the motor was broken because it wouldn't start. Only after several failed attempts did I realize the kill switch lanyard wasn't in place. I replaced it, and each time the motor started faithfully. So, if your motor isn't starting, double-check the kill switch lanyard.

Priming the fuel line on outboards

If your boat has an outboard motor, usually before your engine will start you need to prime the fuel line. This is almost always true when the boat sits for a while (overnight or longer) and fuel drains from the lines back into the tank. To get the fuel back up into the line and into the engine where it can do you some good, use the rubber priming bulb, if your motor has one. Follow these steps to do so:

1. **Look for the priming bulb near the engine.**

   It should be on a black hose about ½ inch in diameter. I once had a bunch of kids boating with me, and one of them suggested it looked like a hand grenade!

2. **Squeeze the ball until you feel it firming up from filling with fuel.**

3. **It usually takes from three to six squeezes to fully prime the line.**

You'll usually have to prime the fuel line only the first time you start the motor on boating day. However, if your boat fails to start later in the day, re-priming the fuel line is a good place to start troubleshooting.

Choking the engine and pumping the throttle on carbureted motors

Some boats start simply at the turn of a key. If yours is one of those, lucky you. You can turn the key, start the motor, and move on to the next section, "Getting Underway." However, plenty of carbureted engines are still being used in boating today. If you're not a bit of a motor head and don't know a carbureted motor from the alternative, ask your dealer if yours is carbureted.

Carbureted motors start only if you pump the throttle to start the gas flowing. Pumping the throttle also chokes the engine, helping get the gas to the engine. If your boat motor is carbureted, follow these few extra steps *before* you turn the key:

1. **Press and hold the fast idle button (also known as the fast idle switch) at the pivot point of your throttle.**

   Pressing the fast idle button allows you to advance the throttle without putting the boat in gear, which makes starting the engine easier. It may not look like a button to you, but if you press on that pivot point, you'll feel the round rubber trim give way, and you may hear a little click.

2. **Holding the button in, push the throttle forward.**

   This step advances the throttle without putting the propeller in motion (which is called *putting the boat in gear*).

3. **Work the throttle back and forth three or four times.**

   This equivalent of pumping the accelerator in an old jalopy causes fuel to squirt into the carburetor so it can do its job — make your engine go.

4. **Turn the key.**

   You may have to pump the throttle back and forth a few times while you turn the key. As soon as the engine gets purring, pull the throttle back to neutral. The fast idle button will reset itself.

   Usually three or four cycles of the throttle is all the pumping and choking your engine needs. If you overdo it, you can flood the engine and it won't start. If that seems to be the case, let it rest for a few minutes, and then turn the key. If it still doesn't start, consult the next section, "Troubleshooting a nonstarter."

5. **If you have any trouble starting your motor again later in the day, repeat these steps.**

   When your engine is warmed up, it's unlikely you'll need to do anything but turn the key on the next startup that day.

Troubleshooting a nonstarter

You're all set to enjoy a lovely day on the water. Everything is perfect. You take all the steps to start your boat's motor — and then nothing happens. Don't despair! In most cases the problem is easily remedied with basic troubleshooting.

Have you ever seen *Slingblade* starring Billy Bob Thornton? In one scene, he steps into a small motor mechanic garage, and after all the experts can't make a mower run, he does so simply by filling the fuel tank. All he does is address the most obvious and easiest possibilities first. Here's how to troubleshoot a starting problem like a pro:

1. **Make sure your kill switch is in place.**

   Remember, even an expert *(c'est moi)* can forget to hitch the kill switch. I cover the kill switch in the section, "Using the kill switch lanyard."

2. **Check the fuel level.**

   It isn't unusual for the gas gauge to fail, so if the motor won't start — and unless you know the tank is full — add gasoline. You may have to return to the fuel station or marina, which may be a problem if the engine doesn't work. You may have to wave down another boater for a tow in.

3. **If the engine turns over but doesn't start, it may be flooded with too much fuel in the carburetor. Give the excess fuel in the carburetor a few minutes to evaporate before trying to start it again.**

4. **If the engine doesn't turn over (you know, that dead battery sound), you may need a jump-start from another battery, a charger, or a portable battery jumper (see Figure 7-2).**

   Batteries discharge in as little as a week or two when the boat sits idle. One of the handiest gadgets you can have to combat a dead battery is an emergency battery jumper. This portable device has battery clamps that attach to the boat battery. The battery jumper recharges when plugged into a wall outlet. I keep one charging up in the garage and throw it in my truck when I head to the lake, just in case.

Figure 7-2:
A portable battery jumper can save the day if your boat battery is dead on the launch ramp.

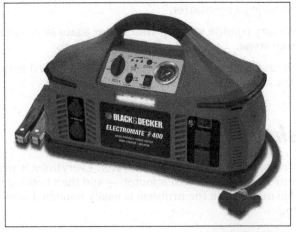

Courtesy of Black & Decker

5. If you get no sound at all, make sure the battery switch is on.

Many newer boats are equipped with battery switches that isolate the battery from electrical systems in the boat and prevent the battery from discharging during storage. You can usually spot the switch near or inside the engine compartment; it's usually red in color and about 4 inches square with a large knob. Turn it to either "on" or "battery one," depending on how the switch is labeled.

If none of the preceding tips get you started, you may have to seek out a mechanic. But I recommend that you run through all the steps a couple of times to be sure you've covered all the possibilities. One of the best, most methodical boaters I know (my father-in-law) put his boat in storage full of fuel. When he returned with his boat to his dock, the boat wouldn't start. He tried everything before he called a mechanic. When the mechanic checked things over, he found the fuel tank empty — someone had siphoned all the fuel.

Getting Underway

When you have that motor purring, you're ready to "get underway" — that's salty talk for "go." The fun part is coming, but if this is your first ride in a boat, you may be a little alarmed the first time you pull away from the dock about something boaters call *bow rise* or *loss of horizon* (see the sidebar "The physics of planing"). You'll also find it's not as easy as it seems to get the boat going smoothly at a safe, steady speed. Don't worry; in this section I walk you through all you need to know to get from point A to point B across the water.

Throttling up for take-off

When driving a car, you use the gearshift to change from forward to reverse, and you manipulate the gas pedal for more or less speed. When driving a boat, both functions are often carried out by the same lever, which behaves differently than you may expect:

- ✔ A boat's throttle lever, unlike a car's gas pedal, doesn't return to idle if you let go. It tends to stay wherever you set it. So, if you're going 50 miles per hour and get bounced from your seat — no, it's not very likely to happen, but it can — the boat will keep going 50 mph until someone or something stops it (unless you're connected to the kill switch lanyard; refer to the section, "Using the kill switch lanyard").

- ✔ Your boat's throttle lever shifts the gears from neutral to forward or reverse.

The physics of planing

Most power boats are built to *plane*, or rise up, on the surface of the water. Exceptions include catamarans, pontoon boats, trawlers, and tugs. These kinds of boats have *displacement hulls,* meaning they remain settled down with much of their hulls below the waterline and they displace water, moving it out of the boat's way as it moves forward. These boats are slower and typically don't have the bow rise you get in planing hulls.

A displacement hull (as seen on the top in the figure) has more of the hull settled into the water at cruising speed. A planing hull (as seen on the bottom in the figure) rides on top of the water and at cruising speed is said to be *planing*.

Planing hulls are made to skim on top of the water. The faster the boat goes, the less of it touches the water. Some boats go so fast that little more than a foot or two of the hull and the propeller touch the water at all. When they're planing on top, they ride level, giving a clear forward view. But as they *climb on plane,* some boats point alarmingly high, obscuring your forward view.

The bow rises as you accelerate. Bow rise happens when your propeller pushes forward on the boat, and the boat is trying to climb up on top of the water with the bow pointing high. As the boat climbs up, the bow rises and blocks your forward view, an effect called *loss of horizon*. Boat builders are getting better at minimizing this effect, but no boat goes without it. Sometimes, boaters make bow rise even worse by trying to start out with their propellers *trimmed up,* meaning that the propellers are tilted upward too high.

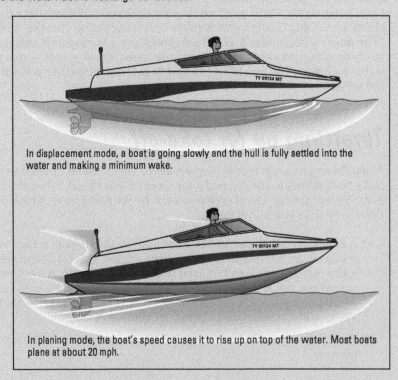

In displacement mode, a boat is going slowly and the hull is fully settled into the water and making a minimum wake.

In planing mode, the boat's speed causes it to rise up on top of the water. Most boats plane at about 20 mph.

Here's a step-by-step rundown of engaging your throttle to get underway and what to expect when you do:

1. **Put safety first.**

   Before shifting from neutral, first check around the boat and be sure it's safe to engage the propeller.

2. **Check the trim of the engine.**

   Before you accelerate, make sure your propeller trim is in the full down position. You can tell by looking at the instrument marked "Trim" on your helm station. The trim gauge should be pointing to the down side of the dial.

3. **Double-check the trim of the engine.**

   It doesn't hurt to just push the down side of the trim switch a few seconds to be sure it's in the right position. You'll find the trim switch on the gearshift lever, and it's usually positioned so that when you grab the throttle, the switch is under your thumb. The sound of the trim motor changes tone when the trim position is all the way down. (See the section, "Adjusting the boat for a great ride," for more on trimming the engine.)

4. **Engage the throttle.**

   Squeeze the handle to release the safety stop, and push the throttle lever forward (or reverse to go backward).

5. **Accelerate smoothly.**

   Choosing a safe, steady speed is more easily done when you can see forward and get a feel for traffic and water conditions. So, on acceleration, give the engine plenty of gas to get the boat up on top of the water and running level as quickly as possible.

6. **Set cruise speed.**

   When the boat levels out, pull the throttle back to a comfortable speed. Most boats plane at 20 mph, and a speed just over that mark is a good target. Any slower and you'll plough along with your visibility blocked by a high bow — you know, the pointy front end — and stir enormous and unnecessary *wakes* (those waves behind you made by your boat cutting through the water).

Maintaining and changing course

When driving a car, maintaining course is easy because you just follow the road. And when you turn, although you may lean into the turn, your car generally stays level (unless you're going way too fast!). On the water, there are no roads to follow, and a boat behaves differently than a car.

The boat leans over when you turn — a fact that may be alarming on your first trip out. Relax, though. This is natural, and it's not a problem as long as your crew remains seated and you look around before you turn. Looking before you turn is normal in cars, but in boating, traffic comes from any direction, making awareness even more important.

The tendency for boaters is to feel like they're all alone in their space on the water. Don't fall into that dangerous trap. Look both ways before you change course; just as cars can on the highway, fast-moving watercraft can come out of nowhere.

Here are some of the most basic differences between a boat and a car:

- A boat responds more slowly than a car to input from the helm and throttle. This is especially true at slower speeds. When trying to guide a boat at slower speeds, it's best to turn the helm a bit and then wait for it to react. This may take a few seconds. If it doesn't turn as far as needed, turn the helm more.

- At slow speeds, the boat wanders. The bow points a bit right, then swings back to the left. The overall result is a straight course, but if you're not aware of wandering, you may try to correct every little movement, which only makes things worse.

  To get a feel for how much your boat wanders, test it. Choose someplace calm with open water, pick a landmark, and steer toward it. When the helm is centered, take your hand off the helm and watch what it does.

- At high speeds, boats tend to turn a bit (because of wind and current) when you're aiming for a straight course. You may think you're holding a straight course, but if you look back, you'll see a slight curve in your wake.

  On short legs of your boating trip, curving isn't a problem. But, if you're heading 20 miles across a bay, you could find yourself lost at the other side. To avoid this problem, choose a landmark ahead and keep the bow pointed toward it. If you can't see a landmark clearly, you need to keep your eye on the compass to hold your course.

Adjusting the boat for a great ride

Adjusting the ride of the boat involves managing the trim while taking into consideration the conditions on the water, as well as pitch, yaw, and roll. How you adjust for wind and waves says a lot about the boater you'll become. Banging yourself, your boat, and your passengers over large wakes is bad for everyone involved.

Understanding pitch, yaw, and roll

Boats can be a little like airplanes: Cars move only forward, back, left, and right, but planes and boats also move up and down, pitch, roll, and yaw. It's your job as captain to manage and minimize the following effects:

- ✔ **Pitch:** Draw an imaginary line through the center of your boat from *port* (that's the left side) to *starboard* (yep, the right side). The bow of your boat pitches up and down from that imaginary line. Naturally, the stern goes up and down, too, making the whole thing act sort of like a seesaw.

- ✔ **Yaw:** Drive an imaginary pin through the center of your boat from the top down (imagine an insect pinned in a collector's box). Your boat can swing right to left around this pin, and that's called *yaw.* It usually only happens when wind and waves push on the boat from one side or the other.

- ✔ **Roll:** Draw an imaginary line through your boat from the bow to the stern. Your boat rolls from side to side on this line when you turn or when waves wash under it from the side. The old expression "Don't rock the boat" speaks primarily of rolling.

Trimming the propeller

Trimming your propeller doesn't involve festive decorations. Rather, it involves raising and lowering the propeller. To adjust your boat for a great ride, trim the propeller for efficiency. It's easy to do, but many boaters forget about it and never get the full enjoyment from their ride. Here's how:

1. **When you accelerate from a dead stop, the trim setting of your propeller should be all the way down.**

   All the way down often means the propeller is tucked a little in and is pointing slightly downward. A marine architect would call this *negative trim,* and it's best used when starting from a dead stop.

2. **As you begin to plane off, coming up on top of the surface of the water and leveling out, trim the propeller up slightly.**

   The idea is to keep the propeller pointing in a line parallel to the surface of the water. When you get it right, the boat feels right — steady but free on the water.

3. **Keep adjusting your propeller trim.**

   Too little trim and the bow is stuffed downward, slowing the boat and making it harder to ride and handle. Too high and the propeller comes out of the water or sucks air from the surface into the prop, which is called *ventilating.* Ventilating causes loss of speed and loss of water supply to the engine, which leads to overheating.

4. **As you cruise at various speeds, adjust the propeller trim to various settings.**

In time you'll be able to detect the sweet spot in trim and instinctively adjust to it. You'll soon find yourself trimming properly without even realizing you're doing it!

Using trim tabs for a balanced ride

You can level the ride using trim tabs to manage roll (see Figure 7-3). Any boat can be equipped with these tabs, and they're so useful that most boats should have them. Trim tabs come in pairs, one right and one left. They actually look like tabs and stick out from bottom of the *transom* (or back of the boat). You control them using a pair of switches near the helm. By using the switches to raise either tab up or down, you can cause the boat to ride more level.

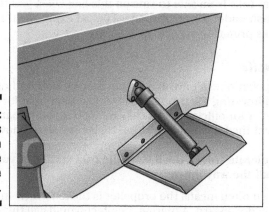

Figure 7-3:
Trim tabs level a boat's ride by lifting the transom.

For example, suppose you have a couple of big people sitting on the port side, and the boat rolls that way. Lowering the tab on the port side lifts that side up (and vice versa, of course). In another example, suppose you're running across a pretty strong wind. You're trying to maintain a straight course, but the boat is leaning noticeably into the wind. Your boat is actually yawing because of the wind, and you're unconsciously correcting by turning into it. Even though your boat is crossing the water on a straight course, it's in a slight turn to counteract the wind's attempt to force you off course. Remember, the boat rolls when it's in a turn. Correct the leaning by putting the tab down slightly on the side of the boat that's leaning down.

Some trim tab controls are marked to tell you which way to push the button to raise or lower the tab. Others are marked to tell you how to push the button to raise or lower one side of the bow or the other. Read the labels on the tab controls so you don't work them backward.

Shutting Down the Engine

Shutting down your boat's engine seems simple enough, right? You just turn the key and turn off the engine, tie up the boat, and say ta-ta for now — kind of like when you pull your car into the garage and walk away; no muss, no fuss. Well, not so fast, matey! You should develop some helpful habits to save you from looking, well, unschooled in boating. Here's a step-by-step guide to calling it a day (or just shutting down to take a dip):

1. **Put trim tabs in the upright position.**

   With the trim tabs up when you shut down the engine, if you change the load balance or anything else onboard, you'll start up next time with no tabs on and be able to adjust properly from there.

2. **Trim your outboard or sterndrive engine all the way down.**

   If you don't do this now, you'll forget to do it when you take off again, and the bow will rise so high you won't be able to see forward and your boat may not be able to get on plane until you lower it. Make a habit of trimming down whenever you turn the engine off, and you won't forget.

3. **Safely stow the key out of sight but not out of mind.**

   You can keep the key in your pocket, but don't go swimming or you risk losing it. One good place to hide the key is in the engine compartment. If you have to go there to retrieve it, you'll remember automatically to check behind the boat to make sure the prop is clear before you start the engine.

Chapter 8

Docking, Rafting Up, and Anchoring

- -

In This Chapter

▶ Docking your boat without rocking the dock

▶ Rafting up with other boats safely

▶ Securing your boat properly with the right anchor

- -

Anchoring is easy, but there's an art to doing it right, and it's an art you can master. And docking? Most people find docking daunting — maybe even destructive at first. Of course, that won't be the case with you after reading this chapter! Finally, rafting up with friends — meaning tying boats together — to hang out also requires some special tactics. Rafting up is bound to become your favorite way to have fun on the water.

Whatever you do, remember a boat is not a car. When you approach another boat or a dock, your automobile instincts may cause your foot to feel for a brake, and even though you already know there is none, before you know it you'll be tappin' your toe in search of it and not slowing down as a result.

You always need to approach docks and other boats thoughtfully and cautiously. Doing so not only gives you time to react to the elements, but also gives you time to react to your useless-on-the-water, land-lubber instincts. Slow and steady is practically a guarantee of success.

In this chapter, you discover not only how to dock your boat but how to approach the dock and tie up your boat securely. I also discuss tactics to avoid performance anxiety when approaching your friends' boats all rafted up in a quiet cove, how to hitch them together, and how to make sure, once you're all snugged up, that you protect your boat from rub rash. For a secluded anchorage on your own in a deserted cove, I tell you how to set and anchor securely, too.

Docking Your Boat Like a Pro

Docking a boat is such a frightening task for some boaters that they actually hesitate to take their boats out at all. In fact, some marine motor companies have developed special engine systems that let boaters dock with the flick of a joystick. These systems cost thousands of dollars, yet boaters are still buying them. I think the new stuff is cool, but docking your boat just isn't that hard. To make a soft, safe landing, all you really need is a slow and thoughtful approach. In this section, I give you the inside track on getting inside the dock — without a ding.

Some more experienced hot-dogs love to charge the dock, slam the shift into reverse, and throttle back hard to stop just short of banging the dock. This technique may be exciting for bystanders, but it's also dangerous for them and the people on the boat. What if the engine stalls with plenty of forward momentum still behind the boat? Don't think it can't happen.

Never approach docking at a speed above idle. In fact, it's often better to shift in and out of gear to go even slower.

When docking, you basically have three choices about how to approach the dock (see Figure 8-1):

- ✔ **Stern-in** (backward)
- ✔ **Bow-in** (frontward)
- ✔ **Alongside** (sideways along the dock)

After you've docked, you need to tie off properly. I tell you how to do that at the end of this section.

Docking stern-in (back first)

Although backing your boat into a *slip* (the boating word for parking space) isn't the favored way of docking, there can be very good reasons for doing so. I once crossed the Gulf Stream with friends who had never boated anywhere but freshwater lakes. When we reached port, I noticed a murmuring of surprise and maybe even disapproval when I pivoted the boat around and backed in. My passengers were probably thinking, "Why in the world would anyone go to that trouble when it's easier to run the bow into the slip?"

The answer became apparent to them when we tied up. Bowlines had to be fastened to very tall pilings, and without the height of the bow to stand on, we would not have been able to reach the piling hooks. Plus, with the stern to the dock, stepping from the cockpit to the swim platform to the dock was as easy as walking into a convenience store. Had the pointy end been facing the dock, everyone would have had to climb to the bow, step over the anchor connected to the davit or bracket that held it, and then high-jump the bow rail onto the dock. Not very convenient. Docking stern-in was more trouble to accomplish, but for the more than 16 hours per day the boat was in port, boarding and using the boat was more convenient.

When to dock stern-in

Backing in can be the hardest way to dock, but it's definitely more convenient for cruisers and cuddies with closed bows. Today, even small runabouts have walk-through *transoms* (the backs of boats) that provide open, secure footing all the way to the cockpit. So plenty of people think backing in is a good idea, and sometimes it is. (To review cruisers, cuddies, runabouts, and other types of boats, turn to Chapter 2.)

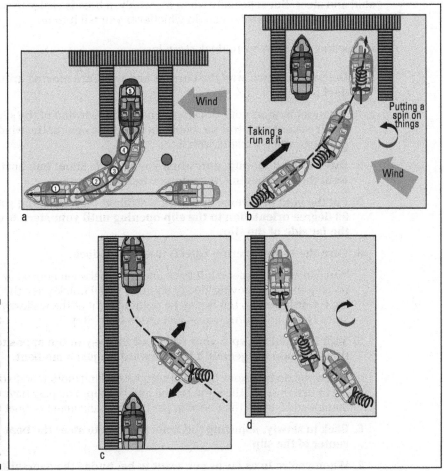

Figure 8-1:
The three common docking positions are stern-in (a), bow-in (b), and alongside (c and d).

Docking stern-in is the best, most convenient, and safest option in the following circumstances:

✓ When the wind is whipping across the opening of the slip

✓ When a current is running across the slip opening

✓ When your boat has a closed deck with a cuddy cabin up front instead of bow seating, making it easier to board from the stern

✓ When prevailing wind and waves are blowing straight into the dock, making it safer for the boat to take the seas on the bow than on the stern

How to dock stern-in

In a lot of ways, docking stern-in is easier than you think. Sure, you have the discomfort of looking over your shoulder as you throttle up and down and shift and steer. But especially when it's windy, a boat is easier to pull than it is to push — the propeller can do whichever you tell it to do.

Follow these easy steps to dock stern-in:

1. **Determine which way the current and wind are moving around the dock.**

   You want to start your docking maneuver downwind of the slip. It's much easier to control the boat when backing *against* the wind or current than when backing with it.

2. **Drive toward the slip, and when your boat is about one boat length from the slip opening, turn downwind 90 degrees.**

3. **Put the boat in reverse and back it straight back, keeping your 90-degree orientation to the slip opening until your stern is even with the far side of the slip.**

4. **Turn the *helm* (steering wheel) toward the dock.**

   You can move the gearshift back and forth between neutral and reverse to keep the boat moving slowly enough. You'll quickly see the boat turning toward the slip, but it may be pointed right at the walkway on the far side. That's not a problem — just move on to Step 5.

5. **Shift into neutral, spin your wheel all the way in the opposite direction, and pop the gearshift into forward for just a moment.**

   When you do this, your boat will stop its backing motion and start pivoting to better orient the stern to pull into the slip. You may have to repeat Steps 4 and 5 more than once to get the ideal alignment of boat to slip.

6. **Back in slowly, adjusting the helm position to steer the boat along the center of the slip.**

7. **When you're in as far as you want to be, nudge the gearshift into forward to stop your motion.**

8. Secure your boat to the dock (see the section, "Tying your boat safely to the dock," later in this chapter for instructions), and bask in the knowledge that you've proven yourself a whiz at one of the hardest parts of boating!

Docking bow-in (pointy end first)

Docking bow-in is so common that most people think backing in is showing off. With the average small runabout (boats fewer than 25 feet in length), docking bow-in is often — but not always — the simplest way to moor your boat. (Did you catch that new term? *Docking* and *mooring* mean the same thing.)

When to dock bow-in

You should dock your boat bow-in when one or more of the following circumstances exist:

✔ Your dock is on a still lake or protected cove that's unlikely to kick up seas (waves) or experience wakes from passing boats that can wash over the transom and flood the boat.

✔ Walkways down either side (port/left or starboard/right) of the boat offer two ways of boarding and minimize the need to board via the transom platform at the back of the boat.

✔ The wind blows across the head of the dock, sending the seas or waves toward your approach. Docking bow-in in this situation is safer for your boat because it takes the turbulence on the bow.

✔ You need the deeper water farthest from the dock and shore to keep your propeller from hitting bottom.

How to dock bow-in

Driving straight into a slip is the easiest thing to do. To do it well, though, you need to go slowly and carefully estimate the impact of crosswinds and currents on your boat's path.

Follow these steps to make driving into a slip a snap:

1. Line up the boat with the slip one to two boat lengths from the slip opening.

2. Put the gearshift in reverse to stop your boat's forward motion, and then shift back to neutral.

3. Watch carefully to see if the wind or current has any sideways impact on your course to the dock slip. You'll be able to see any drift sideways when you've taken off all power.

4. **With the helm aimed straight ahead, shift into forward.**

   However, if wind or crosscurrents push you off course, aim upwind or up current and monitor both forward progress and your drift. In a way, it becomes a game of guessing how much drift you need to account for.

5. **If the boat's forward momentum builds too quickly, shift back and forth from neutral to forward or even from forward to reverse to moderate speed.**

   Go slowly. If you hit the dock at a slow speed, the impact will be mostly embarrassing, but not damaging or life threatening. (Go ahead and forgive yourself right now because sometimes you will hit the dock. It's a fact of boating life.)

6. **Secure your boat to the dock (see the section, "Tying your boat safely to the dock," later in this chapter for instructions).**

Docking alongside (parallel)

Docking alongside is equivalent to parallel parking on the street, but some people feel it's a little easier in a boat than in a car. You have few reasons to dock alongside the dock, and I recommend that you avoid it because it increases the chance that your boat will acquire scrapes and scuffs on the dock side of the boat. But it's not hard to do, and with proper placement of padded fenders to absorb dock knocks, mooring the boat safely parallel with the dock is possible.

When to dock alongside

When should you dock alongside (also known as *docking beam-to*)? When it's your only choice (which is pretty much the only reason most people parallel park their cars). Sometimes the only option you have is to sidle up to a long pier in between other boats. That's almost always the case at a gas dock or courtesy dock found at the boat ramp.

How to dock alongside and between other boats

Sometimes, such as at the short pier of a boat ramp's courtesy dock, docking alongside is as simple as driving straight in, stopping the motion of the boat with reverse shifting, and tying up. But sometimes you're faced with parking parallel between a couple of other boats. Here's how you can do that easily:

1. **Aim your boat at the point on the pier where you want to moor, approaching it at an angle of about 45 degrees.**

   Keep the throttle nice and slow, popping it in and out of gear to go slower if you need to.

2. **When you get within a quarter of your boat's length from the dock, turn the helm (steering wheel) all the way toward the pier and put the engine in reverse.**

   This movement stops the boat's forward motion and swings the stern to the dock at the same time. The bow continues moving toward the pier as the propeller pulls the whole boat sideways. You can coast the last bit of the way.

3. **Just before the stern touches the dock, give the gearshift a short, easy touch of the forward gear to stop the boat and let you tuck fenders between the pier and the boat.**

4. **Secure your boat to the dock (see the next section for instructions).**

Never dock alongside a pier when a current is sweeping you toward the pier. Your boat may be pushed under the dock, injuring you, your crew, and the boat. Always dock on the down-current side of a pier.

Tying your boat safely to the dock

You may never hit anything with your boat — not the trailer, not the bottom of the lake, not a dock piling — but if you don't tie your boat properly, you'll come back to find it scratched and gouged from working against the dock no matter how padded the dock appears.

I've spent years trying to help people moor their boats in a way that prevents docking damage from happening, but new boaters tend to have a hard time grasping the idea that the boat keeps moving even when it's turned off and tied up.

The trick is to give the mooring lines enough slack that the boat can move with the waves but not move enough to be banged into the dock. It takes a combination of fenders and strong docklines. (On a boat, lines are just ropes until they're attached to the boat, and then they're called *lines*.) In this section, I walk you through the steps of tying up a boat perfectly based on how you're docked.

Securing your boat with a four-point connection

When you dock bow-in or stern-in, you can extend four lines — one from each quarter of your boat (port stern, starboard stern, port bow, and star-board bow) — and easily center the boat in the slip and control the motion of the boat. Each of your docklines should already have a loop in one end, and that's what you hook around each cleat on your boat. Put the line loop through the hole in the cleat, and then wrap it around the ends of the cleat for a secure connection.

Here's how to lash your lines to the dock:

1. **For the dockline on the bow, choose a cleat forward of the bow. For the stern dockline, choose a cleat aft of the bow. This arrangement keeps the boat in position at the dock.**

2. **Attach lines to your boat cleats by feeding the looped end of your dockline through the center eye on the boat cleat. Pull the loop through and spread it open and bend it back to the cleat putting it around each end of the cleat. Put one line on each cleat you'll want to tie to the dock.**

3. **Lash your lines around the cleats: Bring the line past the cleat and under the prong farthest from the boat cleat. Then bend it around the cleat under the back prong (see Figure 8-2).**

4. **Make figure-eights: Cross the line over the center of the cleat and around the front of the cleat under the front prong. Cross the line over the cleat again and then around and under the back prong (see Figure 8-3).**

5. **On the last loop, close your fist on the line with your palm up, making a U of the line.**

6. **Make a loop in the line by twisting your hand over so the loose end (boaters call that end the *bitter end*) of the line is underneath, and insert the last wrap under the line (see Figure 8-4).**

7. **Put the loop over the cleat's end and pull on the bitter end to cinch it tight (see Figure 8-5). That lashing will last until you take it out.**

Fasten docklines on all four quarters of your boat, and let out just enough line to suspend the boat in the middle of its slip. That's the key to avoiding damage and keeping your boat from rubbing against the dock.

Figure 8-2:
To lash a line to the cleat, take the line around the farthest end of the cleat and around the side away from the boat.

Figure 8-3:
Wrap the line in a figure-eight around the cleat.

Figure 8-4:
Tuck the last wrap under the line.

Figure 8-5:
Pull the bitter end to tighten the lashing.

Tying up when you dock alongside

When docking alongside the pier, you won't be able to tie your boat on both sides. In this case, you'll need to rely on fenders positioned between the boat and the pier for protection. Here's how to tie up alongside:

1. **Loop two docklines, one onto the boat's bow cleat (front) and one onto its stern cleat (back), and let them both lie in the boat until you need to tie them to the dock.**

2. **Hang fenders at two or three points between the dock and boat to prevent scratches and scuffs from wave and wind action.**

   Your boat most likely has a *midships* cleat (a cleat in the middle), and that's a great place to hang a fender. Lash the fender line onto the cleat, leaving enough rope out that the fender hangs between the dock and the boat. Do the same with the stern cleat. If your boat is long enough and you have more connection points, put out as many fenders as you have for maximum protection.

3. **Adjust the length of the fenders' lines so they can't ride up on the dock or tuck in below, where they won't protect your boat.**

   You can adjust the fender height by adding or subtracting a loop or two around the cleat.

4. **Tie your docklines from the stern and the bow to cleats on the dock.**

   You'll probably find several cleats on the dock; choose the ones that are about a quarter of your boat's length beyond your bow and stern cleats. That distance allows the boat to move up and down with the waves but still keeps it in place.

Many boaters forget to pull their fenders in when they go boating. I expect better from you! Leaving fenders out marks you as a beginner. It's also dangerous because as you speed along the water, the fenders can bounce back into the boat, striking passengers and causing injury.

Undocking and shoving off

Docking your boat and tying it up are all very well and good, but I imagine the time will come when you'll want to undo the process and get back out onto the water.

The following steps help get you untied and safely underway, but there's no hard and fast procedure because as in docking, conditions (where you are, what the water and wind are doing, and so on) always change. The key, as in all boating activities, is to be safe and take your time.

1. Do a safety check, looking all around your boat and checking for prop clearance.

2. Run the bilge fan for two or three minutes to remove gasoline vapors before starting your engine.

3. Take note of wind and current conditions, considering which way they may push you.

4. With the engine warmed and ready for a trot, have your crew untie the downwind or down-current lines first, whether they be port or starboard or from the bow or the stern in a crosswind or crosscurrent.

   A true captain calls these lines the *leeward,* nautically pronounced *lou-word,* and uses *astern* for "from the stern."

5. Have your crew unlash the upwind or up-current lines from the cleats but hold onto them until you're ready to begin moving safely away from the slip.

   Boating lingo for "upwind" is *windward.*

6. Make sure the way is clear outside your moorings, and nudge the boat in gear to pull out.

7. Have your crew pull in the lines and fenders and stow them safely.

 If you're boating alone, the process of undocking and shoving off doesn't change much, but you can expect to be a lot busier than if you had a crew. Follow the same steps, and after moving a safe distance from the dock, put the engine in idle and stow your lines and fenders securely before moving on.

Rafting Up with Fellow Boaters

Rafting up with other boats (meaning tying your boat to others) is a biggie in the book of boating fun, and it's a great way to meet new boating friends. Look around on any lake and you can find a number of favorite spots for it. You probably also see some boats already hitched together.

Raft up carefully by following the guidelines in this section, and you'll make friends and impress people with your expertise!

Approaching a boat or raft at anchor

If you approach another boat the wrong way and cause damage, or if you try to join up with a rafted group that doesn't want guests, you'll make enemies instead of friends. Do two things before you approach a boat or group that's anchored:

1. **Find out if they want company.**

   You can hail them with a friendly shout or raise them on the VHF radio, if you both have one. But no matter how you communicate, establish mutual intent before you approach.

2. **Find out on which side of the boat they want you to approach.**

The captain or crew on the other boat may try to coach you in, but their directions may be confusing and counterproductive. It's best to have a strong strategy for doing it yourself that includes cooperating with the boat or boats you're approaching.

Hitching your boats together

There's no trick to hitching boats together, and it's much like hitching to a dock. One difference, though, is that you use shorter, tighter lines with fenders between the boats for protection. Hopping back and forth between boats simply isn't safe unless the moorings are firm and secure.

Follow these six easy steps to raft up like a pro:

1. **After you and the other boaters have agreed which side you'll be tying up to, position your boat so your bow is facing the same direction as theirs.**

   This positioning makes mooring easier and also makes pulling away later easier, too, because you can back out without having to maneuver around the anchor lines from the other boat's bow.

2. **Approach slowly, shifting in and out of gear to moderate speed.**

3. **When your boat's stern is even with their stern, tap the shifter into reverse to stop motion.**

4. **Tie a couple of fenders to the side of the boat that is against theirs.**

   Your fenders should hang so they nest between both boats, preventing the boats from touching (see the next section for more on using fenders).

5. **Fasten mooring lines to the cleats on the side of your boat that's against the other boat.**

6. **Hand over your mooring lines, and let the other boaters fasten them to their cleats.**

If the other boat is already securely anchored, you don't need to put down your anchor, too. In the event that you do need to drop your anchor, see the later section, "Determining where and how to set the anchor."

Putting fenders at the rubbing points

Fender placement is so critical to protecting boats from damage. I discuss using fenders between your boat and the dock earlier in this chapter, but here are a few more suggestions for fastening and keeping fenders in the perfect position while you're rafted up with another boat:

- ✔ **Fenders need to hang along the most vertical area of your freeboard and the other boat's freeboard.** *Freeboard* is just a fancy term for the side of your boat; a boat with a lot of freeboard has high sides. By positioning fenders between the most vertical surfaces, you can minimize the fenders' movement and increase their effectiveness.

- ✔ **Put fenders out on your boat even if the boat you're mooring with has them out as well.** It's a double insurance policy that each boat has the protection where it's needed.

- ✔ **Keep checking the fenders periodically to be sure the knots are tight and the fenders remain in the best position to protect.** I find so many fenders floating on the water when I boat that I may never need to buy another one!

When your fenders aren't in use, stow them in a clean area free of grit and sand. Sand and grit can become stuck in the fenders, turning them into sanding blocks instead of protectors.

Breaking up the party and the raft

Eventually it comes time to say good-bye and leave the raft. If you're on the outside of a raft, leaving is easy. Just cast off the lines and shove off or idle away to a safe distance before you hit the throttle.

If your boat is positioned between two other boats that don't want to leave, pulling away is slightly more complicated by the fact that when you back out the others will want to be able to pull their boats together and close up your space. Pass lines from one boat over yours to the other one. As you pull out, you and your crew have to guide the lines over your windshield and other potential snags on your boat. Idle away to a safe distance before you hit the throttle.

Be sure to say thanks to those who have helped and wave good-bye as you cruise into the sunset.

Anchoring Your Boat the Right Way with the Right Anchor

This may sound odd to you, but ask most boaters what they do with their speedboats and they'll tell you they drop a hook and hang out. *Hook* is just boater-slang for *anchor*, and the best part of boating, in many boaters' eyes, isn't going fast but stopping. An anchored boat out on the water can be like a private island in a secluded cove.

It's a myth that an anchor holds a boat in place by the force of its weight. In truth, an anchor holds a boat in place by hooking onto the bottom. That's why boaters call it a "hook."

Many kinds and shapes of anchors exist, and they differ in the bottom conditions they're made for. It doesn't matter much what they weigh as long as they sink at a practical velocity.

All anchors have several things in common, which I discuss in this section. I also recommend three anchors I think work best in most situations and one you shouldn't waste your money on.

For safety purposes, it's always good to have at least one spare anchor onboard. And sometimes you just need to drop more than one anchor, so a spare is a must.

Understanding the parts of an anchor

There's more to an anchor than just the hook part. Here's an overview of anchor parts and terms:

- ✔ The actual *anchor* is the metal device that hooks the bottom.

- ✔ A *chain* is attached to the anchor to help the anchor lie down on the bottom so it can dig into the mud or sand or snag a rock. The chain also provides a more secure connection for the part of your anchor tackle that's most vulnerable to being cut by chafing.

- ✔ *Rode* is rope that connects the chain and your boat. Nope, I didn't misspell *rode*. That's the nautical term for rope when it's attached to an anchor. I remember it by this gimmick: "My boat rode all night on the anchor."

- ✔ *Scope* is the amount of rode you let out on your anchor. Depending on conditions, your scope usually is three to five times the water's depth, and sometimes even longer scope is preferable.

✔ *Swing* is the amount of movement your boat experiences at anchor as the tide or wind changes direction. When you're planning to sleep out all night on the hook, you need to make sure your boat can swing 360 degrees around the anchor without hitting the shore or anything else.

Choosing the right anchor style

Different-shaped anchors exist for different duties. Some anchors hold well on mucky bottoms, and some hold better on rocky bottoms. Some waters vary from mucky, rocky, sandy, and weedy bottoms, so if you regularly need to anchor in all conditions, you definitely need to have more than one anchor. You should ask around about the waters you're boating in to get a hint of bottom structure and what anchors work best in your area. Here's a rundown of the most effective anchors and where they work best:

✔ A *plough anchor* (see Figure 8-6a) looks like an old horse-drawn plough. It has a blade shaped to dig under grass and then go deeper and deeper under it. A plough anchor also works well in sand, mud, and gravel, but it works poorly on rock.

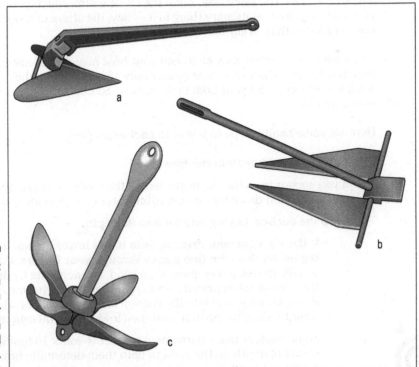

Figure 8-6:
A plough anchor (a), a fluke anchor (b), and a grapnel anchor (c).

✔ A *fluke anchor* (see Figure 8-6b) has two triangular sections called *flukes* and a long shaft to which you fasten a chain and rode. The flukes dig or plough into the bottom as tension is put on the anchor. This type of anchor works well in sand, fine gravel, and mud. It doesn't work well on grassy flats or hard rock because it tends to skim over the grass instead of digging in, and it doesn't always grip rock well.

✔ A *grapnel anchor* (see Figure 8-6c) looks like a device from an action-spy flick: It has a shaft and four or five hooked tines that can snag the edge of rocks or hard obstructions. It sometimes works well on grassy flats, too.

Determining where and how to set the anchor

Unlike parking your car in the garage, an anchored boat isn't stationary. This is important to keep in mind when choosing the place to put down your anchor.

Think of your anchored boat like a dog on the end of a staked rope. He can travel 360 degrees around the anchor point of that rope, and if you get inside his circle, you're his, for better or worse depending on the dog. A boat on an anchor can roam the same way. But if the circle within which your boat can move has any other stationary thing in it — say, the shore or a dock or a rock outcropping — then eventually your boat will hit it.

The wind or the current may shift, and your boat may drift in another direction. Sometimes, when your boat swings only 180 degrees on the anchor, the hook loses its grip and your boat drifts ashore. So choose your anchoring spot carefully.

Here are some handy steps to follow to anchor properly:

1. **Prepare to anchor from the bow.**

   If you anchor from the stern (the back), the anchor can pull the back end of the boat down far enough to let water in, especially in a current.

2. **Drop the anchor, paying attention to its depth.**

   • **If there's a current, drive up into it and lower the anchor, gauging its depth as the line passes through your fingers.** Current usually moves a boat more than wind, so anchoring by driving into the current takes priority over anchoring by driving into the wind. If you're alone, pull into the current ahead of the spot where you want to place the anchor, and then lower it as you drift away.

   Some boaters use a permanent marker to mark 10-foot increments of depth on the rode to help them determine how much scope to let out.

- **If there's a wind but little or no current, drive into the wind to lower the anchor.** Even a calm breeze will swing your boat around, so always drop the anchor upwind from the boat if there's no current.

If you're not boating alone, have a crew member lower the hook and report the depth to you, gauging its depth as the line passes through his or her fingers. He or she can pay out rode while you back away from the anchor (the next step), and then call out the length of the rode.

Minimum rode-to-depth ratio is 5 to 1. So, if your water depth is 10 feet, you should pay out at least 50 feet of rode, counting the chain. That seems like an enormous amount of rope for a shallow spot; maybe on a calm day you could get by with 30 feet, but if you want your anchor to hook up and stay that way, at least 50 feet is what it takes.

3. **When the anchor and rode are out to the appropriate length, back up the boat a bit away from the anchor.**

Keep the engine's force on the rode until you feel the anchor dig in and you quit drifting. Then you can turn the engine ignition to "Off."

It's always best to lower the anchor rather than to drop or throw it. The latter may cause the anchor and rode to tangle, making the anchor ineffective.

If you've dropped your hook correctly, you can relax and pop open a cold drink. And if you don't plan to move the boat until tomorrow, a beer or a cocktail may even be appropriate.

Keeping an eye out for drift while anchored

Even at anchor, you can't quite relax completely. You need to keep an eye open for anchor movement. Once you get your anchor set, take a couple of land bearings — maybe one on each side of the cove or lake or river, with you in between. If you notice any movement at all, keep an eye on things until the movement requires you to reset your anchor or it stops.

Many Global Positioning Systems (GPS) have software in them that lets them monitor your anchor position and sounds an alarm if it moves more than the distance you specify from its original spot, alerting you to the slippage. That's a great device to have onboard, and if you plan to stay out all night, you should be sure to get a GPS with that feature. (See Chapter 10 for more on GPS and other onboard gadgets.)

Weighing (raising) anchor

When it's time to head back to the dock or just explore the waters more, it's time to *weigh anchor* — or pull it up. Follow these steps:

1. **After checking for propeller clearance and running the bilge blower to remove gas fumes, start your engine.**

   You don't want to set yourself adrift by hoisting the anchor and then discovering the engine won't start.

2. **After the engine is warmed up and ready to go, have one of your crew pull in the anchor rode while you drive slowly up toward the anchor.**

3. **If the anchor is stuck to the bottom, have your crewperson turn a couple of figure-eight lashes around the bow cleat and hold the rode while you gently nudge the throttle forward to create more thrust to help pull the anchor loose.**

   If the anchor is really stuck, you may have to repeat this step, approaching the anchor point from several angles.

4. **When the anchor is free of the bottom, your crew member can pull it up, swishing it around in the water to remove mud and weeds before stowing it in the locker.**

The best way to stow the anchor in the locker is to just feed the rode into the locker as you pull in the anchor — don't worry about coiling the rode — and then lay the anchor on top of the rode. If your boat has special hangers for the anchor in the locker, use them.

If you boat alone, weighing anchor while piloting the boat is all your job. If there's no current, you can ease the boat up to the anchor, put the engine in neutral, and walk forward in the boat to hoist the anchor. If there's a current, pull upstream of the anchor, taking care not to foul the rode in the propeller, and pull the rode tight with the motor. This should nudge it loose. Then, with the engine in neutral, walk forward and hoist the anchor.

Part III

With Much Boating Fun Comes Much Responsibility

The 5th Wave   By Rich Tennant

"Don't worry, I brought the charts. Now, what are you, Leo or Capricorn?"

In this part . . .

T he best part of boating is heading away from the ramp or dock for a long day of adventure. But without the right gear and some important knowledge of boating safety, an adventure could turn into more than you bargained for. In this part, I explain the different needs boaters have for navigation electronics, charts, and communications equipment, and then I help you find the right stuff for your boat. I also explain how to handle yourself and your boat in unexpected bad weather or other emergencies.

Chapter 9

Rules Do Apply: Navigating to Avoid Collisions and Confusion

The United States Coast Guard publishes an enormous book of navigation rules that serve one main purpose: help boats avoid colliding with each other. But unless you plan to be a professional boater, neither the Coasties nor the local water cops will require you to know every page of these rules.

If you understand and follow the rules in this chapter, you'll have a head start on passing the rules section of any boater safety course you take — and more importantly, you'll stay safer in your boat. The rules help boaters know what to do when meeting, crossing paths, and overtaking other boaters, and they tell boaters how and when to moderate speed. The rules also explain traffic management schemes that guide you and other boaters along safe channels.

Sharing the Water: Boating Rules

States' boating rules are based on the U.S. Coast Guard Navigation Rules. The overlap makes sense because the Coast Guard has been regulating navigation in American waters since before some states were admitted into the Union. To help you better understand how boating rules work, here's more information on how state and U.S. Coast Guard rules overlap and interplay with each other:

✔ States and the U.S. Coast Guard cooperate to enforce rules in many state waters. However, the Coasties don't enforce navigation rules in land-locked waters that aren't open to commercial waterways, such as stand-alone lakes. The Coasties' primary concern is to protect boaters and commercial interests in waters used for shipping and commerce.

✔ With respect to safety equipment and boat registration rules, individual states often enforce a stricter code than the U.S. Coast Guard does, so you want to make sure you're aware of state rules.

✔ When it comes to watersports such as water-skiing, the Coasties don't make any rules, so individual states are responsible for establishing and enforcing watersports safety rules.

✔ In an accident, the Coast Guard rules form the basis for determining fault and liability of the parties involved.

Bottom line: Some states may have more restrictive boating rules than the U.S. Coast Guard, but in the absence of states' rules, the Coast Guard rules — well, *rule.*

Knowing the Coasties' rules gets you a long way toward being a safe boater, and if you master all 300 pages of them, you'll have gone a long way toward earning a captain's license. You can download a free copy of these rules at `www.navcen.uscg.gov/mwv/mwv_files/NR_Files/navrules.pdf.`

To study individual states' rules, you can visit `boat-ed.com`. This Web site provides boater safety training to satisfy many states' safety education requirements.

A note on terminology: The rules refer to your boat and all other boats as *vessels.* A vessel is any floating thing that you use to transport yourself on the water. A bathtub could be a vessel if you sit in it with a paddle and use it to cross a waterway! You also need to keep in mind the following distinctions:

✔ **Stand-on vessel:** This vessel is often called the "privileged vessel" in the rules. If it were a car, it would have the right of way.

✔ **Give-way vessel:** This vessel is often called the "burdened vessel." It has to give way to progress of the stand-on vessel.

Boating's golden rule: No right of way on the water

The Coast Guard rules were devised for the sole purpose of helping the captains of vessels avoid collisions. These rules set expectations for each captain's handling of his or her craft. But, unlike automobile traffic rules and laws, boating rules have one very important disclaimer: Nothing in the rules excuses a vessel captain for failure to take all necessary actions to avoid a collision.

What this means is that even though a captain may technically follow the rules all the way up until the point of collision, following the rules doesn't relieve him or her of responsibility if some other action could have avoided the collision. In other words, a boater can't stand on right-of-way rules if he could have avoided the collision by yielding or *giving way,* to use the Coasties' vernacular. It's almost like the Golden Rule: "Do unto others as you would have them do unto you."

So the rules aren't set laws that captains can enforce with the horn or their finger or other insulting gestures, like car drivers commonly do. (You wouldn't do that, would you?) However, the rules do set forth terms to indicate who has the greater obligation for maneuvering to avoid a collision: stand-on vessel versus give-way vessel. I define the terms in this section's introduction.

Maintaining a proper lookout

You may think it's kind of dumb to require a boater to maintain a lookout, but you'd be surprised how many boaters let their boats travel in one direction while they look in another. The wide-open spaces of lakes, bays, and oceans often lull boaters into a sense of feeling that they're the only ones out there.

If you collide into another boat, the shore, or a bridge abutment — all things I've seen happen — your citation from the authorities will probably include the line, "Failure to maintain a lookout." Here are the stats on the lookout rule:

- ✔ **Where this rule applies:** In all inland and international waters and in all conditions of visibility.
- ✔ **Exceptions:** None.
- ✔ **Special requirements:** In conditions of poor visibility, maintaining a proper lookout is only possible while maintaining a safe speed. For most foggy conditions or in hard-driving rain, a safe speed is often idle speed. Additionally, if your boat is equipped with radar, you should use it as part of your lookout.

Crossing paths with another vessel

The rules for vessels crossing paths with other vessels are a little like the rules for automobiles meeting at intersections. In boats, the vessel approaching from your *right* is the stand-on vessel and has the privilege to pass first (see Figure 9-1). Following are some basics on the scenario of crossing paths:

- ✔ **When this rule applies:** Whenever a risk of collision exists between two vessels on courses that may cross paths.

✔ **Exceptions:** None.

✔ **Special requirements:** The rules state that if there's any doubt that a risk of collision exists, the risk shall be deemed to exist. Just thinking there's a risk essentially establishes that there *is* one.

✔ **Stand-on or privileged vessel:** This vessel is approaching you from the right. The captain is showing you his or her left side, which is the side bearing the red navigation light (see the later section, "Light colors and locations on the boat"). I like to think of it as "seeing red": When you see red, you stop, just like on the highway.

✔ **Give-way or burdened vessel:** This vessel is approaching you from the left, and the captain is showing you the green navigation light, which effectively gives you the green to go ahead.

When you're the stand-on or give-way vessel in a particular encounter, you can't change your status by changing your course and veering around to one side in order to approach from another angle. Your status in any situation with another boat is determined by your relationship to the other boat at your first sighting of it. That's when you determine your risk of collision.

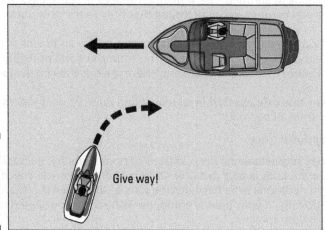

Figure 9-1: How vessels behave when crossing paths.

Give way!

Overtaking a vessel

A vessel overtaking another vessel (see Figure 9-2) doesn't technically have the right or the go-ahead to do so unless the overtaken vessel agrees to it. Agreement is established with horn or whistle signals or via radio, as I outline in Table 9-1.

Table 9-1	Horn and Whistle Signals for Overtaking a Vessel in U.S. Waters	
Number of Blasts	*From Which Vessel*	*What It Means*
1 short	Overtaking	"I want to pass you on your port (left) side."
1 short	Overtaken	The captain agrees to be overtaken on the port side.
2 short	Overtaking	"I want to leave you on my starboard (right) side."
2 short	Overtaken	The captain agrees to be overtaken on his port side.
5 short	Overtaken	The captain either doesn't understand the overtaking vessel's intentions or believes that overtaking is unsafe under the circumstances.

Be aware that the signals for passing in international waters are different than those for passing in U.S. waters. In international waters,

- ✔ **For a portside pass,** the signal is one prolonged blast followed by one short blast.

- ✔ **For a starboard pass,** the signal is one prolonged blast followed by two short blasts.

Here are some stats on the rules for overtaking another vessel:

- ✔ **When this rule applies:** Overtaking rules ordinarily apply only when navigating in a narrow waterway, such as a river, canal, or channel dredged in shallow water, because these waterways are like highways with traffic coming both ways in a relatively narrow space. In open water, it's much easier to veer far away from the overtaken vessel and overtake it without impacting traffic in any direction.

- ✔ **Exceptions:** A vessel coming up from behind your vessel that veers far out to your starboard side and then swoops back in front of you doesn't change status from *overtaking* to *crossing*. It's still an overtaking vessel and must abide by these rules.

- ✔ **Special requirements:** The vessel overtaking has to do so at a safe speed, with the captain mindful of his or her wake. Passing another boat and pummeling it with a large wake is bad manners, not to mention dangerous and against the law.

✔ **Stand-on or privileged vessel:** The vessel being overtaken is always the privileged vessel in the encounter. The privileged captain should not unduly prevent the overtaking boat from passing and should hold course to allow the passing, presuming the captain agreed to it in the first place, which should be the case unless he or she knows of dangers that the overtaking captain can't see.

✔ **Give-way or burdened vessel:** If you're overtaking, you're responsible for getting the stand-on vessel's permission to overtake before doing it safely and without shaking up the other boat with your wake.

To be honest, you seldom hear horn signals anymore. I think that's partly because many boaters don't bother to learn what they mean and therefore don't bother to use them. Unfortunately, it's an unsafe situation. As a safe alternative to sound signals, many boaters today rely on VHF radio communications instead. If you're monitoring your VHF, you may hear a boater call for a "one-whistle pass," meaning he or she wants to pass on the other boater's port side. That other boater may respond by saying that a one-whistle pass is fine with him or her. That's often the only hint of horn and whistle signals on the water today — and it's okay to handle it that way as long as communication and coordination are the goals.

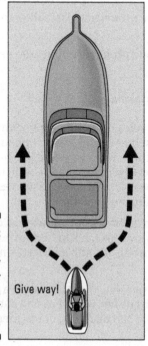

Figure 9-2: How a vessel may pass or overtake another vessel.

Give way!

Meeting another vessel head-on

Vessels approaching each other from a head-on heading are in a *meeting* situation. Both captains should steer their vessels to the right to avoid a collision. Chances are you'll do this instinctively because of your automobile driving habit of staying on the right.

Here's the lowdown on the rules for meeting head-on:

- ✔ **When this rule applies:** Any time vessels are approaching each other from a head-on or nearly head-on heading, the rule applies. If you're unsure whether you're on a collision course with a vessel, the rules say to assume you *are* on one.

- ✔ **Exceptions:** None.

- ✔ **Special requirements:** The rules state that each captain should make a deliberate and obvious course correction so the approaching vessel's captain can see the change and thereby understand the other captain's intentions. If one captain does this before the other one, the approaching vessel is required to follow suit.

- ✔ **Stand-on and give-way vessels:** These terms have no meaning in this situation. Both vessels are expected to show equal consideration to the other in getting by safely.

Keeping your speed in check

For most foggy conditions or in hard-driving rain, a safe speed is often idle speed. When overtaking another vessel (refer to the section "Overtaking a vessel"), you should maintain a safe speed and be particularly mindful of your wake.

For nighttime boating, the first thing you need to remember is to slow down to a safe speed. The U.S. Coast Guard often refers to "safe speed" but never specifies what that is; they simply direct you to choose a "safe and prudent speed," which I'm sure you agree means slower in the dark. Your local state laws, however, may indeed specify nighttime speed limits. I've seen some set at 5 miles per hour and some set at 30 mph.

In the absence of a posted speed limit, a safe speed is a judgment call that must be made by the captain. One thing I've observed about myself in boating is this: If I have a sneaking feeling that something in my piloting is going wrong, a downward speed adjustment usually cures the feeling.

Reading Boat Lights

Boats don't have headlights, and there are no lines on the waterways. It's difficult to see things that get in your way at night or in bad weather, in particular. The rules don't distinguish between low visibility due to nighttime boating and low visibility due to fog, rain, or sleet. They specify operating procedures for boats in "restricted visibility," period.

When it comes to bad weather, I recommend that you just don't boat in the fog or heavy rain, but you probably will, either out of a sense of adventure or because you inadvertently get trapped out in the fog. (I discuss the dangers of navigating bad weather in Chapter 11.)

When boating in any conditions, but particularly in the dark or low visibility, the key concern is seeing and interpreting boat lights. You need to employ your boat's navigation lights to let other boaters know where you are and which way you're headed, and you need to understand the same about them.

There are often many, many lights along the shore, and they tend to interfere with your perception of other boats' navigation lights, a situation that calls for added care. I discuss navigation lights that aren't on boats later in this chapter, in the section "Understanding Navigation Markers."

Light colors and locations on the boat

Your boat lights may not be obvious in daylight, but at night, your lights are visible for miles if they're up to National Marine Manufacturers Association (NMMA) standards (see Chapter 3 for more on the NMMA). In this section, I explain the basic navigation lights and what they mean. You can see a typical configuration of navigation lights in Figure 9-3.

Light configurations for power boats include a combination of red, green, and white lights, as follows:

- ✔ **Red:** This is a bow or side light on the port (left) side of the boat. It's designed to shine in an arc from the tip of the bow to behind the helm station (or driver's seat).

- ✔ **Green:** This is a bow or side light on the starboard (right) side of the boat, where it shines over the same arc as the red light on the port side.

- ✔ **White:** All boats have either one all-around white light or two lights that combine to make a white light visible 360 degrees around the boat. An all-around white light is usually located on the stern or back of the boat.

If two white lights are used, one is usually somewhere near the middle (*midships*) and the other is on the stern.

✔ **Yellow:** Boats towing or pushing other boats are required to display a yellow light facing aft toward the rig being towed. There could be a great distance between the tow boat and the towed boat, so crossing paths too close to a yellow light is a bad idea until you're sure of the position of both the tow vessel and the towed vessel.

Most states have rules about when you need to turn on your lights. These rules often mimic traffic rules, such as turning on your headlights at sunset or 30 minutes before sunset. Check your local boating rules and comply with them.

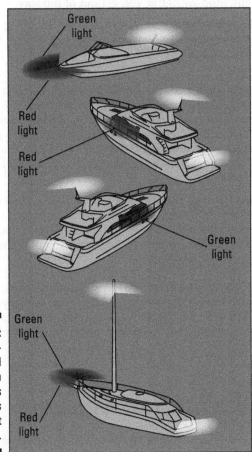

Figure 9-3: The configuration of all navigation lights for boats under about 40 feet.

Interpreting the lights you see

In daylight or clear boating weather, a boat's lights may not be obvious, but chances are, at night you won't see any part of another boat but the lights. Knowing what these navigation lights mean is the trick to safe nighttime navigating. After you've taken a few night excursions, determining what the lights are showing you will become second nature, like reading a traffic light. Here's a rundown of light combinations and their meanings:

- ✔ **A red light and a white light** mean the boat is approaching you from your right. The red light also means you must give way or stay out of the way. Usually when you meet a boat showing you its red light, you treat it like a red traffic light: Stop, or better yet, get out of the way.

- ✔ **A green light and a white light** mean the boat is approaching you from your left. Green means go, and you have the right to proceed. But the rules say don't push it: If you don't think the other vessel will give way, move yourself.

- ✔ **A red and green light visible at the same time** mean a boat is headed directly at you. You'll also see a white light over the colored lights. Don't pause to think too long in this situation — turn hard to one side or the other or, if you're stopped, get moving out of the other boat's path. In a meeting situation, steer to your right; the other captain should do the same. You should both do it decisively enough that you can clearly see each other's intentions.

- ✔ **A white light** means the boat is either heading away from you or at anchor — and you're heading right for it. Unless its anchored or you're overtaking it, you don't need to take action unless the other boat suddenly shows its colored lights as well, indicating the captain has turned around and there may be risk of collision.

Remember that boats don't have headlights. They're actually illegal, and it's also illegal to travel a waterway with a spotlight shining the way. If you're stopped, you're allowed to use a spotlight, but be careful not to shine it at other boats, because it will disrupt their captains' night vision, which is also illegal.

Understanding Navigation Markers

Navigation markers are a lot like the lines on the roadways, stop signs, and yield signs. They have a look and a language all their own, though, and you need to get the basics down quickly or you'll find yourself hard aground or under the hard stare of a Coastie or local water cop. You could even get a ticket for not observing navigation markers.

Some navigation markers are lighted, making them visible at night or in conditions of low visibility, but others aren't lighted, so you need to keep your eyes peeled at all times for markers of any kind. Day markers are unlighted markers that mark safe waterways or places to avoid in your boat. These markers appear on posts and buoys, depending on current, depth, and what the markers need to say.

If you're in waters that you can navigate by unlighted markers only in the daytime, then you shouldn't be out on these waters at night. Although commercial boats and some yachts have night vision equipment and radar that can spot these markers, making navigation easier and safer for them, boating at night in treacherous waters is best left to the professionals (with the exception of an idle speed cruise for the evening).

In this section, I explain the most common navigation markers — lighted and unlighted — and what they mean. When you take your boater safety course, you'll get the full lowdown on all the markers in your locale.

Intracoastal Waterway markers

Certain markers measure about 1 meter across and are posted on wood or metal pilings. When boaters are pointing them out, they often say, "There's the sticks, there." These "sticks" mark a channel that runs from New England around Florida to Texas. It's called the *Intracoastal Waterway,* or ICW.

The two kinds of ICW markers are a red triangle and a green square (see Figure 9-4). The different shapes help you distinguish between these markers even if you can't tell what color they are. The numbers on the marks correspond with numbers printed on charts so that you can tell where the heck you are (I discuss using charts in Chapter 10). So what does each ICW marker mean?

- ✔ **Red, even-numbered triangles** signify the side of the channel closest to the mainland. If you disregard them, you may ground your boat in shallows or encounter other obstructions.

- ✔ **Green, odd-numbered squares** are always closest to the open-ocean side of the channel, even if there's land between you and the ocean, such as an island. If you disregard them, you could hit obstructions or get lost. Green ICW day markers often have matching green lights to help guide the way at night. On a chart, lighted markers are noted by a small, light bulb–like symbol.

Other channel and navigation markers

Local channels that lead into private moorings or community canals are supposed to be marked with triangles and squares that are noticeably smaller than ICW markers (refer to the preceding section). But sometimes they appear to be the same size, which makes it confusing when the channel intersects with the ICW. In that case, you may need to consult a chart.

If you can't distinguish intersecting channel markers because they all appear to be the same size, check to see if the numbers are consecutive. If the last green, square, odd-numbered marker you saw was number 9, the next one should be 7 or 11. If not, then you're probably looking at a marker for the intersecting channel and not the ICW. But that's a little like playing craps, so you should consult a chart — unless you can clearly see where the string of markers leads.

In addition to posted sign markers, channel and navigation markers may appear in the form of buoys and lights.

Figure 9-4:
Red (left) and green (right) ICW day markers.

Buoys

Some intersecting channels and most rivers are marked with floating buoys. They make life easier because these buoys are noticeably different from ICW sticks. Four types of these buoys exist:

- **Both red and green:** Channel entry buoys have red-over-green marks or green-over-red marks (see Figure 9-5). If red is on top, treat it like a red mark. If green is on top, treat it like a green mark. (If this sounds confusing, read on to find out precisely what red and green marks mean.)

- **Red "nun" buoys:** I think these conical red buoys sometimes look like Russian nesting dolls. But somebody else must've thought they look like nuns, because that's the nickname that stuck — I'm sure they meant no disrespect. Red "nun" buoys, shown in Figure 9-6, are even-numbered and mark the outermost right side of a channel or river as you enter it. As you enter a river going upstream, you should keep the nun buoy on your right or starboard side, between you and the shore.

✔ **Green "can" buoys:** No mystery about what these look like: green cans (see Figure 9-7). They mark the left side of a channel or river as you enter it from the sea or other large body of water. Green can buoys are all odd-numbered. Naturally, if you head downstream or return to sea, as the case may be, you want these buoys on your right side.

✔ **White and red or white and orange buoys:** When you see these warning markers, stop, determine what warnings or directions are marked on them, and obey them or risk a collision, a ticket, or both. Here are some examples of warnings indicated by such buoys:

- Keep away from underwater obstructions.

- Keep out of a particular area, such as a swimming area or an environmentally sensitive area.

- Heed special navigation restrictions, such as speed limits or zones that require "no wake" or "idle speed only" operation.

There are two old sayings to help you remember which side of the boat you should keep red and green buoys on as you navigate into a harbor channel or river: "Red right returning" means to keep the red ones on your right when returning to the channel, and "green going out" means to keep the green ones on your right when leaving a river or channel. Leaving a river always involves going downstream.

Figure 9-5:
A red and green buoy marks the intersection of two channels.

Figure 9-6:
A red "nun"
buoy will
be on your
right as you
head into
the channel
it marks.

Figure 9-7:
A green
"can" buoy
will be on
your left as
you head
into the
channel it
marks.

Bridge and other navigation lights

Bridges have lights showing you where it's safe to pass underneath, but you still need to know the bridge clearance, which is indicated on a chart or sign posted on the bridge. Green bridge lights show where it's safe to proceed under a bridge. Red lights indicate the boundaries of safe passage. As you approach the bridge, you'll see both colored lights. Pilot your boat under the green ones.

Partially submerged obstructions like floating breakwaters and other man-made obstructions are required to be marked with white lights.

Green lights on dry land mean you're probably too close to shore and are seeing a traffic light. Backtrack! (I'm sort of kidding, but I have boated in places where you could see traffic lights along the water.)

Chapter 10

Finding Your Way on the Water

. . . .

In This Chapter

▶ Charting your way safely on the water

▶ Using a tried and true navigation tool: The compass

▶ Keeping in touch via VHF radio

▶ Using sonar and radar for safety (and for finding fish)

▶ Navigating with GPS gear on smaller waters

. . . .

Christopher Columbus didn't need any of the navigation devices we have today. He stumbled upon the New World with the most rudimentary tools, and I bet he would have given his right arm for a Cracker Jack spy compass and a sixth-grader's hand-sketched world map homework project. He checked his depths (which is called *taking soundings*) by tossing a lead sinker on a line overboard and measuring the line when the lead hit the bottom.

Today, for less than the price of an MP3 player, you can buy more navigating power than the early astronauts had — and in a very compact package. It's called a Global Positioning System (GPS), it costs as little as $100, and it can pinpoint your position anywhere on earth and clearly display it on an LCD screen. For another $100, you can get sonar so sophisticated you can spot big fish and tell them from the little ones before wetting a hook. More important, with GPS and sonar, you can keep your boat and crew safe from grounding and on the best route to wherever you want to go. Yet many boaters still don't think they need this equipment, and most don't even know how to use a basic compass.

I can't teach you the detailed intricacies of the complex and fine art of sea navigation, but I can get you across a lake. I can tell you what tools you need for safe, simple navigation, where to get them, and how to teach yourself to use them. By the end of this chapter, I hope you'll see the logic of getting (and knowing how to read) a compass and a chart of your waters and maybe even sonar and GPS units. I also tell you what you can expect these tools to tell you. And maybe I can even talk you into a VHF radio, so that you can tell your friends and other boaters that you absolutely do know where you are!

Charting Your Course Over Big and Little Waters

A chart of your boating waters not only helps you navigate more safely, but it can help you more easily discover cool places to take your boat. In the old days of piracy, or just good old kingdom-to-kingdom warfare, charts of unknown waters were among the most important booty. Charts are almost as valuable today.

You may expect to need a chart for traveling offshore — say, to the Bahamas — but you'll also find inland coastal waters like the Intracoastal Waterway (ICW) difficult to navigate without a chart. (Not familiar with the ICW? Check out the sidebar, "Get to know the ICW.") Sure, there are plenty of landmarks, but the channels twist and turn, and even if the route only veers a few degrees, that's enough to put you deep in a sandbar if you don't veer with it.

The hardest argument to win is for buying a chart mapping smaller lakes when a boater often can see every shore from any one spot. You need to keep in mind that even though the water may look flat and easy to navigate, the bottom of the lake it covers may be crazy with rocky outcroppings, long rocky areas called *reefs,* and sandbars. Without a chart, you have to find them by trial and error — a very expensive method.

This section is about what charts can tell you and how you as a recreational boater can use them to keep the wet side of your boat down and the propeller turning. It also tells you how to use charts for fishing and gives sources for finding the fish if you get stumped.

Understanding chart basics

Charts are based mostly on depth soundings and surveying information compiled by the National Oceanic and Atmospheric Administration (NOAA). That information is kept in digital format and updated for changes almost daily. The NOAA's primary charge is to provide navigation information to commercial mariners, so waters non-navigable by commercial traffic aren't always surveyed. Paper charts you buy locally at your marina or marine accessory or tackle store — whether strictly for navigation or with key fishing spots marked on them — most often come from the NOAA data. You can purchase two types of paper charts:

- ✔ **Nautical charts:** Available to help you find your way in most commercial waters

- ✔ **Fishing charts:** Often available for waters that aren't navigable (in other words, they aren't big and deep enough for ships); make a good substitute for nautical charts

Get to know the ICW

The *Intracoastal Waterway*, called the ICW by most mariners, is a popular water route among recreational boaters, but it was initially created in 1919 to aid commercial marine traffic by offering protected waters on which to navigate in rough weather. The ICW runs from the southern tip of Texas, around the U.S. coast of the Gulf of Mexico and around Florida, and up the East Coast to Maine. The route connects many natural rivers and bays as well as manmade canals to make a continuous route around the Atlantic and Gulf coasts.

Funding for the ICW was to come from marine fuel taxes, but the cost of maintaining the route has far exceeded that funding, and in some places, *shoaling* (the result of sand drifting and piling up in waterways, blocking them) has caused the ICW to fill in to depths as shallow as 7 feet. Whenever you navigate — or just plain play in — the ICW, it's a good idea to check with knowledgeable boaters for local information on the condition of the waterway. Note any concerns on your chart.

As you may imagine, charts are obsolete in small ways almost the moment they're printed. Currents shift sands, and storms move islands. For example, during Hurricane Charlie in Florida in 2004, Captiva Island was cut in two, and entries to some ports were filled by the storm's currents. When one channel to a harbor on Captiva Island was redredged, it was 75 feet from its original location! When you're venturing into an unknown area, I recommend that you check in with local boaters (at the marina or marine accessory or tackle store) for local knowledge and compare it to your chart. Despite small inaccuracies, charts are still mandatory for safe navigation because they're the best information available at any given time.

Using navigation or nautical charts

On a navigation or nautical chart, you can virtually visit your new favorite boating waters, visualize the courses to the places you want to visit, and make mental notes of the appropriate channels to use and the boat-crunching rocks and reefs to avoid. Almost everything you need to know about unfamiliar waters is on a navigation chart.

Charts are readily available for *navigable waterways,* which simply are those used by commercial marine traffic. These waters include the oceans, coastal waterways, Intracoastal Waterway, inland rivers, and the Great Lakes. Smaller landlocked lakes not open to commercial waters are considered *non-navigable* (but are almost always still usable for recreational boating) and sometimes aren't as easy to find charts for. That's changing quickly, however, because private entities are compiling maps of non-navigable waterways for consumer and government use.

When you want to know where the channels are, what the markers mean, or how high a bridge over the water is, charts have the answers and much more.

Following is the lowdown on navigational chart contents; knowing what information is on charts makes using them practically self-explanatory.

- **Cardinal directions:** A compass rose printed on the chart tells you how the chart is aligned with respect to magnetic north and true north (see the sidebar "True north and magnetic north" for more details). The compass rose looks a bit like a sundial and is usually printed in rose-colored ink. It's marked in the 360 degrees of all points of the compass, including north, south, east, and west, giving the casual navigator (you and me) a visual guideline for navigating between points. Accomplished navigators use a variety of tools in conjunction with charts to determine exact courses to the next destination on their trips.

- **Geographic "lay of the land":** A navigation chart tells you where land ends and water begins. It clearly identifies every bend in the river, every cove off the shore, and any islands in the region. Coastal cities and community canal systems are all on navigation charts, too. You get landmarks as well as indications of cool places you may like to explore.

- **Depth soundings:** Deep water is white or very light blue on charts, whereas shallow water is a progressively darker shade of blue (it's darkest where it's most shallow). Numbers scattered throughout the water are depth soundings that indicate how deep the water was at mean low tide when the depths were last measured for charting purposes.

- **Local channel markers:** Out in a channel, red triangles with even numbers and green squares with odd numbers mark each side of the channel. Your job is to go between them, keeping green on the right going out and red on the right returning to port. The number of each marker is reflected on the chart so you can find yourself on the chart by the marker number. (Turn to Chapter 9 for coverage of channel markers and other navigation laws.)

- **Intracoastal Waterway (ICW):** A popular water route among recreational boaters, the ICW runs from the southern tip of Texas, through the Gulf of Mexico, around Florida, and up the East Coast to Maine. This waterway is marked by red, even-numbered triangles and green, odd-numbered squares on stationary pilings. These ICW markers are similar to but usually larger than local channel markers (see Chapter 9). When you stay between the red and green marks, the green marker will always be closest to the open ocean, and there will usually be land between you and the ocean. The number, shape, and color of each marker is reflected on the chart, so if you're near buoy number three, for example, you can find it on your chart and know your position.

- **Buoys:** Floating buoys sometimes mark channels in lieu of triangular and square markers on pilings. They're numbered and marked on charts for the same reasons as other channel markers.

From the outside, a cuddy is easy to spot thanks to its closed deck on the bow.

Close the deck on a bowrider and you get a cozy cuddy cabin like this one.

Deck boats offer spacious seating similar to that of pontoon boats, but the fiberglass hull provides the sporty ride of a bowrider or cuddy.

Deck boats have an open bow for spacious seating up front. It's accomplished by widening the beam, or width of the boat, at the bow.

The best part of boating is finding your own private spot and dropping an anchor for an afternoon of swimming and hanging out.

Rugged and sporty, inflatables offer spacious cockpits and plenty of passenger carrying capacity.

Inflatable boats like this Zodiac perform beautifully on lower horsepower and are easily towed behind smaller vehicles.

Pontoon boats offer the most seating and deck space per foot of deck. New models with high horsepower also

Walleye boats have trolling motors and livewells like bass boats, but they're built with a deeper freeboard and often a windshield to handle rougher waters and cooler weather.

The best fish and ski boats blend both skiing and fishing features together in a boat that lets boaters enjoy both sports without compromise. The casting decks on this fish and ski boat can be covered with sun pads, and the trolling motor has been removed to streamline the boat.

Flats boats can float in just 1 foot of water and have a poling platform for the angler to stand on to quietly maneuver the boat with a pole while fishing.

Bay boats like this Ranger are similar to center consoles but have a shallower freeboard to ease casting and can run in less than 2 feet of water.

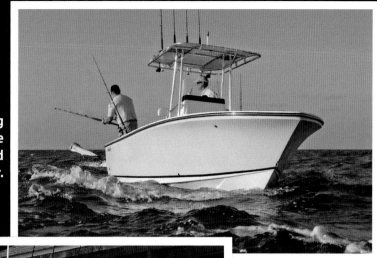

Rugged center console offshore fishing boats and many bay boats have deep cockpits for deflecting spray and handling rough water.

Walkarounds, also called express boats, are equipped for serious fishing but also have many comfort features for overnighting and day cruising.

This center console boat is in full action — and loaded up for a day of fishing — on the water.

A pointed bow and open deck with seating are the hallmarks of a bowrider. The transom platform offers a fun hangout at anchor, but stay away from it when the motor is running.

The cuddy is just as sporty as a bowrider, but thanks to the closed forward deck, a cuddy cabin below offers sleeping accommodations.

✔ **Obstructions:** Wrecks, reefs, and rock piles are marked on charts and their depths noted. Some obstructions have physical markers on them in the water, and information about the markers and their meanings is noted in fine print on the corresponding mark on the chart.

✔ **Bridge or power line heights:** Most power boaters don't have to worry about clearance for most bridges and power lines. But some lines and bridges are low even for boats without sails and masts. That's why all overhead obstructions and their heights over the water are noted on charts. (On a bridge itself, a clearance gauge indicates the exact clearance height at any given tide.)

For most casual boaters, just knowing the lay of the land, depths, obstructions, and channels is enough for safe boating. But the more you use a chart when boating, the more you imprint that information in your mind's eye. You'll soon find many other interesting details in charts that may help you navigate more effectively. There's much more to navigating waterways and charts than I discuss in this section, but considering that most casual boaters don't even have a chart, let alone know what it can tell them, you're a step ahead of those misguided navigators if you use charts.

Using fishing charts

For inland waters, I've found that the best charts are printed for fishermen. You may be hoping to avoid an underwater obstruction, but anglers absolutely want to find one because such obstructions usually hold fish.

Many inland waters are considered non-navigable and therefore may never have had navigation charts made for them. Oh, you can boat in these waters, and you should, but like an oversized pond, there's no way to get your boat outside the shores except with a trailer. So a 5,000-acre lake in northern Minnesota may not have a navigation chart, but the U.S. Geological Survey (USGS) maps it, and that information is used to produce fishing maps with surprising detail.

Sometimes actual navigation data, like channels, markers, bridge height, and other structures, is sadly lacking from fishing charts. In that case, you should use a navigation chart in conjunction with a fishing chart.

Here's a little of what you can expect from fishing charts:

✔ Fishing charts usually (but not always) have all the information of NOAA navigation charts — if NOAA charts on the particular waters exist.

✔ Some fishing charts are based on USGS information. The USGS surveys aren't conducted with navigation in mind but rather focus on terrain features. Maps based on this information may not have sound navigational information.

USGS–based maps often have more detailed depth information than nautical charts and show contours of the land under the water.

✔ Being created by fishermen, for fishermen, fishing charts mark historically productive fishing holes, points, bays, and sometimes underwater springs bringing in cool water that can attract fish in the heat of summer.

Where to buy your charts

Charts are usually available from marine and tackle retailers. You can also buy them from the government, and in some communities, I've found accurate navigational charts as promotional giveaways paid for by local advertisers. Here's a rundown of some sources:

✔ **Local sources:** Most boating communities have charts available through marinas, tackle stores, or boating accessory stores.

✔ **Free sources:** Local chambers of commerce may have basic navigation maps with at least rudimentary detail available at no charge.

✔ **Online sources:**

- www.nauticalcharts.noaa.gov: This Web site identifies sources for downloadable charts and local sources for buying charts. These sources are often digital operators who print out a chart when you request it, resulting in a chart with up-to-the-minute changes.

- www.fishinghotspots.com: This company has an extensive selection of fishing maps, with pretty good navigation information, too. The site lets you purchase charts for many coastal, intracoastal, and inland waterways that are printed on waterproof paper that can stand up to tough abuse.

Finding True North (And the Way Home) with a Compass

Fewer and fewer boaters know how to use a compass. And fewer and fewer boats come with a compass as standard equipment or are ever equipped with one later. With often two GPS units available onboard for redundancy and a handheld stowed for backup, it's easy to see why a compass may seem needless.

I, too, felt that compasses were unnecessary until I once went 25 miles off-shore in a new boat on a mostly sunny day and followed my course on the GPS. I fished for several hours, moving at random but mostly easterly, when scattered clouds joined to form threatening thunderheads and hid the sun. When I turned for home, I noticed the GPS wasn't working. My untried compass was the only way back.

I set the boat on an easy idle in a straight line, pointing at what I hoped was the west, and watched the compass settle. It agreed with my choice, and I nervously hunkered down for the 30-minute ride to get back in sight of land. If the compass had failed due to my negligence in not checking its accuracy, I could've traveled farther into the Atlantic, run out of gas, and drifted until someone noticed I was gone.

That confession made, in this section I tell you what to look for in a compass and how to get some basic directions from it — in other words, what I should have done on that cloudy fishing day. Then please do what I say, not what I did!

Discovering how a compass works

A compass won't tell you how to get home. All it can do is point north by aligning itself with the earth's magnetic poles — one to the north, one to the south. Fortunately for navigators, pointing north is something even inexpensive compasses do with reassuring regularity. Here are a few more details to brush up on to master your compass:

- ✔ **Cardinal directions:** North, east, south, and west are called the *cardinal directions*. They're arranged on the compass dial, which is called the *card*, in a clockwise fashion.

- ✔ **A matter of degrees:** There are 360 degrees counting from zero, which is north, to 90, which is east. South is 180 degrees from north. West is 270 degrees from north. The compass dial is divided into degrees so you can plot a course in any direction *between* any two of the cardinal directions.

- ✔ **Always points north:** When you turn your boat, your compass card rotates to always point north. The adjustment pulls the direction of your course into view on the compass and aligns it with the mark on the front called a *lubber line* (see Figure 10-1).

Navigating with a compass

Using a compass isn't as hard as trusting it. There's much more to compass navigation than I can tell you here, but hopefully this section helps you see the possibilities and at least crack open the compass instruction manual to bone up on navigating the way Columbus did. If you don't already have a compass, I may even get you thinking of shopping for one.

For using a compass in the most rudimentary way, you first need to check it for accuracy against known landmarks. In this section, I fill you in on how to do that and then tell you how your compass can help you find your way while boating.

Checking your compass for accuracy

Every time you launch your boat, the first thing you should do is check your compass — assuming that your boat came with a compass or you bought one. Here's how:

1. **Point the boat toward something you know to be a specific direction in degrees from your position.**

   Suppose the harbormaster told you the enormous water tower outside the harbor is on a course of 110 degrees from the harbor inlet. Point your boat in that direction and watch the compass. It should settle on 110 degrees, which is between east and south (yep, call it southeast).

2. **After traveling maybe a quarter mile toward that landmark, check your course on the compass. It should be holding at the expected degree.**

   In this example, you should travel toward the water tower and check that your compass holds at 110 degrees — if the harbormaster was correct.

Figure 10-1: A compass shows your course in alignment with the center mark, called the lubber line.

3. **Reverse your course and head back to the harbor in what's called the** *reciprocal course.* **The reciprocal course is the original course plus 180 degrees.**

   In this example, your compass should swing to 290 degrees (110 degrees + 180 degrees = 290 degrees). Sometimes your compass can vary more from magnetic north in one direction than in another, so this test of the reciprocal course helps give you a feel for compass variations.

4. **If your compass is off by more than a couple degrees from the expected degree on the outbound course, and if you're planning to travel great distances out of sight of land, you should adjust it according to the directions packed with your compass — or risk missing your destination by much more than a mile.**

Letting your compass lead the way

Like most boaters, you may go on visual references in all but the most adverse conditions, and in adverse conditions like fog and blinding rain, I hope that you stay in port. But if you're caught away from port when bad weather rolls in, you may find yourself relying on your compass to find your way home. Here are some tips for using it:

- ✔ **Familiarize yourself with landmark headings, and mark them on a chart.** Check these landmarks against your compass and jot down notes on locations. Sometimes the information is offered by other sources you trust, like a charter captain or a marina operator or harbormaster. Suppose your favorite waterfront hamburger joint, the Clown, is at 90 degrees or due east from the ramp. Find the Clown on the chart and jot down "90 degrees from the ramp." Do this for all the most visible landmarks, and soon you'll be able to find them with your compass even when they aren't visible because of darkness or fog.

- ✔ **Your reciprocal course from a charted landmark will take you home.** Take the course to the landmark and add 180 degrees to find your course back to port. If you're at the Clown when a fog rolls in, take the 90-degree course plus 180 degrees; your course back is 270 degrees or due west.

- ✔ **Travel at a prudent speed.** When poor visibility requires navigation by compass, proceed slowly so you have as much time as possible to maneuver to avoid an oncoming boat. Keep one eye tuned to your sonar, too, just to make sure you don't ground yourself. (I talk more about sonar later in this chapter in the section, "Scanning the Unseen Depths with Sonar.")

True north and magnetic north

Few people are aware that the true north pole is quite a long way from the magnetic north pole and that the magnetic north pole keeps drifting ever so slightly away from the true north pole every year. Some scientists theorize that eventually the poles will swap ends, north for south, causing quite a disturbance for the inhabitants of earth. But don't worry, the poles aren't apt to swap ends for thousands of years.

But beyond its value in a trivia contest, the earth's shifting magnetic pole does have a practical application to mariners. A great mariner or even just a recreational boater interested in having a very accurate compass should follow some very specific steps to be sure his or her compass is properly aligned to magnetic north and not reacting to magnetic fields in the boat. Each compass comes with the directions to adjust it for maximum accuracy and to compensate for the local difference between true north and magnetic north.

Choosing the right compass for your boat

Some boats come with compasses installed, but if yours doesn't, your budget and the complexity of your boating will determine the kind of compass you should buy. Even though today's $10 compass is likely better than the one Columbus used, you don't want to handicap yourself with inadequate equipment. Here are some practical guidelines to help you choose the right compass based on the way you boat:

- **In smaller inland waters:** Less detail in a compass used in small lakes and rivers is okay, because most of the time you'll be navigating by visual references. Naturally, a compass for this sort of boating will be the least expensive option.

- **In larger waters or night boating:** The more you rely on your compass, the more detailed it should be. On larger waters, a more detailed compass is important. But even if you boat on smaller waters, you may boat frequently at night, making a larger, more detailed compass useful. A compass with a card divided in 5 degrees or even a full 360-degree card is best because you may not have clear lights and landmarks to navigate by. Compasses in this class are naturally a little more expensive because of added detail, but they're still affordable.

- **On large, choppy lakes, oceans, and bays:** If you're making 5- to 10-mile runs from shore to shore, it's not unlikely you'll wind up on the wrong side of the lake in a blinding rain. Choose a compass with a metal base and a large lighted dial. Better compasses are more stable (less jiggly or jumpy to read), easier to read, lighted . . . and just look really cool on the helm station — you know, where the wheel, ah, helm is! Even at a premium price, this kind of compass is a good value for the safety it provides.

Understanding the Value of VHF Radios

I think few boaters worth their salt would go out without at least a handheld *VHF* (very high frequency) *radio*. I may cut you some slack if you boat on a small lake in the north woods of Wisconsin *and* if none of your peers have a VHF radio — *and* if you carry a cellphone programmed with emergency-responder numbers. But if you boat in any coastal waters or on waters frequented by commercial traffic, you're doing yourself — and your fellow water people — a disservice by being unequipped to communicate with them. In this section, I help you choose the radio that's right for you and give you some tips for using it.

Turning on and tuning in

VHF radios aren't expensive, and you have a few good choices to consider, plus additional options for your radio antenna. Not surprisingly, the more you spend, the more features you get and the better the service.

Handheld VHF radios

Handheld radios are easy to find and convenient to use. Here's what you can expect:

- ✔ **Cost:** Usually about the same as an average MP3 player.

- ✔ **Rechargeable batteries:** Most handhelds have base stands with chargers. Some have an AC adapter plug with a charger that plugs into the wall. Either works fine.

- ✔ **Many channels:** Handhelds have all or nearly all the channels of a fixed radio, including channels to receive NOAA regional weather forecasts.

- ✔ **Built-in antenna:** The beauty of handhelds is their simplicity. You don't have to pay an installation charge for the antenna or the radio.

- ✔ **Transmit range:** Most handhelds can transmit and receive calls for 5 miles, but their range is limited by mountainous or hilly terrain.

- ✔ **Disadvantage:** The limited range of a handheld VHF radio makes it best for inshore use and for offshore boating, as a backup to a fixed radio.

Fixed VHF radios

Fixed radios are the best way to go if you have the cash and space in your boat. Here are some things to consider:

- ✔ **Cost:** You can purchase a VHF radio for the price of a nice dinner at a restaurant, but you also need to budget for an antenna and maybe installation costs, potentially tripling your investment, depending on your equipment.

✔ **No batteries to recharge:** Fixed radios run on the batteries already in your boat.

✔ **Maximum channels:** Fixed radios usually have all the channels available, plus an ability to scan them silently for transmissions and then stop on the active channel.

✔ **External antenna:** An external antenna requires installation, but the added height of the antenna improves transmitting and receiving range.

✔ **Transmit range:** Fixed VHFs have more transmitting power and longer range. It isn't unusual for a fixed radio with an antenna rising 10 feet to reach out 25 miles or more.

✔ **Disadvantage:** If boat trouble occurs due to battery failure, chances are there won't be enough juice to run your radio, either. (This makes a good case for keeping a charged handheld VHF onboard for backup.)

DSC-equipped VHF radios

Most fixed radios now have a function called *digital select calling* (DSC). Connect one of these radios to a GPS (which I discuss later in this chapter), and the radio will monitor your latitude and longitude. Register your DSC-equipped radio with the Federal Communications Commission (FCC), and then if you get into trouble, you can use a very handy panic button to make your radio continually transmit your position and the fact that you have declared the need for assistance, making it possible for help to find you quickly. Other DSC radios on other boats in the area will repeat the signal, automatically multiplying your chance that responders will hear you. To register your DSC radio, visit `boatus.com/mmsi`.

Antennae for fixed radios

A fixed VHF radio requires the installation of an external antenna. The antenna often has more impact on the quality of transmission and reception than the radio itself. Here are some things to consider when selecting and installing an antenna:

✔ **Antenna height:** The higher your antenna, the longer the distance your radio can transmit and receive signals. A larger boat has the stability to handle a taller, heavier antenna without breaking it, whereas smaller boats react more to chop and seas and transfer the stress to the antenna. A 6- to 8-foot antenna is ideal for most boats under 40 feet.

✔ **Mounting location:** A 6-foot antenna mounted on the side or gunwale of a boat doesn't have the longer range of one mounted on the hardtop shading the passenger area. Always mount an antenna as high as you can.

✔ **Mounting bracket:** Buy the heaviest mounting bracket you can find for your antenna. Plastic brackets may seem fine on inland waterways, but just head over a cruiser wake once without slowing down, and the jolt may make the bracket snap off. Choose a bracket that lets you raise and lower the antenna when transporting your boat.

✔ **Cost:** An antenna can cost up to three times the price of your radio, depending on length, strength to resist whipping back and forth in chop, and the quality of the wiring components. Choose a stronger one than you think you'll need because if you break an antenna and you don't know how to replace it yourself, the cost of professional installation can be triple the cost of the antenna. Add another $50 or so for a strong bracket.

Communicating between boats

There's a protocol to speaking on radios, and many other boaters will be quick to broadcast their objection to any infraction of the protocol. When you call another vessel, obeying protocol makes things easier for everyone.

Getting the right VHF channel

You can monitor the dozens of available VHF channels, but you should transmit only on the few I list here:

✔ **Channel 16:** This channel is for emergencies and ship-to-ship calling. Most commercial ships and recreational boats monitor this channel. When you call another boater on this channel, the protocol requires you to agree to switch quickly to a noncommercial, nonemergency channel. When you're boating, your radio should always be on and tuned to channel 16 to hear emergency advisories or respond to others' emergencies.

✔ **Channels 71, 72, and 78:** For noncommercial calling, these are the channels you should switch to for conversation.

✔ **Channels 78A and 79A:** These channels are for noncommercial communications *only on the Great Lakes.*

When you're entering a marina or passing under a drawbridge, the harbormaster or bridge tender will be monitoring a specific channel for your call. Directions to use these channels are usually posted on a bridge or commercial signage posted by a harbormaster.

For a complete listing of VHF channels and their uses, visit www.navcen. uscg.gov/marcomms/vhf.htm.

Calling others on your VHF radio

As I say in the preceding section, you can call another craft on channel 16 to get its attention, but you should quickly switch to a noncommercial channel to continue your communications.

When calling ship to ship, your call should sound something like the following. Suppose your boat is named Little Boy and you want to call a boat named Big Boy:

1. **On channel 16, say, "Big Boy, Big Boy, Big Boy, this is Little Boy, over." If you're calling a boat that's not expecting your call, repeating the name helps limit the number of callbacks by giving the other skipper a better chance to hear what you said.**

2. **If you don't know the boat's name, then the skipper doesn't likely know yours. You may address your call to "Sea Ray 300" or "Big blue boat" or some other descriptive term and say, "This is Little Boy off your port bow."**

3. **Big Boy should respond, "This is Big Boy. Switch to channel 71 [or 72 or 78], over." If you called for "Big blue boat," the skipper may respond with the boat's real name.**

4. **You should say, "Switching to 71."**

5. **Over on channel 71, you can proceed with your conversation normally.**

The radio frequencies and airways are governed by the FCC, and laws require you to use the radio politely and without profanity and to yield the channel if someone has a more pressing need. In other words, use common sense and good manners, and don't yack away on it as if it were a closed cellphone circuit.

Transmit an emergency message using the ship-to-ship protocol I explain in the preceding steps, but substitute "Mayday!" for the other ship's name in life-threatening or boat-threatening situations and "Pan-pan!" for less-urgent situations. Also include your position and the nature of your emergency. Chapter 12 contains a complete dialogue for sending emergency messages.

Scanning the Unseen Depths with Sonar

Sonar is so inexpensive and so useful to boaters that many boat builders make it standard equipment. If your boat doesn't have it, you can buy inexpensive sonar units with monochrome LCD screens for around $100 or spend thousands on units capable of penetrating thousands of feet of water and returning detailed images of the bottom contour and fish in between.

Recreational-quality sonar is so detailed that volunteers using it are often responsible for finding stolen cars abandoned in the depths or recovering accident victims. But for most recreational boaters, sonar's primary benefit comes from helping you avoid grounding. This section tells you how to choose the sonar unit that's right for you and get the best use of it.

Whether you get into fishing or just use your sonar for a convenient method of staying out of trouble, read your sonar owner's manual. It tells you all you can expect your sonar to reveal and how to get it to give more detail in its readings than you can imagine.

Seeing how sonar depth finders work

If you saw the movie *The Hunt for Red October,* you saw sonar in action. The lake or ocean bottom returns most of the signals, but if a fish (or submarine Red October) swims between the lake or ocean bottom and the transducer mounted on the bottom of the boat, it gets painted on the screen at its respective position. It seems like a miracle, but sonar has been available to sport fishermen since the early 1970s. Today a dozen or more companies make good sonar equipment.

Sonar depth finders transmit a signal through a transducer on the bottom of the boat. Think of a transducer as an antenna sending and receiving a signal. The sonar system works something like this:

1. The *sonar unit* creates a signal or ping.

2. The *transducer* mounted on the bottom of the boat passes the signal into the water in a cone shape. For the transducer to work correctly, it has to be in contact with the water, and no air can be between the transducer and the water. Your installer will handle that for you.

3. When the ping echoes back, the transducer hands it to the sonar unit, which calculates the time lapse between when the ping was sent and when its echo returned. With that information it can accurately calculate the distance the ping traveled to the bottom.

4. The depth is displayed on the screen. Depending on the unit you have, it may just display a number in feet or meters, depending on how you program it, or it may give you a graphic drawing of the contour of the bottom of the lake or ocean.

Choosing the right sonar unit

Sonar units can be as inexpensive as $75 for a monochrome LCD display perfectly suitable for most lakes, rivers, and saltwater bays. A top-of-the-line unit that can draw detailed graphs of the bottom contours and fish deep in the ocean can cost over $2,000, though. Some are so detailed they can draw a clear image of a sunken boat, log, or — well, whatever's down there!

Sonar units get progressively more expensive as you include more of the following features:

✔ **Larger screens:** Big screens are more fun to look at (just like your TV) and give a better view of the bottom.

✔ **Color LCD screens:** Color gives a more detailed image of the bottom structure, giving anglers a better idea of what's below.

✔ **Bright displays:** Screens that can be easily read in bright sunlight cost more than those that are dimmer.

✔ **Dual-beam transducers:** Multiple-frequency pings enhance sonar's ability to operate efficiently in shallow *and* deep water, giving a more detailed image in both.

✔ **Digital transmitters:** The more frequencies the better — at least, that seems to be the latest trend to get greater detail in sonar imaging, which is primarily important to anglers. Digital sonar transmitters add more frequencies and detail.

✔ **Multiple transducers:** Some sonars have multiple transducers and computers to analyze and compile the data. These tranducers look forward and down, and some scan 180 degrees from port to starboard. The latter kind can tell you if fish are hovering 30 yards or more from where you're fishing and let you go cast bait on them.

Using sonar

If you're unfamiliar with waters, you can avoid grounding by traveling at a prudent speed and paying attention to your depth sounder (sonar unit). A sounder's screen may look like something from an airplane cockpit at first, but sonar really is easy to use and understand. Here are some tips to keep in mind for working your sonar system:

✔ **Let an automatic sonar unit do its thing.** Most sonar units are automatic, which means that the unit determines how much power — called *gain* — it should transmit based on depth and other factors it detects in the water. It also automatically adjusts settings to eliminate interference and change the scale from, say, zero to 30 feet to zero to 60 or 90 or 120 feet as you move to deeper water. All you do is turn on the unit.

✔ **Be alert for a shallow water alarm.** Some sonar units have a shallow water alarm that beeps when your boat enters water shallower than a preset depth you select.

✔ **Be aware of your unit's time lag.** Keep in mind that sonar has a time lag between the moment the depth is actually sounded and the report of depth. This lag is tiny, but at 45 miles per hour, if your sounder suddenly reports a depth change of 20 to 10 feet, don't wait for it to reach 5 feet to slow down. Chances are, if a sandbar is coming up that quickly, you're already in 5 feet of water or less.

Spotting fish with sonar

Anglers were the first recreational boaters to appreciate sounders because they help find sunken logs or boats or other underwater obstructions that fish like to hang around in. They can even spot fish.

Fish love to hang out at the edge of drop-offs or around logs. By cruising slowly along a likely shoreline with your sonar going, you can quickly discover whether such fish-attracting obstructions are there. On the sonar screen, they'll jut up abruptly from the bottom, often looking like a cross section of their actual shapes.

Fish appear on sonar screens as marks floating over the obstructions or the bottom. Sometimes you'll find fish suspended far above such obstructions or farther offshore but at exactly the same depth as the obstruction. You'll have to ask the fish why they do this — I certainly don't know.

Using GPS Chart Plotters

The *U.S. Global Positioning System (GPS)* is a navigational miracle. With a basic $100 receiver to collect and analyze signals from GPS satellites circling the earth, you can pinpoint your exact location on earth — within a few feet. GPS units are so inexpensive that they're commonplace in cars and even more commonplace in boats.

This section gives you a basic idea of how GPS devices work and how you can use them while boating. Of course, you can't use one if you don't have one, so I prepare you to go shopping for one, too.

How GPS units work

Mariners used to navigate by the sun and the stars. Based on centuries of observation, they knew where to expect the stars to be. Using a tool called a *sextant,* they measured the angle of the triangle created by the horizon, the heavenly body, and their boat's position. They then used a trigonometric calculation to determine roughly where the boat was in relation to a star or the sun. It *was* a rough calculation, too, often only good to within dozens of miles. GPS uses nearly the same math but has a much better system of arriving at a position. I won't go into the math, but it helps to have a basic idea of what's happening with what components when you turn on your GPS.

- ✔ **Satellites:** At least 24 satellites are in the U.S. GPS system, and they orbit the earth in a predictable pattern, transmitting their position to GPS receivers on earth.

- ✔ **Receivers:** A GPS receiver can receive signals from all the satellites within the horizon or sight of the receiver's position on the earth. Receivers have to be in sight of the sky to receive a signal, meaning they often don't work indoors or in the cabin of a boat.

- ✔ **Calculating a position:** A computer in the GPS receiver calculates its position, based on the information received from the visible satellites, and displays latitude and longitude.

- ✔ **Leaving a trail:** The GPS information is useful only if you keep the unit running and let it leave your trail marked on the screen. You can then follow that trail back by watching your position change on the screen and keeping your position aligned with the trail.

- ✔ **Chart plotters:** GPS units with navigational charts preloaded in them will coordinate your position or latitude and longitude with an animated chart on the screen, and you can easily visualize your exact position and watch it change as your boat travels onward. Some GPS units also can display charting information, but you have to plug in a card that carries the data. Various manufacturers make these charts; Navionics (www. navionics.com) and C-Map (www.c-map.com) are reliable GPS chart providers if your GPS doesn't include charts.

Choosing the right GPS for you

GPS units are getting more and more inexpensive, but their prices climb as you start adding features such as the following:

- ✔ **Larger screens:** Big screens are easier to understand in a moving boat.

   Your helm station has limited space for a GPS chart plotter, so you need to keep that in mind and not buy a screen that you can't use.

- ✔ **Color LCD screens:** Color adds some cost, just as in sonar depth finders. Color screens give you a clearer picture of bottom contours and navigational markers, and some even display satellite maps in full color. A color screen gets dim as direct sunlight floods it but can be shielded from direct sunlight in order to provide a more detailed image of chart features.

- ✔ **Bright displays:** Color screens easily read in bright sunlight cost more than those that are dimmer.

In an open boat with no cover for shade, a monochrome LCD display is the easiest to read — and the least expensive.

✔ **Charts:** Some GPS units have all the charts you'll ever need built right into them. Others have more basic maps, and to get the detail you need, you have to get chart cards, which are electronic storage devices that plug into the unit. Charts cost extra in some GPS units.

✔ **Fixed mount units:** Most GPS units have an external antenna that has to be in sight of the sky for consistent accuracy. Plan to mount the antennae at any convenient place where it has an unobstructed view of the sky. Some GPS units have integrated antennae and don't require external ones as long as they have a clear view of the sky from the helm.

✔ **Combination units:** Some GPS units also have sonar systems built in. Such a unit combines functions on one screen by splitting the screen, kind of like a TV with picture-in-picture capability. Some combo units are capable of displaying navigation, sonar, and radar all at once. (I talk more about radar in the section, "Letting Radar Spot Things Far in Advance," later in this chapter.)

Many a boat is navigated by a handheld GPS. The integrated antenna and portability mean handhelds work fine in open boats. Plus they're cheaper, run on AA batteries for 20 hours or more, and don't require installation, making them useful for hiking as well as boating. You can get a 12-volt power cord for your handheld GPS to plug into the boat's system and avoid batteries altogether. You can even get an external antenna, but by then you're jacking the price up to the level of some fixed units.

Finding your way with GPS

If you have a GPS chart plotter loaded with a local chart, you can simply turn it on, give it time to establish communication with satellites, and then see where you are on the map. But you can do a lot more with such a device to make boating more fun and safe. Here are some tips and suggestions for getting the most out of your GPS:

✔ **Turn on your GPS while you're prepping your boat for launch so it will be ready when you launch.** GPS units take up to five minutes to establish communications with satellites. If a GPS unit is turned off and transported several hundred miles, communication often takes even longer next time it's turned on.

✔ **Use the GOTO function.** If you have a chart installed on your unit, *GOTO* is a function that lets you use a mouse-like device to scroll the cursor on the on-screen chart over a place you want to go to. Then you press *GOTO,* and it sets the course, plots a line to it, and shows you when you're off or on course.

✔ **Familiarize yourself with the Man Over Board (MOB) function.** MOB is sort of like a panic button you push when somebody (or maybe just a baseball cap) falls overboard. You'd be surprised how difficult it is to spot something again after you turn your boat around. MOB marks the spot on a chart to help you return to it easily.

✔ **Follow trails and tracks.** Your GPS leaves tracks, or what I call a breadcrumb trail, on the screen to mark where you've been. It's a beautiful thing because you can retrace the trail on the GPS and get back again. If your boat icon on the screen strays from the line, you can easily steer it back in line with the trail.

✔ **Record waypoints.** On your GPS, you can record the position of spots you like or spots you think you'll want to return to. You can even name these spots and give them a customized little picture or icon to reflect home, fishing hole, ramp, fuel, food, or whatever else. Later, you can highlight them with the cursor and, at the push of a button, set a course for the waypoint.

✔ **Watch the speedometer.** A GPS can display your speed because it not only knows what your position is but how fast it's changing. It's actually more accurate than most speedometers on boats!

Letting Radar Spot Things Far in Advance

Most recreational boaters don't need radar, but the bigger the boat, the more likely it is to have radar onboard. It has to be mounted well overhead of the captain and crew to give a clear signal and avoid hitting people with the radiation it transmits, both of which are good reasons to avoid radar on smaller boats. Offshore fishermen and women love it for spotting unseen flocks of birds diving for baitfish — a sure sign of hot fishing action. For example, I have radar on my 25-foot offshore fishing boat.

In this section on radar, I give you the layman's 411 on how it works, how you may find it useful, and what to look for in a radar for your boat.

How radar works for you

Radar works on the same principle as sonar (refer to the earlier section, "Scanning the Unseen Depths with Sonar"), but it works above the water instead of under it, sending out horizontal pings and waiting for echoes to return. Radar calculates the time between transmission and the time the echo is returned and then calculates how far the echo traveled. It then plots that on the radar screen, showing how far away other boats or land or other obstruction is. Some radar arrays let you automatically track a target. That's handy when you think a boat may be approaching you and doesn't know you're there. Radar helps you visualize the other boat's course and its possible crossing of yours.

The radar array spins 360 degrees, fanning signals around the boat that travel to infinity unless they hit something that returns the signal in the form of an echo. The signals see things in every direction and far beyond the ability of the human eye, even with binoculars.

Radar can see when you can't; it shows you things in fog, dark, and even blinding rain that you can't see unassisted. Its value in adverse conditions is inestimable. Birds, boats, land, rain squalls, and even navigational markers you can't see in the dark show up well on radar. When you're forced to travel in fog, nothing beats the peace of mind radar gives.

Choosing the right radar for your boat

Radar devices are smaller than ever and getting more and more inexpensive. So it's not surprising that captains of progressively smaller boats take advantage of it these days. But there are some limiting factors to consider before you buy a radar system:

- ✔ **Radar mounting:** You need a radar arch or hard top over your boat's cockpit on which to mount the radar array. This placement gives the signal enough height to be effective and keeps the array from pointing the radar signal at passengers. If you don't have an arch, you can have one mounted on your boat at a cost of several thousand dollars, which may be prohibitive.

- ✔ **Radar power:** Your radar range is partly dependent on its power and partly on the installation and height of the array. Consult a navigation electronics installer when you consider radar for your boat to make sure the power is optimal for your boat.

- ✔ **Helm display:** A radar screen is needed to display a radar array's information. If your dash has room for a GPS and sonar and radar, you're all set. If not and you want radar, choose a GPS/sonar unit capable of displaying radar, too.

Chapter 11

Navigating Bad Weather

. . . .

In This Chapter

▶ Finding weather forecasts for your boating day

▶ Taking heed of small craft warnings and advisories

▶ Adapting your plans to forecasts and weather conditions

▶ Handling your boat when you're stuck in bad weather

. . . .

*I*t may seem pointless to include a chapter about boating in bad weather when most likely you'll try to avoid it. But there's a real chance that you could get caught in bad weather — in fact, if you boat long enough, you definitely will. If you're a fisherman, you know the fish often bite best during the approach of a weather front, so you may just choose to dodge in under an approaching front, hook some fish, and go home. But believe me, if you've been caught in your boat in a thunderstorm once, you'll avoid them at all cost and in spite of any expected reward.

This chapter is about keeping yourself out of weather trouble and how to plan your boating around great weather. I show you where to go for boating and marine advisories so you can maximize safe weather conditions and avoid unsafe conditions. And, because eventually you *will* be caught in a storm, I explain how to proceed to shelter as quickly and safely as possible, as well as how to forge through stormy seas in the event that you face them head-on.

Tuning In to Marine Forecasts Before You Go Out

Weather manages to surprise even the experts, even though meteorologists calculate their forecasts after analyzing ground radar, satellite imagery, and uncountable data from numerous ground stations. Sure, the experts still get it wrong, patterns take an unusual shift, and a storm diverts to a different location than expected. But the odds are that most of the time the weather forecasters will get it right, and your odds for safe boating are better if you follow their advice.

In general, you should start checking the kinds of sources I discuss in this section a few days before your boating trip. That way you can watch fronts come through on radar and satellite maps and develop your own feel for what your boating weather will be.

Finding local marine forecasts has never been easier. In addition to local news sources, you can access 24-hour weather channels, numerous government and private weather forecasting Web sites, and radio broadcasts transmitted around the clock. Even some Global Positioning System (GPS) units can receive real-time weather forecasts (I discuss GPS in Chapter 10). In this section, I outline the sources of weather news available for boaters and offer suggestions on which sources provide the best information for your region.

Checking weather on the Web

The Internet is chock-full of weather-reporting Web sites. Most are based on information from the National Oceanic and Atmospheric Administration (NOAA), the federal agency responsible for monitoring atmospheric conditions, weather, and the health of oceans and oceanic fisheries.

When preparing for a boating outing, check the following sites, which I've found to be the most useful and accessible:

- ✔ www.weather.gov: The National Weather Service site, maintained by NOAA, quickly links you to the marine forecasts for any coastal or Great Lakes region. To get to marine forecasts, click "Marine" on the left menu bar. A map pops up with red dots on the chart that immediately connect you to forecasts in the region. The regional forecasts provide all the basics you'd get from the newspaper or local news *plus* all the information boaters need, such as wind, waves, approaching fronts, and other changes expected in the weather. The information is almost exhaustively detailed but totally useful for safe navigation.

- ✔ www.wunderground.com and www.weather.com: Their information is based on data compiled by NOAA, but they package it in an easier-to-access format, making them very popular with boaters even though they're not as detailed.

These commercial Web sites provide

- • Coastal reports, including saltwater bays and coastal waters up to 20 miles offshore by region

- • Great Lakes reports containing weather and wave conditions

- • Inland weather reports that can help you predict inland water conditions, because conditions that are unfavorable for any land-based activities are equally so for boating in lakes and rivers

Using VHF and weather radios to monitor weather on the water

NOAA broadcasts weather 24/7 on various radio bands, giving the most up-to-the-minute marine and inland advisories. You can get these forecasts on your VHF marine radio, which I recommend you buy. But, a household weather radio also carries these broadcasts.

Special VHF channels, accessed by touching a button on your VHF radio marked "WX," carry weather broadcasts regularly. Local Coast Guard stations notify listeners on channel 16 whenever weather predictions are apt to change. Keep your VHF radio on channel 16, and for the details on a particular announcement, simply press the WX button again. (I discuss VHF radios in more detail in Chapter 10.)

Inexpensive weather radios receive just the weather channels and often offer the added feature of sounding a weather alarm from the National Weather Service before automatically turning on and reporting severe weather forecasts. In coastal areas, weather radios report on marine conditions as well.

Locating weather information on your GPS

A new form of weather information has emerged that links certain GPS systems with satellite radio providers like XM and SIRIUS.

Only certain brands of GPS units interface with satellite radio providers' weather services, and each requires a special module to be connected to the navigation system.

Here are a few brands offering satellite weather interface at the time of this printing:

- **Garmin:** Garmin GPS systems link with satellite weather to give all the weather information available from ground radar, satellite imagery, and NOAA weather buoys almost as soon as it's measured and transmitted. In addition, XM Radio provides NOAA information that measures water temperatures, phytoplankton content, and other factors to predict where fish that seek certain conditions may be found.

- **Raymarine, Furuno, Northstar, and Lowrance:** These GPS systems link with SIRIUS Satellite Radio to display what the providers call real-time radar and satellite imagery, in addition to the latest information from NOAA weather buoys, giving the state of winds and seas through SIRIUS Satellite Radio.

These systems conveniently overlay satellite weather information right on your GPS chart plotter screen, coordinating radar and satellite images over the chart of your location. XM Radio also identifies promising fishing grounds on your chart plotter so you can navigate directly to those waters.

In time, I expect many other brands and models to begin *connecting* to satellite weather information. For offshore and Great Lakes boaters, the capability can be so useful that it makes a very wise investment both for added fun (especially for anglers) and increased safety.

Knowing about Warnings and Advisories for Small Crafts

A *small craft* isn't defined by its weight, length, or *beam* (width), but instead it's any boat (including large ships and yachts) that can be adversely affected by the conditions of the waves or seas, wind, and precipitation like fog, rain, snow, sleet, or hail. Is your boat a small craft? The short answer is yes. If you're reading this book, you're going to be piloting a boat that should heed a small craft advisory.

Chances are that as a pleasure boater, when an advisory is issued, you aren't going to ask the question, "Is it okay to go?" Your reaction will be more like, "Sure doesn't sound like much fun. Why go now?" The latter is the appropriate response to a small craft advisory.

Taking small craft advisories seriously

Nothing puts the brakes on a day of boating like a small craft advisory telling you that a prudent boater would keep off the water. Watch and listen for these advisories in whatever source you use for your weather information (Web sites, weather radio, GPS, and so on).

Your check of weather and boating conditions prior to leaving the dock may show that conditions are great for boating, but the Coast Guard may issue a small craft advisory over the VHF radio when you're already out on the water. Keep yours tuned channel 16 to pick up any advisories that develop.

Small craft advisories are advice, not commands, and you have to exercise judgment about the conditions, your experience, and your capability to handle them in your boat if you decide to go out (or stay out) anyway.

Knowing regional advisory differences

Small craft advisories are issued for the Great Lakes, U.S. coastal waters, and the high seas — waters beyond U.S. jurisdiction. The conditions that trigger these advisories vary by region and are set by the NOAA. The regional definitions in this section include information from www.noaa.org.

General elements that factor into an advisory include the velocity of the wind and the size of the waves. In each of the following regions, certain local areas within a given region have more or less restrictive definitions, and you should check them at your nearest Coast Guard station. If you think the language is a little stiff, you must have skipped Chapter 9 on the U.S. Coast Guard's rules of the road — or sea! You can download a free copy of the navigation rules at www.navcen.uscg.gov/mwv/mwv_files/NR_Files/navrules.pdf.

- ✓ **Eastern region:** Maine to South Carolina, including Lake Erie and Lake Ontario, are combined in this broad region. In general, small craft advisories are issued when "sustained winds or frequent gusts range between 25 and 33 knots and/or seas or waves 5 to 7 feet and greater."

- ✓ **Central region:** On the Great Lakes from Minnesota to Ohio, "sustained winds or frequent gusts between 22 and 33 knots inclusive, and/or seas or waves greater than 4 feet" form the threshold of an advisory. This region includes all the Great Lakes.

- ✓ **Southern region:** This enormous region ranges from the coast of Georgia, around Florida, all along the Gulf of Mexico to Texas, and the Caribbean. Advisories are generally issued in conditions of "sustained winds of 20 to 33 knots, and/or forecast seas 7 feet or greater that are expected for more than two hours."

- ✓ **Western region:** This region extends from California to Washington. Advisories are issued for "sustained winds of 21 to 33 knots, potentially in combination with wave heights exceeding 10 feet (or wave steepness values exceeding local thresholds)."

- ✓ **Alaska:** An advisory is issued for "sustained winds or frequent gusts of 23 to 33 knots. A small craft advisory for rough seas may be issued for sea/wave conditions deemed locally significant, based on user needs, and should be no lower than 8 feet."

- ✓ **Hawaii and Samoa:** Advisories are issued in the presence of "sustained winds 25 knots or greater and seas 10 feet or greater."

- ✓ **Guam and the Northern Mariana Islands:** "Sustained winds 22 to 33 knots and/or combined seas of 10 feet or more" trigger an advisory.

Taking Precautions When the Forecast is Bad

Superb, detailed, and up-to-the-minute weather information is out there to be nabbed by anyone with a laptop or a VHF radio. You no longer have to look at the sky and wonder "Red sky at night, sailors in fright" — or was that "sailors' delight"? (By the way, that old saw works only in tropical regions anyway.) This section poses some common-sense strategies for dealing with the uncertainties of the weather.

Tweak your departure or destination plans

Many boaters go out with a false sense of security, assuming that because a weather forecast predicts thundershowers at 2:00 p.m., they're safe to boat for the morning at least. That's often not the case. Plan simpler, shorter boating if forecasts show conditions deteriorating later in the day. Or postpone your boating outing and go to a movie instead. There's always another day to boat.

I've had to disappoint my crew when we expected to boat to a favorite destination and looming weather interfered. Even though visible signs were good, with blue skies, light winds, and a gentle breeze, a forecast calling for deteriorating conditions held us close to home. We've never regretted playing it that way. Predicted foul weather usually sets in as scheduled or even a little early, and had we not made a habit of staying tuned to the forecast, we would have been trapped in dangerous weather more than once.

Head for port at a hint of lightning

Lightning is always a threat in any kind of rainy weather, and it can appear to come from nowhere. Gentle rains with no breeze, light clouds, or no clouds are all conditions that have produced lightning.

If you're out on the water and hear thunder in the distance, you're in range of being struck. On a vast expanse of water in conditions that favor lightning, a boat may be a prime target.

Don't expect that because you don't see any lightning, there's no risk. Definitely don't go out boating when lightning is present because once you're out in it, you can't protect yourself and your crew except to get back in port and to shelter quickly and safely. Handling your boat in an unsafe manner can pose a much greater risk than the lightning itself.

For more on thunderstorms and lightning, see the later section, "Understanding the power of thunderstorms and lightning."

Anticipate sudden weather changes

Keep in mind that a forecast — even one for the best boating conditions — can change. If the boating forecast is a good one and you decide to head out, take your weather radio with you or keep your VHF tuned to channel 16 to get updates or notices to switch to the weather channels for more information.

Secure or relocate your boat in named storms

Nobody boats in the face of hurricanes or tropical storms — at least not on purpose. Occasionally someone in a sailboat without enough sense or at least enough seamanship to get out of the weather gets trapped in such storms. Mercy on their souls — and on the souls forced to attempt to rescue them.

You won't be out in this weather, but you may want to consider securing your boat where it's stored or moving it to a safer place in advance of a storm. Insurance providers often require boat owners to do so. Prior to a big storm, take the following precautions to secure your boat:

- ✔ **Remove your boat cover.** I know it sounds crazy, but listen up: Hurricanes are defined as having winds over 74 miles per hour. If that wind speed is sustained for a period of hours, it will shred your cover, and the flapping pieces, snaps, and zippers could further damage your boat. Even a tropical storm-strength wind of 39 to 73 mph can damage a cover — especially those not designed for trailered boats.

- ✔ **Batten down the hatches.** It's an old saw from Errol Flynn movies, but there's truth in it. Anything loose in your boat should be stowed in a lockable locker. Seat cushions or carpet held in place by snaps should be stowed away or tied down so wind can't get under it and spirit it away.

Dealing with Weather Conditions

In addition to knowing how to find out about weather in general, you should know about the *kinds* of weather that concern boaters.

Gauging wind, waves, and seas

In coastal and ocean waters, waves are called *seas*. In the Great Lakes and any other inland waterway, waves are just waves. They're usually driven by wind and, in the coastal areas, by the tide as well. *Wakes* are another form of wave created by the passing of boats. Here are some more details you need to know about wind and waves to boat safely in varying weather conditions:

- **Wave height:** Waves are measured in height by the distance from the wave *trough*, or low point between waves, to the peak of the wave. When the NOAA issues a statement that waves or seas will be 4 feet, they base that information on an average of readings taken from weather buoys anchored in the ocean. When gauging whether you can handle 4-foot seas — and many recreational boats can — remember that it's an average: In the period of time during which the average wave height was calculated, at least one wave could well have been twice that height. An 8-footer may not capsize you, but it could easily capsize you if you're not watching for it. And what fun would rough seas like that be, anyway?

- **Wave period:** The NOAA may also report the *wave period,* which is the time it takes the peak of one wave to pass and the next wave to arrive. Even if there's no report, you can expect distinct and important differences between Pacific and Atlantic wave periods. In the Pacific, small craft advisories are issued when the wave heights reach 10 feet, yet in the Atlantic it takes only 7-foot seas to trigger an advisory. Part of that has to do with the longer wave period in the Pacific. It's much more difficult to manage 7-foot seas closely spaced — as you crest one wave, you plunge down the side of it into the trough and instantly, while you still have downward momentum, another wave rises before your bow. To understate it, that makes for a pretty wet ride.

- **Winds:** Winds are divided into 13 categories defined long ago by a noted seaman, Sir Francis Beaufort. In the Beaufort Scale, winds of 18 to 24 mph are considered a *Fresh Breeze.* However, just 1 mph over that threshold steps into the category of winds in which small craft advisories are issued. While it may be technically okay to go out in an appropriate craft when winds are 1 mph over the Fresh Breeze threshold, you can count on the ride being less than fun. (See the sidebar "The Beaufort Scale" for more about the story of Beaufort and his scale.)

Understanding the power of thunderstorms and lightning

Poking around on www.noaa.gov is one of the best ways to brush up your meteorological skills — and gain a respect for the power of bad weather. Together, knowledge of the weather and respect for its power will make you a better boater.

The Beaufort Scale

What's a little wind on the water? In 1805 Sir Francis Beaufort, an Admiral in the British navy, wanted to define winds in terms of what a casual seaman might observe. You can see a table that clearly presents his findings in terms of marine and land conditions online at `www.spc.noaa.gov/faq/tornado/beaufort.html`. Even though Beaufort was a decorated seaman whose greatest contribution to navigation was in hydrographic charting of unknown waters, he's still better known for his definitions of the forces of wind still used in meteorology today.

As a boater, gauging wind descriptions from the comfort of your home even without a weather radio is easy — just visit `lwf.ncdc.noaa.gov/oa/climate/conversion/beaufortland.html` for the same table but with observations of conditions on land in the face of such wind speeds, courtesy of the National Weather Service. Comparing your observations to the small craft advisory thresholds listed earlier in this chapter can tell you whether weather conditions suggest you take a pass on boating that day.

According to the NOAA, about 100,000 thunderstorms occur in the U.S. every year. About 10 percent of them are severe, with destructive winds. There's no way to predict whether a storm will be severe in advance, so you should be cautious of all storms and especially their effect on boating. Here are some other things I learned from the NOAA (at `www.nws.noaa.gov/om/brochures/ttl.pdf`):

- ✔ Thunderstorms are formed when moist air that is warmer than surrounding air rises thousands of feet. At that altitude, cooler atmospheric conditions cool it rapidly, causing moisture to condense and fall as rain. Lightning is nearly always present, and often hail is as well.

- ✔ Lightning kills 80 people and injures 300 per year. Consider your vulnerability to lightning when you and your boat are on a broad expanse of flat water and are the most prominent, highest structure for maybe miles around. There's very little you can do to protect yourself from lightning except hope for the best, so don't get caught in it.

- ✔ Hail can be uncomfortable in normal pea- to quarter-sized pieces. But larger hail, like the size of golf balls or baseballs, can also fall at a speed of 100 mph. Certainly it will damage your boat, and it could also injure or kill you or your crew.

Navigating through fog

In most cases there's no good reason to navigate in fog. Although there are ways to lower your risk in doing so, boating in fog is always a little risky. Specific rules for navigating in fog are spelled out by the U.S. Coast Guard in their publication *Rules of the Road*. Most state boating laws are based on these rules, which you can find more about in Chapter 9.

I'm sure you've driven your car in fog, but as a responsible boater, you need to know how to drive your boat in fog as well as recognize conditions that are likely to produce fog.

Recognizing fog-generating conditions

There are a variety of scientific explanations for how fog is formed in the atmosphere, but here's the gist of what you should know for boating and navigating:

- ✔ The kind of fog that most often impacts boaters (and often automobile drivers, too) occurs when cool air drifts downward and meets warmer moist air.
- ✔ Fog often happens at night as air over the land cools, and the fog is drawn to water by warmer air rising from the water's surface.
- ✔ Fog often burns off as the sun climbs and changes the weather dynamics.

Fog isn't always predicted accurately, but the conditions that cause it are, and those conditions are reported on most weather forecasts. You just need to know what to look out for.

When you have a choice of not boating in dangerous weather such as high winds, storms, or fog, my recommendation to you — and my personal practice — is to avoid boating in it altogether. Fog is something you usually meet at the dock, and you can easily wait it out by remaining ashore.

Observing foggy rules for boaters

Despite your efforts to avoid boating in fog, you may encounter times when you go boating and find fog between you and safe harbor. In those cases, you need to know the rules for handling it.

The Coast Guard's rules for boaters don't actually specify rules for navigating in fog. They take the much broader approach of specifying rules for navigating in restricted visibility — which can include heavy rain as well as fog. Here are the high points of these rules:

- ✔ **Safe speed:** Conditions like fog and rain obviously restrict visibility, and the rules require you to slow down to a safe speed. They don't specify what that speed is, but you're expected to make a reasonable choice based on how quickly you can see and react to oncoming traffic or obstacles. Generally, if fog restricts your visibility to 50 feet, you should go no faster than a speed that allows you to avoid an obstacle like another boat, piling, or buoy. To complicate matters, you also have to consider the speed of other oncoming vessels; for example, an object moving toward you can eat up a 50-foot visibility perimeter faster than a fixed object you're moving toward.

Although the Coast Guard doesn't define *safe speed,* trust me, it's always less than 10 mph.

✔ **Sound signals:** The Coast Guard's rules address sound signals in fog because lights aren't much of a guide in restricted visibility (see the next bullet). When moving through areas of restricted visibility, you should make one prolonged blast of the horn or a whistle about four to six seconds in length. You should make this signal every two minutes.

✔ **Lights:** Even though running lights aren't visible very far in fog, they're often visible farther than solid objects — even if only a few feet farther. You should turn your navigation lights on when boating in fog.

✔ **Radar:** Radar goes a long way toward identifying other traffic, buoys, navigation aids, and navigation hazards. But it isn't as foolproof as the ability to see where you're going and what's around you, and you should still maintain a speed under 10 mph even if you're able to navigate using radar.

✔ **Special sounds:** If you find yourself in the waterway and unable to make progress safely, you should sound two prolonged blasts of the horn or a whistle of four to six seconds long with not more than two seconds separating the blasts.

When it comes to navigation rules you should obey, following the rules I outline in this section will give you a leg up on 90 percent of the other boaters out there, but the U.S. Coast Guard Navigation Rules are the final authority. You can download a free copy of them at www.navcen.uscg.gov/mwv/mwv_files/NR_Files/navrules.pdf.

Handling Your Boat in a Storm

Even if you faithfully watch forecasts and monitor weather conditions, it's likely that you'll eventually get caught boating in a storm.

On any lake or bay, a thunderhead creeping in suddenly sends boaters running like the devil for cover. On busy waters, all the boats may streak back toward one narrow bay opening and may get there all at the same time. There's something about a storm that triggers the flight mechanism in boaters, and while that may be the right course of action, doing so without caution is not.

If you've followed all the safety precautions I discuss in Chapter 12 regarding safety gear, you'll be able to keep a level head. In this section, I outline what to do in a weather emergency.

Handling your boat safely in a storm isn't hard if you keep a level head, but that doesn't mean you should ever purposely take the risk!

Preparing your crew

Getting prepared for the last thing you expected is the first thing you need to do when faced with a storm. Here are three steps you should take immediately before making a beeline to homeport:

1. **Double-check that your crew is equipped with life jackets. If they aren't wearing them, command them to don jackets immediately.**

2. **Have everyone secure loose items that could bounce around or blow out of the boat because of the wind and waves.**

   Beach towels or swimsuits hanging from railings should be secured inside the boat. If a towel were to fall into the water and foul your prop, you could find yourself dead in the water when the storm strikes.

3. **Make sure all your passengers takes a secure seat, and let them know that it's important they remain in it no matter the conditions.**

Riding out the storm

If you're forced to take precautions in dealing with foul weather, it's probably because you've gone out in spite of the forecast and what the meteorologists warned about has come to pass. But it could be you've just skipped the forecast and only recently noticed the weather has crept up on you. Or, in rare cases, perhaps the forecast simply didn't anticipate the storm.

Regardless of who's to blame, here are some options to consider when you have to ride out the storm on the water:

✔ **Wait it out where you are.** If a storm appears between you and your port, dock, or launch ramp, don't make a run for it. According to the NOAA, thunderstorms move up to 30 mph. Instead of running through the storm, gauge the motion of the storm to see if it will pass you by before you head in. On open water, that's often easier than you may think. Many times, I've been able to easily skirt storms because, without land obstacles in the way, the beginning and end of a rain squall (unless it's a full-blown weather system you shouldn't have left home in anyway) is easy to spot and track. If there's no observable and clear definition of the squall, secure everything and everyone in the boat, sit low to the deck, and work your way in at a safe speed.

✔ **Head offshore or away from port.** I've known boaters on Lake Erie who fished far offshore and decided it was safer to head away from port to Canada to wait out the storm than to try to make their way through it. They gassed up in Canada and returned stateside when the threat passed. Never bulldoze through thunderstorms unless you want a truly harrowing and unnecessary experience.

✔ **Adjust your speed to seas and visibility.** You won't be the only boater panicked by a storm. If you're caught in the storm, heading to port or the ramp in poor visibility at maximum speed is more dangerous than sitting still in the water until the threat has passed.

✔ **Radio your position to the Coasties.** If a storm overtakes you and your situation becomes alarming, notify the Coasties of your position and your course of action. They may be able to keep tabs on you and wait for your periodic reports. Maintaining radio contact means that if your boat becomes disabled, the Coast Guard can begin searching for you in the vicinity of your last communication.

✔ **Use a cellphone.** On inland waters where agencies are less likely to monitor VHF radio frequencies, use a cellphone to call a friend, family member, or marina operator. Marina operators are often the first to be sought for advice when people are delayed by a storm.

✔ **Know when it's an emergency.** If your boat is taking on water, it's an emergency. If your boat is disabled, you may be in an emergency, or you may just be experiencing a frightening inconvenience — it depends upon the way your boat is handling the weather and whether you think there's risk to your crew. Review the procedures in Chapter 12 for making mayday and pan-pan calls.

Handling your boat in rough seas or waves

If you're caught in a storm out on the open water, one of the hardest things you have to do is navigate heavy seas or rough waves. Avoiding seas or waves is the better part of safe navigation, but when you can't, knowing what seas can do and what you should do in the face of them can save your life.

Many times navigation isn't possible in seas or heavy waves, and all you can — and should — do is hold your position into the waves so they pass under you as gently as possible. Pounding into them, often dipping the bow into the next wave, will eventually swamp your boat and stall your engine, increasing the danger. Letting seas take your craft from behind is even worse.

Your ocean-going boat is designed to take the seas head-on easily under power. Here's how strong seas affect parts of your boat and cause hazards:

- **Bow:** Its sharp stem (the peak of the bow stretching down to the keel) is designed to pierce head seas, or waves that come at you from the front of the boat. The flare of the hull is designed to deflect the waves away while lifting the boat over them. In large waves, as the boat crests a wave, it plunges down the face of it into the wave trough. If the speed is too great, the next wave could pour over the bow, swamping an open boat.

- **Freeboard:** The sides of the boat above the waterline are designed to keep the water out. *Freeboard* isn't the sides of the boat but rather the distance on the sides between the waterline and the *gunwales* (the top edges of the boat). When quartering seas hit your boat from behind at a 90-degree (or so) angle and turn it so that heavy seas hit the sides directly, the waves can push and roll the boat, risking upsetting it.

- **Stern:** The *stern* or back of a power boat is relatively square and flat. For outboards and sterndrives, this shape gives the boat more stability under power, especially when turning. However, in *following seas* — that's the nautical term for waves that come from behind — the force of waves can push the boat, causing it to heel or tilt over hard to one side.

If your boat goes dead in the water in rough, stormy seas, the safest recourse is to fasten an anchor to the bow and throw it overboard. Have every passenger sit on the floor as close to the center of the boat as possible because as the boat turns, it will heel or roll heavily to one side, and getting the load centered and low helps combat that. Even in water far deeper than your anchor can reach, the drag of the anchor, chain, and *rode* (the rope on an anchor) should turn the boat's bow into the seas so it can better ride them.

Dealing with head seas

Head seas are what your boat is designed to handle in normal operation. But in stormy seas, special challenges require special tactics.

Head seas hit your boat at the bow — the highest part of the boat. High, stormy head seas can still break over the bow if you don't adjust your speed for them. Sometimes the waves are so bad that they can still break over the boat even when you've slowed down as much as possible, making a strong case for watching your weather forecast in the first place.

Take head seas cautiously. They'll pass under your boat from the bow, and if you press forward too fast, as you crest one wave you'll slide down its face into the trough, leaving yourself vulnerable to the next wave. Take each wave as slowly as possible until you're certain how the boat reacts to them. Chances are 5 to 10 mph is the best speed you'll be able to make over head seas, but you should take care when adjusting the speed.

Dealing with quartering seas

Quartering seas come up under the stern or back of the boat from an angle instead of dead on, like following seas (see the next section). Most boats behave awkwardly in quartering seas, and the larger the seas, the more awkward their behavior.

When quartering seas come behind the boat from the starboard (right) side or the port (left) side, they not only push the boat ahead but also push the stern aside. The risk is that they'll push the stern so far aside that your boat takes the seas broadside. Then the danger is that the boat will turn over.

Follow these steps when facing quartering seas:

1. **Trim the propellers up slightly to a level or "zero-degrees" trim. Rougher waters may require a slightly higher trim setting to one or two degrees up.**

2. **As the wave comes under the boat, steer away from it to counteract its push to the side.**

3. **As you enter the trough, straighten your course but be prepared to quickly steer away from the next wave.**

Over a great distance, these seas will push you off course. Correcting for that may not be possible, and you may be forced to head for a different port.

Dealing with following seas

Following seas that come directly from behind are great under power — if you handle them properly. Following seas of small craft advisory proportion can be pretty exciting, though.

Following seas come in under the boat and lift it. If the wave period is short, however, the boat's motion from the past wave may fight the lifting, and the wave can press against the boat, pushing it or splashing over the transom and swamping the boat.

Under power, you should keep the boat moving at a pace equal to the speed of the waves, if their height makes it unsafe to cross them. In outboards and sterndrives, trim the propeller to an angle that pushes directly in line with the boat's keel; which is called *zero-trim angle*. In some cases, when the seas overtake the boat, it's best to have the propeller trimmed upward slightly to combat the lifting of the waves and hold the bow up to prevent nosing into the next wave or trough.

Changing course in stormy seas

Changing course in stormy seas is a tricky maneuver. So tricky, in fact, that experienced boaters try to avoid it at all costs. If you have no choice in the matter and you have to turn in stormy seas, in following or head seas, you can retain control by managing the speed of your craft and trim of your propeller so waves come under the boat directly and with a minimum impact. But when turning around in seas, there's a brief moment when the boat's keel is aligned with the crests of the waves. If that happens in the trough between waves, things work out fine. If it happens as a wave crests under the boat, the force of the wave can turn over your boat.

This turning maneuver takes timing and coordination and a cooperative crew seated on the floor near the centerline of the boat to lower the boat's reaction to the seas. The trick is to make the turn quickly in the trough and be pointing at the next wave before it crests under the boat. Here's how:

1. **Gauge the speed of the waves and adjust the speed of the boat to be nearly equal to the speed of the waves.**

2. **Inform your crew of the maneuver, and have them sit on the floor near the center of the boat.**

3. **As the boat levels out in the trough, simultaneously turn and apply additional throttle to speed the turn.**

4. **As the boat finishes the turn, straighten the helm (steering wheel) and pull the throttle back to a slow setting.**

5. **Adjust your speed to the new rhythm of the waves.**

Turning the boat around in seas is a tricky and even dangerous maneuver. It's often better to find a safe port in the direction the seas are taking you, if you can. Sometimes, the seas are lighter closer to land, and you can make a course correction in calmer seas even though you may be farther from home.

Chapter 12

Preparing for and Handling Boating Emergencies

In This Chapter

▶ Preparing for a variety of eventualities

▶ Knowing how to deal with common emergencies

▶ Calling for help on the water

▶ Deciding to stay with or abandon the boat

▶ Attempting basic temporary repairs

*A*ccidents are often preventable, and the best first aid is being prepared for the unexpected. The goal of this chapter isn't to tell you how to be an EMT (emergency medical technician) or a *Baywatch* superhero. The point of this chapter is to help you know when and how to act on your crew's behalf in the most prudent way when an emergency arises.

In this chapter, I give you some tips on being prepared by explaining how to have and check the right equipment, how to handle some common emergencies, and how to correctly call for emergency assistance.

Being Equipped for Dealing with Boating Hazards

Too often, boaters are ill-prepared for accidents. They leave the dock without properly fitting life vests, working fire extinguishers (or none at all), or even an anchor onboard. I've rescued boaters and "put out fires" in several incidents where they were having problems because their equipment was outdated or poorly fitted and failed when they needed it. Being prepared means having the right equipment onboard and making sure that equipment is shipshape, as we boaters like to say. Being prepared also means planning ahead and sharing those plans with others onshore so that someone always knows what you're up to.

Checking your safety equipment

In Chapter 4, I describe the essential safety gear you need and how to make sure you obtain quality stuff. These items include:

- First-aid kit
- Anchors
- Fire extinguishers
- Life jackets
- Life preservers
- Paddles

For some reason, many boaters consider this safety gear optional. What a mistake! And now *you* know better.

Every time you go out on your boat, you need to check your safety gear to make sure it's in good, working condition. Follow these recommendations and check out Figure 12-1:

- Before each trip, make sure your communication devices (cellphone and/or VHF radio) are charged and working properly.
- Check your fire extinguisher to make sure the charge gauge indicates it's ready for action.
- Check that the anchor, *rode* (the anchor rope), and shackles that hold the rode to the anchor are secure and the rope isn't frayed.
- Even if you don't expect your crew to wear life preservers, hand one to each person so he or she can make sure it fits before leaving the dock.

Federal law requires children under the age of 14 to wear life jackets at all times while boating. This law applies in all states unless the state has its own minimum age requirement for life jacket wear. In boating, state laws take priority over federal law, so make sure you check the rules where you boat.

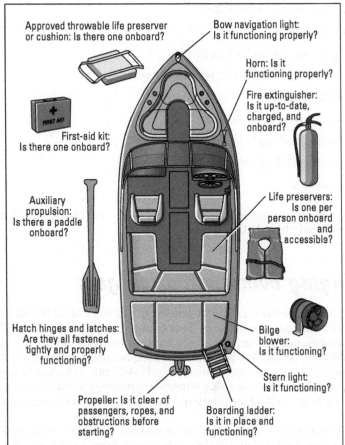

Approved throwable life preserver or cushion: Is there one onboard?

Bow navigation light: Is it functioning properly?

Horn: Is it functioning properly?

Fire extinguisher: Is it up-to-date, charged, and onboard?

First-aid kit: Is there one onboard?

Auxiliary propulsion: Is there a paddle onboard?

Life preservers: Is one per person onboard and accessible?

Hatch hinges and latches: Are they all fastened tightly and properly functioning?

Bilge blower: Is it functioning?

Stern light: Is it functioning?

Propeller: Is it clear of passengers, ropes, and obstructions before starting?

Boarding ladder: Is it in place and functioning?

Figure 12-1: Check your boat equipment and safety gear every time you head out on the water.

Stowing a first-aid kit

A first-aid kit can't carry everything needed for an appendectomy or a heart attack, but you should at the least stock the same type of basic medical supplies you have at home in your medicine cabinet.

While the potential always exists for a serious medical emergency to arise when you're boating, 99 percent of what you'll run into on your boat will be manageable if you keep handy all the basic supplies for relieving discomfort and injury. Here's a list of gear I keep on the boat in my first-aid kit:

  ✓ Adhesive bandages

  ✓ Antibiotic ointment

  ✓ Antihistamine for bug bites or allergic reactions

- ✔ Aspirin or other painkiller
- ✔ Bug repellent
- ✔ Cortisone cream for bug bites
- ✔ Elastic tape for binding wounds or sprains
- ✔ Medical tape
- ✔ Seasick remedies and antacid
- ✔ Sterile gauze pads in several sizes
- ✔ Sterile rolled gauze
- ✔ Sunscreen

Before you go boating, grab your first-aid kit — and check its contents — so you'll be ready for what ails you.

Bringing communication gear

You should have the equipment needed to call the United States Coast Guard or other local rescue operators. This equipment may include a VHF radio in some places, but on many smaller inland waters, a cellphone for a call to 911 is sometimes better. Ask your local boating acquaintances which they use and suggest. Or do like most boaters and take both. I discuss how to properly call for help on the water using whatever communication device you choose in the section, "Calling for the Help You Need," later in this chapter.

If you're going into more remote areas without communication, you're dependent on your boat and motor for a safe return. Even though you can often count on friendly boaters for a rescue should your boat fail, you also should be prepared to go it alone.

Reaching out with a VHF radio

VHF radios are special radios operating on bands reserved for marine communications. Before the cellphone, many boaters inland and offshore used VHF radios daily, and you could walk the docks of any marina and hear radio chatter. Today, the proliferation of cellphones makes that experience rare.

So why buy a VHF radio if you think nobody's listening? Because when trouble comes, the rescuers *will* have one and will be able to talk to you — and they won't need to know your phone number to call you. Even though they may not easily see you because your boat's just a small speck in the sea or other large body of water, you'll be able to see their chopper or rescue craft and talk them in with signals to turn right or left or north or south.

A waterproof, handheld VHF radio can be your best safety device. With it, you can continue to transmit mayday calls even if you're in the water. When you see rescue boats or aircraft, you can hail them on the radio — they'll be listening, trust me. In fact, handheld VHF radios are in retailer West Marine's list of top ten popular gift items. I think keeping one in the boat is essential to peace of mind and safety.

Calling on your cellphone

Cellphones were once looked down upon as a primary communication device for boaters. But in areas where there's adequate coverage, more boaters rely on them than on VHF radios. If your cellphone works in an area, you can rely on 411 for information and often 911 for emergency response. However, not all response centers can get a position from your cellphone, so a GPS or a chart is necessary to give rescuers your position.

I don't have to tell you that being stranded along a highway with no way to call a tow truck or ambulance is frustrating, if not scary. You bought a cellphone for that very reason, right? Well, your cellphone may not work on the lake, just like it may not work along a remote section of highway. And it sure won't work more than a few miles offshore on the ocean. If your cellphone gets wet, it may not work, either. So take care to keep it dry.

Taking navigation tools

The second most frequent cause for initiating search and rescue missions (boats dead in the water is the first) is grounding, according to a report by the U.S. Coast Guard. Accidents because of faulty navigation tactics are the easiest safety failure to correct. It's easier to navigate safely today than ever before because the entire world has been mapped and remapped. All that information is available on charts and Global Positioning Systems (GPS). A combination of charts and a GPS device makes boating safer. And don't forget your trusty compass when the batteries in your GPS go dead. See Chapter 10 for more details on navigation equipment.

Finding your way with GPS

Getting lost leads to running out of gas or running aground. Both strand you at inconvenient, often dangerous times and places. A GPS device is the ideal solution for keeping trouble at bay. You can buy a handheld version complete with basic maps for as little as $100.

For boating in unfamiliar waters — all waters are unfamiliar for new boaters — the better the GPS device you can afford, the more likely it is to save you from trouble of both the mechanical and life-threatening sorts. In fact, I heard that one propeller repair shop manager, who worked on the Georgian Bay of Lake Huron, said that the GPS equipment that boaters are using is so accurate it's killing his repair business. They simply aren't running into the rocks as much. Seeing as the Coast Guard reports the number-one cause for initiating search and rescue missions is for boats dead in the water, saving a propeller could be saving a life.

Don't think of a GPS as a handy substitute for a paper chart and strong local knowledge. Every GPS I've seen has a disclaimer on the power-up screen saying, "Don't rely on this device as your sole source of navigation information." I've been on the water many times when GPS has failed.

Even if you're boating with a GPS guide, look behind you frequently as you meander along. On your return trip, the landmarks will be familiar.

Following a chart with the help of a compass

Even if you spring for a GPS, don't go boating without a chart and a compass as well. Keep the chart folded open to the area you're in, and note your progress along the way, penciling in landmarks you see. I've had to come home on a compass when my GPS failed, as mechanical things are bound to do, and my notes and marked landmarks ensured me that I was on the right path.

You may think talk of charts and GPS units is goofy when you're planning to boat on a lake in which you can see the entire shoreline from any one spot. But most waters have hidden hazards revealed only in a chart. You may never need to rely on a compass on a 500-acre lake, but you should get in the habit of doing so anyway. Soon, you'll want to adventure in other waters that may not be so tame.

Filing a float plan and checking insurance

The best way to make sure you'll be missed if you become stranded is to tell people when and where you're going and when you will be back! A *float plan* is the boater's version of the flight plan that pilots file to indicate their departure times and locations, their destinations, and their estimated landing times. They do this so that if something goes wrong and they don't show up, people have an idea of where to begin a search.

You can call reliable friends or relatives and give them your float plan, but keep in mind that they may all get it confused when trying to remember it later. It's better to write your float plan on paper and give it to two or three friends or relatives, or send them an e-mail with the information. Make sure they receive it by following up with a phone call. Tell them you'll contact them when you return. That way if you don't, they can call the rescue authorities.

Double-check your boat insurance and make sure you have enough towing insurance to get you back from the farthest point at which you may break down. In ocean situations, a tow boat has to find you, hitch up, and pull you back. That can take hours and even a few thousand dollars. Make sure you're covered so you can easily secure the help you need.

Tackling Types of Emergencies

When an emergency arises, it helps to remain calm. And it's easier to remain calm when you know the right steps to take to deal with the emergency. In this section, I walk you through some of the most common categories of calamities you may encounter while boating and offer tips on how to manage your boat and your crew in case of equipment breakdowns, fire, groundings, and more.

By the way, during an emergency, if you have other capable people onboard, assign them tasks such as gathering kids together, double-checking life jacket buckles and adjustments, and, if you have to abandon ship, getting supplies together that you'll need while adrift. In fact, these are great tasks to assign *before* you leave the dock or boat ramp. That way you minimize the confusion in communication in the event of an emergency.

Communication is the key to keeping your crew calm and helpful. If some crew members don't seem to be functioning well, assign other crew members to keep them on the right track. Nothing stokes the flame of panic like a vacuum of information.

Equipment failure

So often boaters head out of port for one reason: to get away from everything, including other people. Whether you're boating alone or with a crew, you have to be prepared to handle emergencies. On a small Northwoods Wisconsin lake, it's not so hard to get help by just waving your arms. But if you're miles up a desert lake in Utah or far out to sea when things break down, you may be hours from rescue.

If you have room on your boat, take along spare parts that commonly fail, like an extra propeller, hose clamps, and wooden pegs or wax seals to repair leaks should they occur. In Chapter 20, I explain in detail what a good mariner carries in order to handle tight spots caused by equipment failure or leaks.

Fire

Boat fires are usually a result of a mechanical malfunction, although it's possible for a collision to result in one, too. Most fires start in the bilge around the engine where fuel vapors and electrical components create the perfect storm for fire: volatile fumes, heat, and an electric spark. If they ignite and you can't put it out quickly, fire becomes pretty hard to stop because the resins that give fiberglass its strength and shape are flammable.

If your boat's on fire, here are the basic steps to take:

1. **Double-check that all crew members are wearing life jackets, and give the handheld VHF radio to an adult.**

2. **Get people off the boat and away from it as quickly as possible. Use a lifeboat if you have one handy; otherwise, they should jump into the water wearing their life jackets.**

3. **Extend a long line from the boat and have the crew swim to the end of it and hang on for as long as the boat floats or until you put the fire out.**

   It will be much easier for the Coasties to find everyone near the burning boat. Make sure everyone can easily let the rope go if the boat goes down — you don't want to go with it!

4. **With everyone off the boat, and only if you feel confident that you can safely do so, try to put out the fire with fire extinguishers.**

   Many experts believe if you can't put a fire out in 10 seconds, you need to get off the boat in less than 60 seconds. That's why some captains' first response to a fire is to get passengers off the boat.

   If you suspect fire in the engine compartment, *don't open it to check.* Opening the hatch could let in oxygen and stoke a small fire in the closed compartment into a big one.

   Many boats have a see-through fire port — a clear silicone peep hole — on the engine compartment. You can see if fire is inside, and if it is, you can puncture this port in order to poke the nozzle of a fire extinguisher in and douse the flames. If you don't have a fire port, they're easy and inexpensive to install. Other boats have built-in extinguisher systems that let you deploy them without lifting the engine compartment hatch. Automatic fire extinguishers usually are installed by the boat factory and are reserved for larger boats. However, European safety standards commonly require them in boats once thought too small, so it's now not surprising to find automatic fire extinguishers in boats as small as 20 feet long.

5. **If you can't put out the blaze, or if the boat is already sinking, join your crew in the water. Or, if you're *sure* the fire's out, bring the crew back onboard to await assistance or limp to port.**

My good boating buddy Ted Lund comes from Key West. He told me of a trip on his dad's charter boat when it caught fire. His father's first command in responding to the fire? "Get off the boat, son. Jump in the water." Which Ted did, immediately. They put the fire out, but the boat could have exploded.

Truthfully, I hate even bringing up fire in a boat. I've never seen it happen, but I know more than one person who has experienced it. Those boats were all much older boats and probably didn't have the superior safety building techniques now required to achieve the coveted NMMA (National Marine Manufacturers Association) certification. Boats with that certification are always built to a high standard of reliability and safety.

Grounding on hazards below the surface

Grounding is essentially a collision with the ground or other object beneath the water's surface, such as a sandbar, large rock, or even a large tree stump. Some groundings are gentle and the boat simply grinds to a halt. But they can be abrupt, too, knocking people around in the boat more like a collision. The point is that a grounding brings your boat to a halt. Sometimes, you contact the ground, pass over the shallow spot, and find your boat disabled but floating on the other side.

Here are some steps to follow in the case of a grounding:

1. **Make sure your whole crew is safe. Address any injuries or, if you have a capable crew member, assign someone else to handle injuries while you check out the boat and your situation.**

2. **Make sure the boat's situation is as stable as it can be.**

   • If you're grounded, stay that way and check for leaks. Don't unground the boat until you're certain it doesn't leak. Chances are if it does leak, you can't fix it and you need to wait for help.

   • If you're afloat or adrift in a current without engine power, drop an anchor. Your collision with the ground could leave you floating, but your propeller or engine could be damaged and unserviceable.

   • If you have power and you're leaking, get to shore as quickly as possible.

3. **Assess your need for help. If you need help, use whatever tools you have (VHF radio, cellphone, flares, or waving rags) to summon it and sit tight. Otherwise, do what you need to do to ensure you're seaworthy (there are no leaks, you have engine power, and you can control the boat) and head in to port.**

Note: When you're safely back on shore, you may need to notify the local authorities of your grounding accident. Most states have a damage threshold amount that must be exceeded before reporting is necessary. In the case of injuries, reporting is always required. Even if your boat isn't damaged, in environmentally sensitive places like the Florida Keys, damage to the bottom of the water body must be reported and mitigated by your insurance.

Collision with another vessel

The considerations to keep in mind and act on when you have a collision with another vessel are basically the same as those for a grounding (refer to the preceding section). The crucial difference is that, with a collision, another boat and another crew are involved. The circumstances bring special responsibilities such as the following:

- ✔ No matter who is at fault, see that all passengers in *both* boats are as safe as you can make them.
- ✔ Call rescue help if needed.
- ✔ Call state, municipal, or federal water patrol authorities on a VHF radio or cellphone (usually such a call is required by law). Follow their directions.
- ✔ If damage is minor, both boats are still seaworthy, no injuries are involved, and you have been cleared by the authorities to leave the scene, then exchange the same kind of information you would if you were involved in a fender bender, including names, driver's license numbers, insurance info, phone numbers, and hull registrations. You may find you need to be in touch later.

Distracting the captain never ends well

Most U.S. Coast Guard accident postmortems indicate that serious and sometimes fatal accidents are often the culmination of a series of events that began with one innocuous and seemingly unrelated event.

For example, a boat passenger gets his finger pinched in a hatch. The captain leaves the helm to help him, forgetting that the motor is idling in gear. While their heads are down as they try to open the finger-jamming hatch, the boat meanders into a roped-off swimming area and a swimmer is injured by the boat's propeller.

Distractions in a boat are common. The best way to avoid them is for the captain to remember that, while the boat is running, his responsibility is to control it. Even when the boat is adrift and not under power, it's the captain's job to keep it safe by signaling others, dropping an anchor, or even paddling the boat safely into port.

Weather

Sudden violent weather can sneak up on you when boating, and sometimes you don't have time to get to port safely before it arises. I've seen even smaller lakes whipped up into dangerous whitecaps by squalls; the worst thing boaters can do when that happens is to try to run like the wind to get home. Better to hunker down low in the boat and travel to the nearest shelter to sit things out. Duck into a cove or a nearby marina to wait. Even tucking in around the downwind side of a point or bend in a river can offer more safety and protection than the open water. I explain in detail the tricks for handling bad weather in Chapter 11.

Personal accident or injury

The trick to good first aid is found in the Hippocratic Oath: "Do no harm." If you don't know what to do, it's better to do nothing unless the threat to life is immediate. An overheated crewmember needs to be cooled and his or her thirst quenched. You need to know the signs of heat stroke (nausea, vomiting, fatigue, dizziness) so you can help him or her before thirst and heat become a problem. Arterial bleeding has to be stopped or slowed by applying pressure, or medical attention may unfortunately not be needed later. But is removing a fish hook really something you should try to do?

Check with your boating guests in advance to make sure they bring along any time-sensitive medications they need. Asthmatics should have inhalers or other meds, and diabetics should have at least one extra insulin injection onboard along with plenty of appropriate food for the outing. When you're boating with new guests who may be a little sensitive to outdoor risks, keep the outing simple and close to home — at least until you know they're up for more adventure.

Calling for the Help You Need

You've seen those movies where people drift around in lifeboats, delirious and drinking ocean water and trying to eat seagulls, right? Well, that's *not* where you're going with your boat. At least, not if you read this chapter. Sure, I know more than a couple of boaters who had to spend the night out in their boats, but in your power boat you're probably not going into the endless sea lanes of the South Pacific.

There's no guarantee that you won't need assistance, though. If you boat long enough, it's almost a statistical certainty that eventually you'll at least need a tow in.

The two types of calls for help you want to be familiar with when you're boating are

- **Mayday:** The international call for distress when the boat or someone's life is in immediate danger
- **Pan-pan:** An urgent call for help when the boat or a human life is not immediately threatened

Unless immediate assistance is mandatory to save the boat or save lives, never use mayday.

Whether you've made a boating mistake or not, don't be too embarrassed to ask for help. And don't worry about being slapped around verbally for goofing up with the wrong call. I've never seen anyone more gracious than marine rescue personnel.

Making a mayday call

Mayday calls on a VHF radio can only work wherever other boaters and water safety enforcement personnel monitor the VHF band. The U.S. Coast Guard seldom monitors VHF signals far from waters navigated by commercial boats. In most inland waters, local or state law enforcement personnel are your go-to guys in an emergency.

In port, inquire about who handles emergencies on the boating waters and determine how to communicate with them. If VHF radio is used in your area, follow the steps in this section for making a mayday call. If emergencies are handled through a 911 dispatcher, you make that call with your cellphone, just like you would at home.

Follow these steps to call a mayday on the VHF radio:

1. **Turn the VHF radio to channel 16.**

   That's the channel the Coasties monitor — and the channel most other boaters monitor, too.

2. **Press the transmit button and say "mayday" three times.**

   Be calm when you say it, even if you don't feel that way. And don't yell into the microphone; it tends to make your transmission unintelligible.

3. **Clearly state who you are.**

   - **If your boat has a name,** say it. For example, if your boat were named *Unfortunate,* you would say, "Mayday, mayday, mayday! This is *Unfortunate,* this is *Unfortunate.*"

   - **If your boat doesn't have a name,** say something descriptive like, "This is little white Sea Ray." (Sea Ray is a brand of boat.) This information can help rescuers spot you when they approach.

4. **Give your location.**

   - **If you have a GPS,** give your latitude and longitude — it really makes things easier. (If you don't have a GPS for your first mishap, I'll bet you'll be shopping for one soon.)

   - **If you don't know your location,** give the closest thing you know. For example, you may say, "We passed under the big green bridge about ten minutes ago" or "We left Neophyte Harbor headed north- west two hours ago." Anything like that will help narrow down the search area. If you have a chart with you, refer to it to give better landmarks.

5. **If you don't hear a response, don't give up. Keep trying.**

6. **When you get a response or even if you don't get a response, give your position and the nature of your emergency.**

   Tell the Coasties in as few words as possible why you're in danger. Just because you can't hear a response doesn't mean someone isn't listening to you.

Making a pan-pan call

"Pan-pan" is what you say when you need help but your situation isn't life-threatening. If you need pan-pan–level help, use the same procedures as for a mayday call except substitute the word "pan-pan" for "mayday": "Pan-pan, pan-pan, pan-pan!" That tells rescuers that you won't get home without help, but the situation is stable and your passengers are safe.

For example, you would make a pan-pan call if

- You're aground on a sandbar.
- You're out of gas.
- You're broken down.
- You're lost.
- There's thunder and lightning all around you.

However, one of these situations *could* turn into something mayday-worthy if the delay in your return to port could cause injury. For instance, if you have a diabetic onboard who's about to go into insulin shock, then your mishap that led to an inconvenience has resulted in a mayday.

Remember, it's up to the boat captain to decide whether it's a mayday or not. It's unlikely you'll be criticized for erring on the side of caution. But, generally speaking, I wouldn't want to tell a rescue swimmer that he jumped out of a helicopter just because you were going to miss a plane to Phoenix if you didn't get home by 7 p.m.!

Sometimes you'll just pull a boneheaded move (don't take offense; I've done it myself, I freely admit) and run out of gas or jam up on a sandbar or — well, you get the picture. If one of these things happens and you're inconvenienced but not endangered, there are at least three nationwide boat-towing services that will bring you fuel or tow you in. Good boat insurance will cover the expense (find out more about insuring your boat in Chapter 3). Look into the three top national marine towing services by visiting these Web sites:

- ✔ seatow.com
- ✔ www.vesselassist.com
- ✔ www.boatus.com

Other means of getting attention

Three kinds of help are available to you out on the water: official help, private enterprise help, and Good Samaritan help. On inland waterways, you're most likely to get a Good Samaritan. If your life or that of your crew is in peril, the U.S. Coast Guard or other state or local rescue or enforcement agencies will be there to help you.

Here are a few ways to get the attention of a Good Samaritan:

- ✔ **Flares:** In many waters, three safety flares are required safety equipment onboard. Don't fire them unless you believe someone is in visible range. Various kinds of flares are available at marine stores, and each has specific and simple directions for usage.

- ✔ **Waving a rag or flag:** It's true, flying Old Glory upside down is a distress call. But you also can wave a rag or a paddle or anything to get a Good Samaritan's attention.

- ✔ **Empty-handed wave:** If you don't even have a shirt on your back, wave your hands from side to side, crossing them overhead. Do it repeatedly until the Good Samaritan notices.

If you see a boater giving a distress signal, you absolutely have an obligation to offer assistance. If you're aware of a life-threatening situation on the water and fail to act to save a life, you can be culpable in the loss of life. At the very least, you should stand by and raise help on a radio or cellphone.

Deciding whether to wait for help or head for shore

Waiting for help in an emergency isn't easy. Even on land, rushing to the emergency room or waiting for an ambulance can be a tough judgment call. When boating, here are a few instances when waiting is either necessary or at least a better choice:

- Your motor doesn't work (you aren't going anywhere anyway).
- Moving an injured patient is too painful or otherwise dangerous.
- The rescue authorities have asked you to wait for assistance.

Sometimes waiting for help isn't feasible, though, such as when you're not sure help is coming. Here are two instances when moving toward shore and help is preferable, if you're able to:

- You have no indication that anyone heard your call for help.
- Any injured parties are stable and able to handle the motion of the boat.

Don't feel compelled to take action merely to expend nervous energy. If help is on the way, it's best to wait for it. Heck, the Coasties may be planning to give your friend in need a chopper ride. You wouldn't want to cheat him or her out of that, would you?

Deciding to Abandon Ship

"Abandon ship!" You've heard the words used jokingly a million times. But as a boat owner, now you have to think about what those words really mean. If you have an emergency on your hands, will it require you to leave your boat? If so, your main objective is to make sure your crew is calm and prepared with life jackets on.

Emergencies like a small boat overturning in high seas or winds or a grounding that fractures the hull and swamps it are extreme cases when life jackets are all that stand between you and drowning. That's why keeping them handy, if not wearing them, at all times is so important.

In all cases but fire onboard, staying with the boat — even if it's swamped — is the best rescue scenario. If the boat is overturned, staying in it isn't possible, but staying near it is the best and safest course. It's easier for rescuers to find the overturned boat than bobbing heads in the water. If your boat is under 23 feet long and is certified by the NMMA, it's designed *not* to sink even when fully flooded, giving your crew a safe place to await help. Some boats over 23 feet are also built not to sink, and that's a reassuring advantage.

As captain, you need to understand how to handle emergency circumstances and help your crew deal with the situation. Keep these steps in mind when you decide to abandon ship because of a sinking ship:

1. **Forgive me for saying this again, but make sure everyone's wearing a life jacket.**

2. **If the boat is sinking, help everyone stay calm. Stay with the boat until it's obvious it's going under.**

3. **Make sure those assigned to grab emergency supplies (VHF radio, water, flares, and food) do so.**

4. **Jump into the water, and stay together. If the water is cold, you can minimize cooling by huddling together, which also assists everyone in staying afloat.**

In cold water below 60 degrees Fahrenheit, you only have a few seconds or a minute or two (depending on the temperature) before cold water causes shock that robs you of your ability to coordinate your motions to stay afloat. If you can't at least rely on a life jacket in that time, your chances of survival are poor at best. That's why I always wear a life jacket and make my crew do the same when boating in cold water.

Ocean or Great Lakes boaters in particular are wise to keep a small inflatable lifeboat onboard. Stow it forward, as far away from the engine as possible. When it's apparent that abandoning ship is imminent, deploy the lifeboat by following the instructions on the bag (which you should have read and familiarized yourself with earlier).

Attempting Temporary Repairs

If you've had an accident that isn't serious, there are no serious injuries, and you have the know-how and tools, you can attempt temporary repairs that will allow you to get safely back to port. In this section, I cover some tips and tactics for assessing damage and repairing or recovering your craft so you can either get back to boating or at least get back to shore. Keep yourself and your crew calm, and you can often keep an accident from being anything more than an inconvenience.

Assessing the damage

When an accident occurs, you need to look around yourself, look to your crew's safety and mental state, and try to maintain the integrity of the boat and crew.

For a normal outing in a runabout, it's not likely you'll have special tools or materials handy to permanently patch a hole, but if your boat is properly equipped to the letter of the law, you should have the tools to put out a fire, and you may also have plenty of resources onboard to stop it from taking on water.

Fixing what you can

When you've settled the safety and security of your crew, made contact with local rescue authorities, and identified the damage to the boat, it's time to play MacGyver and whip out your Swiss Army knife to get things patched up. Here are some things you can try:

- **Plug leaks.** Improvise if you have to, but try to stop the water. Rags, plastic bags — heck, sometimes even chewing gum — can get you back to the dock. Stuffing towels or garbage bags in the hole can slow the flow.

  Through-hull fittings are a common point for taking on water. They can break off or corrode, allowing water in the hull. Keep tapered wooden pegs onboard to drive into these openings, or fill them with wax from a plumber's wax ring (Chapter 20 discusses your options for materials to plug leaks).

- **If your propeller is broken and you carry a spare, try to get the boat in a safe position to change the propeller and get underway again.** Spare propellers are a great safety item to carry if you have room. Find out more about changing propellers in Chapter 15.

Boating is about as safe a sport as exists, but when you turn on the local news at the end of a holiday weekend, you often hear about a boating accident. To a non-boater, it can look like a bunch of self-destructive idiots are out there on the water every weekend. Yet, for the number of boats registered each year — over 12 million — the number of accidents is low, and the sport is likely safer than snow skiing, motorcycle riding, or bicycling.

Still, if you play the game long enough, accidents will happen. Not necessarily fatal ones, but problematic ones. Personally, I've been run into by another boat, and I once crunched a concrete pier hard enough to damage the boat. It happens.

Minor equipment failure can have major consequences

Malfunctioning equipment is a safety concern, no matter how unrelated to safety or how inconsequential it may seem. You may not plan to be out after dark, so knowing that your navigation lights don't work may not bother you. But a breakdown that leaves you stranded on a busy waterway after dark can make you a serious hazard to other boaters, not to mention yourself.

Make sure your boat is shipshape. Everything on a boat needs to be in place and functioning. You never know what minor equipment failure could tip the first domino that leads to an accident. Here are two examples of real accidents and their surprising causes:

✔ **The case of the missing spare anchor:** Bill and his boys were returning from bottom-fishing far offshore. They snagged their only anchor and had to leave it on the bottom. Returning to their harbor was always dicey for them because currents were fast and the inlet choppy. They'd been in calm seas all day, and none of them were wearing life jackets when they reached the choppy inlet.

The motor conked out. Ordinarily, Bill would simply have had one of his boys deploy the anchor while he sorted out the engine problem. But their anchor was lost and they didn't have a spare. The current swept them into an outlying jetty and capsized their boat. Fighting the current, Bill and his boys barely made it to safety — and they lost their boat and gear.

An anchor is considered safety gear because it lets you control the boat when the power fails. Bottom-fishing is a common way to lose an anchor, and Bill should have had a spare onboard for such a case. Or, knowing they didn't have one, Bill and his crew should have returned to harbor earlier to hit the inlet at slack tide when it was less treacherous.

✔ **The case of the loose ladder fitting:** The Andersons and Wilsons decided to drop anchor and enjoy a sunny day from a quiet cove. They spent all afternoon paddling around the cove, drinking refreshments, and playing cards. Half the crew was still swimming and the other half were onboard when they decided to return to the dock.

Just as Mr. Anderson began to hoist the anchor, the boarding ladder broke and the swimmers couldn't get back on the boat. Mr. Anderson had the anchor halfway in and lashed it down to a deck cleat so he could assist the swimmers. He'd been planning to fix that loose ladder fitting for months.

With all crew safely onboard, he put the throttle down and got up on plane when suddenly the anchor, still dangling from the deck cleat, reached the end of its rope and sling-shotted into the boat, injuring the Wilsons.

A boarding ladder is a key piece of safety gear that enables passengers who fall or jump overboard to return to the boat. The Andersons saw it mainly as a swimming convenience and so weren't too concerned about the loose fitting. Even a loose hinge breaking at an inopportune time could have distracted Mr. Anderson from securing the rogue anchor that caused the injury.

Part IV
Keeping Your Boat Shipshape

The 5th Wave   By Rich Tennant

"Can I have a big motor with it so the zebras can water-ski?"

In this part . . .

There's more to boating than just leaning over the helm with a heroic look on your face while the wind toys with your hair. Sometimes you have to roll up your sleeves and get busy making the boat shipshape. In this part, I explain what kind of service work generally needs to be done on your boat and when it needs to be done. If you're a do-it-yourself kind of boater, I give some specific tips to help you decide if you should get a service manual and tackle boat maintenance yourself, and I walk you through the steps of some maintenance procedures.

Chapter 13

Keeping Up with Routine Boat Maintenance

In This Chapter

▶ Preventing engine problems with simple maintenance

▶ Checking and changing fluids

▶ Charging your battery properly

▶ Keeping your boat looking spiffy longer

*B*oating isn't free, but it's not the most expensive family pastime you can enjoy, by far. If you compare it to a day at a theme park or a weekly round of golf, it's usually cheaper fun. To tilt the scale even further in the direction of value, many boaters learn to handle some of the most basic boat maintenance themselves. Yet, more than the dollar savings, many boaters weigh the *time* savings of hauling their boat to the shop and waiting for the mechanic to get to it. Sometimes the work needed is simple and fast enough that the mechanic concludes in a day or so. Other times, there's no way to explain why it takes the mechanic so long.

This chapter can't take the place of a step-by-step engine service manual or your particular engine's owner's manual, but it does give you a job list of tasks that need to be done and lets you know how uncomplicated the work is. If you store your boat on a trailer or in a marina that will let you service your own boat, I hope you'll dig into this chapter and be motivated to get a little grease on your hands and keep a little more green in your pocket.

In this chapter, I break down the service work that various engine types require and explain the basic processes involved in performing the work. I list the tools you need to do the work, including handy gadgets to ease the work. And I give you cost comparisons between servicing your boat and servicing your automobile, so you have a standard by which to compare the payback for doing it yourself.

Checking and Changing Your Engine's Oil

I was shocked when a friend told me that a mechanic charges nearly four times the cost of an automobile oil change to change her boat's engine oil. It's remarkable, especially when you consider that the oil, filter, and other supplies usually cost the same for a boat as for an automobile and the work is no different.

This section walks you through the general steps of changing your engine's oil. If you've ever changed the oil in your car, you'll catch on to the process immediately. If you've ever checked your car's engine oil, it won't be hard to apply this information to the marine engine in your boat. If you're a take-it-to-the-shop sort of person, that's okay — at least you'll know what your recreational time is worth.

Your engine owner's manual tells you how frequently the oil should be changed. That frequency is based on hours of operation, instead of miles driven, as you're used to with your car. The hours of operation interval can be different for every engine and therefore is something you should consult your owner's manual to determine. And, just like when your car manual says to change the oil once per year or every 5,000 miles, your boat's engine manual says "change the oil once a year or every X hours of operation." If you use your boat a lot, you may need more than one oil change per year. And as I say in Chapter 14, you should change the oil before you put it in long-term storage for the winter.

Lubing up four-stroke outboards

Like your automobile engine, four-stroke outboard engines have an oil reservoir and an oil pump that lifts oil from the reservoir and distributes it around the engine to lubricate the moving parts so they don't destroy themselves with friction. Over time, heat and friction degrade the oil, and some of it is lost as it seeps into the engine's combustion chamber and gets burned along with the fuel. In some cases, fuel slips into the oil reservoir, diluting the oil and also degrading its ability to protect the engine from abrasion.

Although the individual steps remain the same from boat to boat, the locations of the dipstick, oil filter, and reservoir drain plug are different on each engine. The following sections detail what tools and supplies you need and how to perform the work on four-stroke outboards.

Tools and supplies

The tools list for changing your oil is simple and not very expensive. You need the following:

- ✔ **An oil filter wrench** to remove and replace the oil filter. This tool is available at any auto parts store.

- ✔ **A 12-inch adjustable wrench** to remove the reservoir drain plug. Avoid the shorter 8-inch wrench, which may not provide enough leverage to unscrew a tight drain plug.

- ✔ **A container, bucket, or jug** to capture the old oil as it drains.

- ✔ **A long-necked funnel** to pour new oil into the engine without spilling it.

- ✔ **An ample supply of rags** to make cleanup easy and to help prevent spills.

Not just any engine oil will meet the standards approved by all boat engine makers. Your engine owner's manual may specify a certain brand and grade of oil, but competing brands or formulas may be perfectly acceptable as well. Oils are formulated and graded for their ability to do the job of lubricating under certain conditions. (For a deeper understanding of oil formulations, I discuss formulas in the sidebar "Premium or bargain oil: Does it matter?") Here are some additional things to know about the oil you use:

- ✔ **FC-W:** This is the standard of oil required to sustain your engine's operation and warranty if you change the oil at the recommended intervals and maintain it at the levels prescribed in your engine owner's manual. The FC-W code appears on the engine oil label if it meets that requirement.

- ✔ **Quantity:** Your owner's manual specifies how much oil should be added in quarts or liters. Most oil marketed in the United States is bottled in quarts or gallons, and your engine manual specifies quarts, so you should naturally follow the quart measurements when adding oil.

- ✔ **Oil weight or grade:** Oil is graded in weights, such as 30W (W is for weight). In addition to watching for the FC-W logo, you also should select the grade of oil specified in your engine owner's manual.

- ✔ **Brand:** Some misinformed mechanics will tell you that your engine warranty is voided if you don't use the same brand of oil as the brand of your engine. That's patently false. Not one engine maker I know of requires that their brand of oil be used.

Oil filters remove bits of metal worn from the engine during normal use and also filter out sludge and other contaminants that reduce the oil's ability to protect the engine from friction and heat. You should change the oil filter every time you change the oil. The two types of oil filters available for four-stroke outboards are

✔ **Automotive engine oil filters:** Some four-stroke outboards are actually built with engines also used for automobiles. As a result, often automobile filters fit the outboards and can be used for substantial savings. Many Honda outboards, for instance, use the same filters used in Honda automobiles. Check with your marine mechanic or an auto parts store to scope out compatibility.

✔ **Marine engine oil filters:** Some four-stroke outboards use filters specifically designed only for them. Your marine dealer should tell you whether this is the case, but you can also find out from your owner's manual.

Checking the oil

The locations of the dipstick used to measure the engine oil level, the reservoir drain plug, and the oil filter vary with all four-stroke outboard motors, but all such motors have them. If you can't spot these parts easily (Hint: They usually have a bright yellow handle on them!), consult your owner's manual.

You should check your engine's oil level before you start the motor at the beginning of the day. Remove the dipstick and look near the end of it. Marks on the stick will indicate whether it's full or you need to add oil. If the oil is down to the "Add oil" level on the dipstick, add some oil just like you would for your car, checking the level intermittently so as to be sure you don't overfill it.

Changing the oil

Oil-changing procedures may be slightly different from boat to boat — and you may find one brand of outboard engine more or less convenient to work on than another — but the basic process of changing the oil is universal. Oil change frequency can vary from boat to boat, as well. You need to consult your engine operator's manual for the exact oil change interval.

The best place to change the oil is with the boat on the trailer in your own driveway. However, with an extractor pump, which allows you to pump out the oil through the dipstick tube and into an attached container that's drum-tight, you can even do it in the water with no risk to the boat or environment. Here's how to change your oil:

1. **Gather the tools, oil, filter, and rags you need to change the oil.**

2. **Unlatch the latches on the engine cowl that covers the motor, and remove the engine cowl. Set it in a safe place where it won't be damaged.**

3. **Locate and remove the oil dipstick to open the reservoir from the top so that it doesn't air lock and prevent the oil from draining.**

4. **Locate the engine drain plug and position the collection container under it to catch the used oil as it drains.**

5. **Remove the drain plug, and let the oil drain into the container until it stops flowing.**

6. **Locate the oil filter and unscrew it by hand or using a filter wrench.**

   It looks like a beer can screwed to the engine. If you need a visual reference on a beer can, check the contents of your left hand — it *is* a weekend, after all!

   Be careful when removing the filter; it contains oil, so hold it upright until you can empty it into your container for recycling.

7. **Set the used filter aside for disposal.**

   Some communities offer oil filter recycling programs; contact your city hall or consult a mechanic in your area about these programs. If no recycling program exists, dispose of the filter and the oil as recommended by your community's sanitation managers.

8. **Replace the drain plug, and hand-tighten it, but don't lean into it with your body. You don't want to over-tighten it and risk stripping the threads.**

9. **Before installing the fresh oil filter, dip your finger into the old oil and rub a little of it around the rubber gasket on the top of the new oil filter to lubricate it so it seats firmly to the engine. Then screw on the filter.**

10. **Replace the oil dipstick.**

11. **Remove the oil cap on the top of the engine (it says "Oil fill" or something similar). Using the funnel, replace the engine oil in the quantity and grade specified by your owner's manual.**

12. **Double-check to make sure there are no drips from the drain plug or filter. If there are, retighten things.**

13. **Using the dipstick, check the fresh oil to make sure you didn't underfill or overfill.**

    If the dipstick shows that you still need to add oil, that's easy enough to do. If you accidentally add too much, you can use the extractor pump to remove it.

14. **Replace the engine cowl, and latch it on.**

Dealing with oil in two-stroke outboards

Two-stroke outboards don't have an oil supply in the engine. Instead, they draw their lubricating oil from tanks located either in the cowl, as is the case with most outboards under 115 horsepower, or in the bilge (that's boat-speak for bottom of the boat). When the engine is started, oil is drawn into it in a similar way as fuel. Some of the oil is diverted to the inner workings of the engine, and some is burned with the fuel.

You don't change the oil in a two-stroke outboard, but you do have to add oil every time you add fuel.

If you don't add oil, your two-stroke outboard engine usually detects the low levels and sounds a beeper, and at the same time shuts down the engine or limits its running speed automatically so you can limp home for oil without damaging your engine. If your engine fails to detect low oil levels (older engines don't always have this safety mechanism) and continues running normally, excessive heat and friction will destroy your engine very quickly. So follow the procedure in this section every time you refuel your two-stroke outboard.

Tools and supplies

You don't need any mechanical tools to add oil to your two-stroke outboard, but a funnel is handy to add oil without spilling. You also don't need to change an oil filter because there isn't one! The oil circulates through the engine only once and then is burned with the fuel, so it doesn't get filtered.

Like four-stroke outboard oil, two-stroke outboard oil must meet certain standards to properly protect your motor. The industry minimum standard is set by the National Marine Manufacturers Association (NMMA) in cooperation with marine engine manufacturers. The standard is called TC-W3, and any oil you use should bear that code on the label.

Adding two-stroke oil

With a two-stroke outboard, you don't need to change your oil — just fill up your oil reservoir every time you fuel up. It's too easy not to do it yourself — the trick is remembering to do it.

If you have a 90-horsepower or smaller motor, locate your oil tank in the engine cowl. If it's a larger motor, look in the bilge under the hatches in the sole (that's boat-speak for the floor inside the boat). Remove the lid, insert a funnel, and pour in the oil. External tanks located in the bilge are translucent, so you can see how much you're adding. Tanks in the cowl, however, need careful monitoring as you pour so you don't overfill and spill.

Changing inboard and sterndrive engine oil

Regardless of the brand of sterndrive or inboard engine you own, the engine was probably made by General Motors (GM) and burns gasoline. Very few sterndrives are made with diesel engines, and nearly all go to European markets where diesel fuel prices are subsidized by the government. These GM gasoline engines were first built for automobiles, and some will continue to be used in GM cars for many years. The process for changing the oil in them is exactly like the process of changing the oil in automobile engines.

Tools and supplies

If you change your car's oil, you already have the tools you need for this job. All the tools necessary for changing four-stroke outboard oil that I cover in the earlier section, "Lubing up four-stroke outboards," also work on inboard and sterndrive engines.

However, there's one thing that makes changing inboard and sterndrive engine oil harder than changing automobile engine oil: Draining it out without spilling it in the bilge. It's almost impossible to put a catch pan or container under the motor and then remove it without spilling the used oil when you're done.

Most Mercruiser-brand motors built since 2005 have a clever drain tube on the engine that can be pulled through the bilge's drain plug hole so the oil is drained directly into a container to be taken for recycling. I wish they all had that handy feature! If your engine isn't equipped with the drain tube, I suggest you use an oil extractor pump made by Moeller Marine and available through marine stores like www.westmarine.com. The pump makes it extremely easy to pump out the oil through the dipstick tube. This extractor also serves as a used oil container that's drum-tight, so you can transport it to a service station to recycle the oil. This extractor costs about the same as an automobile oil change and can be used over and over, so it's a must-buy if you're going to service your own boat.

Gasoline-powered marine engines need 5 to 7 quarts of oil, depending on the size of the engine. Because they're automotive engines, using filters and oil from an auto parts store is fine if you buy quality brands — and it may save you some cash over buying products made just for boat engines.

Consult your engine owner's manual to determine what weight of oil you need to use. Both of the following common sterndrive brands have GM engines:

✔ Volvo Penta recommends 15W-50 engine oil.

✔ Mercruiser recommends 25W-40 engine oil.

Because marine engines are usually operated in warm and even hot weather, you should use heavier oils than you do in auto engines. In hot weather, even a *cold* inboard or sterndrive engine is at a higher temperature than a cold auto engine.

Your inboard or sterndrive engine is made by a car manufacturer and then *marinized,* or made ready for marine use, by the marine engine manufacturer. The oil filter fitting on your engine is often the same as one on a comparable car engine. Your engine manufacturer naturally recommends an oil filter of the same brand, and you can be assured it's a good fit for your engine. However, you can buy an oil filter at an auto parts store if you prefer it to a marine shop, and if you buy a quality brand-name filter, you can rest easy that it will do the job quite well. Plus, you may save a little money.

Checking the oil

Checking your marine inboard or sterndrive engine's oil is just like checking your car engine's oil, which is logical given that most engines are made by GM. Here's what you need to do:

1. **Locate the dipstick (it should have a bright yellow handle with a ring in it to put your finger through), and pull it out.**

2. **Wipe off the stick with a rag and reinsert it all the way into the reservoir.**

3. **Pull the dipstick out again.**

4. **Look at the oil sticking to the end of the stick, which has a mark with the label "Full" and "Add" or words to that effect.**

   If the oil is right at the "Add" mark, you need to add oil — usually just 1 quart. If it's below the "Add" mark, pour in another quart and check it again after a couple of minutes. Allow time for the oil to run down into the reservoir. If oil is still below the "Add" mark, add another quart. Keep in mind that you should have checked it sooner and avoided risking damage to your engine.

Changing the oil

Here are suggestions for changing your oil in an inboard or sterndrive without spilling a drop:

1. **Remove the oil fill cap or the dipstick on top of the engine.**

   The oil fill cap says "Oil fill cap" or words to that effect, so you can't mistake it. Removing either the cap or the dipstick before you drain the oil eliminates the possibility of an air lock that can slow the draining process.

2. **Insert the extractor tube from the Moeller Extractor pump (see "Tools and supplies" earlier in this section for more on this pump) into the dipstick tube and pump the oil out of the engine.**

   If you don't have this pump, buy one or have your dealer change your oil.

3. **Locate the oil filter on the side of the engine, and place rags under it. Set a container near the engine to put the old oil filter in.**

   Some oil filters are mounted on the boat near the engine and have hoses connecting them to the engine. These remote oil filters are usually easier to change and more accessible.

4. **Try to loosen the filter by hand by turning it counterclockwise. If it doesn't budge, loosen it with the filter wrench. Carefully remove it — it will be full of oil. Pour the oil in your catch bucket, and dispose of the filter or recycle it as I explain in the earlier section on four-stroke outboard oil changes.**

5. **Dip your finger in the old oil and rub a little oil around the rubber seal on the new oil filter so it will seat tightly and smoothly. Screw on the new filter.**

   If you removed the old filter by hand, tighten the new one by hand. If you use a wrench, don't over-tighten the new filter — just make it snug.

6. **Place a funnel in the oil fill hole on top of the engine, and carefully pour in fresh oil. Keep a rag handy in case of spills.**

   Most marine engines require 5 quarts of oil, but some may require 6 or even 7. Consult your owner's manual or local dealer if you're unsure of the quantity.

7. **Replace the oil cap, and check the oil level to be sure the appropriate amount is indicated on the dipstick.**

8. **Look carefully around the oil filter for signs of oil leaking. If all is oil-tight, you're ready to go boating.**

On inboard and sterndrive boat engines, I've seen mechanics remove the boat's drain plug, remove the oil drain plug, and let the oil run into the bilge and then out the bilge drain into a bucket for disposal. I've even seen them let oil run out on the ground, too. Never let the oil run into the bilge, because you can never get it completely cleaned out. Every time your bilge pump runs, it will pick up the oil residue and pump it out with the bilge water *into* the water, leaving an oily sheen. It's a bad practice — and it's illegal.

Premium or bargain oil: Does it matter?

Most people know what engine oil is for, but few beyond the scientists who blend and validate it actually know whether its chemical formula stands up to the claims made by advertising. My readers at *Boating Life* magazine often ask me whether premium oil is really worth the money. Until I was able to wrangle a tour through the Shell/Pennzoil blending plant in Texas and the private lab that does validation testing for them and for the National Marine Manufacturers Association (NMMA) that sets minimum standards for some oils, I didn't know how to answer this question.

My takeaway from the tours was this: You may get really good oil from a bargain brand. In fact, it's possible the bargain brand is bottled in a premium-brand facility. What you don't get with a bargain brand is the exhaustive validation testing required not only to prove the oil works as intended but also to substantiate advertising claims. In short, I may not always buy the most expensive oil, but I will buy oil from brands that have the clout and the incentive to prove their blends work through such validation testing.

Changing the oil in a jet-drive engine

The process for changing oil in a jet-drive engine is the same as for an inboard or sterndrive engine. However, jet-drive engines don't have the handy oil drain feature in newer engines made by Mercruiser, so you use an extraction pump instead of draining the oil from the bottom of the engine. Here are a few points unique to this jet-drive job:

✔ Jets are made to run at much higher revolutions per minute (RPMs) than other marine engines. This puts an extreme challenge on your oil, so I suggest you carefully follow the oil specifications when replacing the oil in your engine.

✔ You aren't likely to find oil filters for your jet-drive engine at the auto department of a parts or discount store. Get the correct filter from your dealer.

Beyond these two concerns, the tools and process of changing oil are much the same as for inboard and sterndrive engines, so consult the previous section, "Changing inboard and sterndrive engine oil."

Changing Gear-Case Lubricant and Transmission Fluid

The propeller on sterndrives and outboards is attached to a drive shaft that extends from the gear case. The gear case is sealed and contains gear-case lubricant that protects the bearing from wear. This lubricant should be changed once a year — usually when you winterize your boat. (I explain winterizing, or preparing your boat for long-term storage, in Chapter 14.) Inboard engines have transmissions, which need regular attention, too.

This section is about how to change the gear-case lubricant in your outboard or sterndrive engine and how to manage the transmission fluid in your inboard engine. Gear-case lubricant is fairly easy to handle yourself, taking only minutes. Best of all, doing it yourself can save a bundle of time and money. Transmissions, on the other hand, are more complicated to work with.

Changing gear-case lubricant

If your boat has a sterndrive or outboard motor, you can change the gear-case lubricant yourself. This section explains what you need to do the job and how to go about it.

Tools and supplies

You need only one or two tools to change your gear-case lubricant, and the correct ones depend on your engine. Here are some considerations:

✔ Some boat gear cases have one or two plugs you can remove with a large standard screwdriver.

✔ Some gear cases have plugs that require a hex wrench to remove them. A *hex wrench* is sometimes called an *Allen wrench;* it's L-shaped with six sides and fits in screw heads with hexagonal sockets. Hex wrenches usually come in complete sets of varying sizes and aren't expensive. You can select the wrench that fits your engine's gear case drain plug.

✔ An *adjustable wrench* is handy for those gear cases that are opened with a standard screwdriver. The plugs often become tight from corrosion, and tightening an adjustable wrench on the blade of the screwdriver so you can use the wrench as a handle often helps remove the plug more easily.

✔ To catch the old gear-case lubricant, use a bucket or other container capable of holding 2 quarts of fluid with room to spare so you can move it without spilling it.

✔ Gear-case lubricant, like oil, comes in various weights or grades and ordinarily comes in squeeze tubes. Your gear case should hold one or two tubes of the correct oil specified in your owner's manual.

How to replace the gear-case lubricant

Changing the lubricant in the gear case is a snap. Follow these steps:

1. **Place a bucket under the gear case to capture the lubricant after you remove the drain plugs.**

2. **Locate the two drain plugs in the gear case: One is directly on the bottom of the case and the other is higher up, just over the bulging part of the case.**

3. **Remove the top drain plug and then the bottom plug, using either the standard screwdriver or the hex wrench, depending on your engine.**

   You open the upper plug to prevent an air lock and the bottom plug to drain the gear case.

4. **Let the gear case drain into the bucket until empty.**

5. **Insert the end of the new tube of lubricant into the bottom drain hole, and squeeze it until the tube is empty.**

   It helps to roll the tube from the bottom like a toothpaste tube.

6. **When the first tube is empty, place a finger over the top drain hole to seal it and create an air lock that lets you insert a second tube of lubricant, if necessary. Continue adding lubricant until some runs out of the top drain hole.**

7. **Place your finger over the top hole, and screw in the bottom plug without spilling.**

8. **Tighten the bottom plug firmly, and then screw on and tighten the top plug.**

When you drain your gear-case lubricant, what comes out gives you a lot of information about the health of your boat's gears and gear-case seals.

✔ If the grease is milky, water is present and the gear-case seals need to be replaced.

✔ If visible water comes out, your gear-case seals are letting in water and you need to get your boat to your dealer before taking it back out onto the water.

✔ It's normal to see tiny, fine metal filings stuck to the magnetic gear-case plugs. However, particles the size of ice cream sprinkles indicate that serious internal damage is occurring in the gear case, probably because of improper lubrication or possibly damage from grounding your boat. Have it serviced before heading out onto the water.

Upper gear cases in sterndrives

Sterndrive engines have a lubricant reservoir attached to the engine that lets you monitor the gear-case lubricant level. A tube connects this reservoir to the gear case.

The upper gear-case reservoir adds an extra step to the process of changing gear-case lubricant, but it eases the process of keeping an eye on lubricant levels because you can easily see the level in the reservoir on the engine. If you have a sterndrive, here are a couple of steps to add to the steps for gear-case lubricant that I describe in the previous section:

1. **Remove the cap of the gear-case lubricant reservoir, which should be clearly marked, to be sure the reservoir drains fully along with the lower gear case.**

2. **After draining the lower gear case (following the steps in the previous section), check that the upper reservoir is also completely drained.**

3. **After refilling the gear case, add additional lubricant to the level indicated on the upper reservoir. It doesn't refill from the lubricant you squeeze into the gear case itself.**

If you own a classic sterndrive boat — that is, one built before 1988 — the upper gear case has to be drained separately from the lower gear case, and you don't have that handy reservoir to keep an eye on levels. However, you'll find the fill hole capped with a screw just like the lower gear case. Now and then, remove the cap with a large screwdriver and make sure the lubricant level is up to the screw hole. If it isn't, add lubricant according to your dealer's recommendation.

Checking and changing inboard transmission fluid

Instead of a gear case, inboards have a transmission that needs to be serviced periodically. Unfortunately, the process for changing transmission fluid is more involved and difficult to manage than checking and changing gear-case lubricant. You can check the transmission fluid level yourself, but have your marine mechanic change the transmission fluid each spring when you first take your boat off mothballs and then again later in the boating season, at your mechanic's recommendation.

Checking the transmission fluid is as simple as checking the oil. Here's how:

1. **Locate the transmission fluid reservoir.**

   On some inboards, the transmission is forward of the engine. On others, the transmission is aft the engine (*aft* means behind, toward the back of the boat).

2. **Unscrew the transmission fluid dipstick, which looks like a screw-down cap and is marked somehow to tell you it's for the transmission fluid. Remove the dipstick and wipe it clean with a clean rag.**

3. **Reinsert the dipstick, and then remove it and note the level of the fluid on the stick, which indicates whether you need to add fluid or not.**

   In some cases, removing the cap lets you visually check the fluid level inside the transmission. If you can see the fluid, you have enough.

4. **If needed, use a funnel to add transmission fluid as recommended in your owner's manual.**

Other Sterndrive Lubricants You Should Monitor

If your boat is a sterndrive, you need to keep an eye on one or two other fluids in addition to the engine oil and gear-case lubricant. These additional fluids include power-steering fluid, if your boat has it, and hydraulic engine trim fluid, which all sterndrives have.

I can't tell you how important it is to maintain proper fluid levels in your engine. Well, actually I can. Operating any of the functions on the boat with low fluid levels can quickly damage the component, costing hundreds of dollars in repairs. It takes only a minute to make sure these levels are full.

Checking the power-steering fluid

Most sterndrive engines built since 2004 are equipped with power steering. On the front of the engine is a reservoir marked, as you may have guessed, "power-steering fluid" or similar language to that effect. The container lid has marks on it for "Full" and "Low" or "Add."

Check the power-steering fluid every time you boat. If needed, add fluid as directed in your owner's manual. Often the correct fluid is indicated on the reservoir cap.

Checking the hydraulic engine trim fluid

All sterndrive engines are equipped with hydraulic trim to adjust the angle of the propeller up and down for a better ride. (I discuss using your engine trim in Chapter 7.)

As with power-steering fluid, there's a reservoir for trim hydraulic fluid on the engine, and it's marked so you can identify it. Note the "Full" and "Add" or "Low" markings on the side, and when necessary add fluid as prescribed by your owner's manual.

Protecting Your Engine from the Effects of Ethanol

Mixing ethanol with fuel has become a mandatory step in trying to reduce dependence on fossil fuel. Unfortunately, ethanol is bad for engines, particularly for marine engines manufactured before 2004.

This section helps you understand the negative effects ethanol fuel can have and what you can do to defend your boat engine against them.

Understanding the negatives of ethanol

You may be for or against using America's food crops to make ethanol for fuel, but your position on the issue doesn't change the fact that fuel will be laced with ethanol for some time to come. You need to be aware of ethanol's damaging impact on engines so you can protect your engine. Here's a breakdown of the key effects:

✔ Ethanol absorbs water vapor from the air, causing water to collect in the bottom of your fuel tank. That water can be drawn into your engine and destroy it completely. This is much more of a risk in a boat than in a car because a boat sits for long periods of time, often with a partial tank of fuel, which leaves more air to hold dangerous water vapor.

✔ Ethanol delivers less power per gallon than regular gas, causing your engine to work harder yet deliver less horsepower. That can lead to your engine overheating if your cooling system isn't up to snuff.

✔ Ethanol can dissolve or decay some rubber fuel lines, plastic fittings, and gaskets in older boat motors built before 2000 and also in some motors built more recently.

✔ Ethanol has dissolved fiberglass fuel tanks — and you'll hear about it if you hang around a marina much. But, for your peace of mind, boats with fiberglass fuel tanks are generally older and larger than the power boats discussed in this book — so don't worry much about this one!

Dealing with the effects of ethanol

You can't do anything about the reduced horsepower your engine delivers when burning ethanol, but there are things you can — and must — do to prevent engine damage from ethanol.

✔ **Keep your boat's gas tank full.** A full tank reduces the contact fuel has with air and reduces ethanol's ability to absorb water vapor into the fuel.

✔ **To prevent ethanol and the water it draws into the gas from turning your fuel into varnish or gum, add fuel stabilizers like Pennzoil Fuel Stabilizer, PRI-G, or Sta-bil to your gas every time you fill up.** I'll make an exception for this if you burn a tankful of gas in your boat every two weeks or less, in which case your fuel isn't sitting long enough to worry about.

✔ **Have a fuel/water separator installed on your boat, if it doesn't already have one.** Your fuel/water separator should have a 10-micron filter media in it to efficiently capture water in the fuel. A fuel/water separator looks a lot like an oil filter. It's mounted inside the engine compartment with the fuel line from the gas tank running into it and the fuel line to the engine running out of it.

Check the fuel/water separator every week or so by shutting off the fuel supply to it with the faucet-like valve located near the separator. Then unscrew the separator canister — it's just like unscrewing an oil filter — and carefully empty it and inspect the contents. If you see any sign of water in it, check your separator every time you fill up your boat or every time you leave your boat unattended for a week or more. If you find the filter full of water, you need to empty the water in an environmentally safe place and replace the separator filter.

✔ **Run your boat often to keep the fuel fresh and oil circulated throughout the engine.** Nothing is better for a boat than frequent use along with normal maintenance.

Monitoring Engine Gauges

Automobiles have become so reliable that most people don't know what all the lights and symbols on their dashboards mean. Marine engines are approaching that level of reliability, but there's still a ways to go. And because it's hard to thumb a ride home when your boat breaks down, it's always important to keep an eye on indicators and gauges at the helm and keep an ear out for engine troubles when you're on the water. Your instrument indicators and gauges are there both to reassure you and warn you, so make sure you get a feel for the following common ones:

✔ **Buzzers and beepers:** Buzzers and beepers are installed on most boats fewer than ten years old to tell you when something is going wrong. When you hear one, stop and check all fluid reservoirs on your engine. Look at the temperature gauge to see if it's overheating, reduce your RPMs to minimum speed, and limp in to a mechanic.

✔ **Oil-pressure gauge:** An oil-pressure gauge tells you whether oil is circulating properly to your engine. If you see that number fall below what the operator's manual says is normal for your engine, you'd better slow down and limp in to a mechanic.

✔ **Smart instruments:** Smart instruments are instruments that can read computer codes sent by your engine's onboard computer, if it has one. Some motor companies call this computer the *engine management module* (EMM) or *electronic control module* (ECM) or something along those lines. When the module detects something going wrong with the engine, it sends a specific code to the instruments telling you the engine is overheating, low on oil or other fluids, or otherwise malfunctioning. These systems are expensive but give great peace of mind to journeying boaters. They often tell you exactly what your engine needs to solve its problem. Unfortunately, these systems are available only for newer engines, and retrofitting usually isn't possible.

✔ **Speedometer:** A speedometer isn't much good alone for detecting engine problems, but when you compare speed to RPMs and detect a slower-than-usual speed at a given RPM, you're noticing loss of power, which is a good reason to visit your mechanic.

✔ **Tachometer:** A tachometer tells how fast the engine is running in RPMs by way of a sensor that detects how fast the crankshaft is turning. The *crankshaft* is the part that transfers the power of the fuel burning in the engine to the propeller shaft and in turn to the propeller. If your engine begins to lose RPMs, that's a sign something is going wrong inside the engine. The quicker you get it to a shop for repair, the better.

✔ **Temperature gauge:** A temperature gauge monitors the engine temperature. Most gasoline engines and diesels are designed to operate at temperatures under 180 degrees (check your engine's manual to be sure). If you see a temperature running higher than the norm, it's time to slow down, return to port, and see your mechanic.

✔ **Voltage meter:** A voltage meter tells how much voltage your battery has. If it's less than 11.5 volts, don't shut off the motor because you may not get it restarted. The culprit could be your battery or *alternator,* the part on your engine that recharges your battery.

Maintaining Your Boat's Battery

Even if you turn out the running lights, turn off the stereo, and shut down every other thing that can use battery juice, your boat battery can still run down between weekend outings. Marine stereos, for instance, continuously draw a little bit of power to keep programmed radio stations in memory. So, to keep your battery at its best, a battery charger is essential.

When a boat won't start, it's usually because the battery has run down. It's easy to avoid that frustrating delay and, in the process, keep your battery working better longer. Boats are harder on batteries than cars are, so I share some special considerations to bear in mind to make sure your boating outing doesn't end before it starts. In this section I give you the lowdown on using chargers, as well as how to know when you need a new battery.

Note: Electric trolling motors like those used on bass and walleye boats (described in Chapter 2) usually require a *deep-cycle battery.* Unlike your primary marine battery that's closer to your car battery, deep-cycle batteries work better when they're fully drained before recharging.

If you have a charger you bought ten years ago for your car or motorcycle battery, I recommend that you look into buying one of the new automatic marine chargers available today for your boat. These new chargers use computer wizardry to measure the charge and condition of your battery, and they automatically match the charging current to the battery's needs. When the battery reaches full charge, the charger completely stops putting out current, with the exception of an occasional test pulse that it uses to analyze the battery's current condition. When the charger detects a decline in current, it ramps up again and recharges.

In the old days, an automatic charger constantly pushed current to a battery even though undergoing a constant current tended to reduce the battery's capacity power over time. Even a small amount of charging current from these older chargers can wreck a battery if left on too long.

When you buy a new battery charger, make sure it

✔ Has a meter to tell you the condition of the battery. Some meters are in the form of a gauge with a needle, and some come with a multicolor LED readout. The LED readouts are easier to interpret — one color indicates the battery is fully charged, another indicates the battery is charging, and another indicates it's partially charged. These colors take away the guesswork.

✔ Is specifically designed for marine applications. These models are built with more resistance against water and corrosion, and they'll work on your car or motorcycle, too, if you find yourself in a battery bind.

✔ Has a maximum output of 10 amps unless you want to wait all day for your battery to recharge. *Amps* are a measurement of how much current the charger puts into the battery. Less power means more time waiting for the recharge.

The four types of marine battery chargers to consider are

✔ **Solar:** Best for keeping a small charge going to the battery during storage. This charger is just enough to keep the battery topped off and doesn't require a wall plug to operate! But solar chargers only work in direct sun, so they aren't much help in a boat stored under a roof.

✔ **Built-in:** Work just like portable chargers but are waterproof and remain in the boat. All you have to do is plug the 110-volt lead into the wall socket, and the charger monitors and properly charges the battery.

✔ **Portable:** Carried to the boat, connected to a battery, and then plugged into 110-volt power. This charger connects to just one battery at a time, and you have to monitor the charging process and move the battery charger to subsequent batteries as needed.

✔ **Battery packs:** Not really battery chargers but rather jump-start devices. Packs have their own 12-volt power and can store it for long periods of time without being plugged in for a recharge.

Getting power from the sun with solar chargers

Solar chargers are just what they sound like, and they're very handy for keeping a battery charge maintained over long periods of storage. Shown in Figure 13-1, this charger's positive red lead and negative black lead bolt right onto the battery terminals. When you store the boat for long periods, you can temporarily attach the solar panel to your boat or boat cover, and the sun will keep your battery fresh and ready for the next adventure.

Figure 13-1:
Solar
chargers
are handy
to maintain
battery
power dur-
ing storage.

Courtesy of PulseTech Products Corporation

Using built-in chargers to save time and work

Built-in chargers are made to fasten inside the boat, usually in the bilge or engine compartment, and remain there for the life of the boat. They're water-proof and have a 110-volt lead that plugs into a wall socket and two or three pairs of charging leads. These systems are ideal for boats with more than one battery; instead of lugging the charger and transferring it from dead battery to dead battery, you keep all the connections in place and the battery char-ger does the work of determining which battery to charge.

Rescuing the day with a battery pack

A battery pack holds a small 12-volt battery with a wall plug to recharge it. It holds a charge for months and is a great device to keep in your tow vehicle. If your boat battery is dead, you can hook up the battery pack and voila! When your boat starts, you can stow the battery pack and let your motor recharge the battery, which takes about 30 minutes of running time.

Using a battery charger

Batteries that aren't recharged regularly and kept fully charged tend to lose their charge potential. Each time you let your battery drain of power, it loses some of its ability to store electrical power. The best thing you can do for your boat battery is use it frequently so the engine alternator keeps it charged and in top shape. You can expect two or three years of use out of a marine starter battery if you avoid frequently discharging it completely.

Using a battery charger is easy:

1. **Turn off the battery isolator switch, if your boat has one, to isolate your battery.**

   This step prevents items on the boat from sapping the charge current and prevents charge pulses from going into the boat's system.

   Most boats made since 2000 have one or more battery isolator switches (see Figure 13-2) located near the batteries, either in the engine compartment or behind a small door near the *transom* (the back wall of the boat). Some single-engine boats have one battery for the engine and one for the *house,* or all the things onboard you need to run. Turn isolator switches to the off position whenever you secure your boat to the trailer for storage so that nothing accidentally left on in the boat can drain your battery.

Figure 13-2:
A typical battery isolator switch.

Photo by Randy Vance

2. **Attach the red clamp from the charger to the positive post on the battery.**

   The positive post has a "+" mark and a red cable bolted to it. Always hook up the red post and clamp first to reduce the chance that sparks could cause a fire.

3. **Hook the black clamp to the negative post on the battery.**

   The negative post has a "–" mark and a black cable attached to it.

4. **Plug the charger's 110-volt power cord into a wall socket.**

   All battery chargers come with a 110-volt cord for electricity and battery cables with red and black clothespin-type clamps to connect to your boat's battery.

5. **You may have to wait 15 minutes or so for the battery and charger to get a "dialogue" going so that charging can commence.**

   The indicator gauge or LED on the charger indicates that the charge is taking place, unless the battery is sooooo dead that it can't detect enough current to determine its own status. If the charger indicates that the battery is faulty, the battery may be ready for the recycling dump or fully discharged with no readable current, in which case, unfortunately, an automatic charger won't help.

Replacing a worn-out battery

After a couple of years of boating bliss, your starting battery will need to be replaced. If you wait until it refuses to hold a charge from one day until the next or until you hear it turning the engine slowly after being fully charged, you've waited too long to change it. When the time comes, swap the old one for a new *marine* starting battery. Marine batteries are made with sturdier components than automobile batteries to resist damage from the occasional complete discharge and to hold charges longer between uses.

If your boat isn't equipped with an electric trolling motor, you can skip this tip. If you do have a boat with electric motors, be sure to replace your batteries with deep-cycle batteries. Deep-cycle batteries are designed to be nearly fully discharged and recharged repeatedly without damage. They're bigger and heavier than other batteries and store more power.

Washing, Waxing, and Preserving Your Boat's Good Looks

That gleaming finish on your boat is more fragile than the shine on your car. The finish coat on your boat is called *gelcoat,* and it's porous and absorbs moisture instead of repelling it like the clear-coat finish on your car.

The porous gelcoat means that things that get on your boat, like bird droppings and road grime from trailering, will soak into it if they aren't removed quickly and with the correct soaps. They can leave stains that are difficult and sometimes impossible to remove if you don't act quickly.

You may be tempted to get out your car washing and waxing products to spiff up your boat, but this section tells you why that's a bad idea. I help you select the best boat-friendly cleaning tools and products because there really is a difference between washing your car and washing and protecting your boat.

Getting the right boat-cleaning tools

You can wash your boat with a rag, but it will take about 3 hours, and you can dry it with a towel, but that will take about 12 hours. Special boat-cleaning tools are designed to ease the labor, lessen the risk of damaging your hull, and get you back to boating faster. Following are some goodies you'll find very handy for a Sunday-afternoon spiff-up of your boat; all should be available at your local marine-supply store:

- ✔ **Boat brush:** For general hull cleaning, use a soft-bristled boat brush with an adjustable-length handle. The soft bristles don't scratch the boat, and they don't absorb and hold grit that can be rubbed back into the gelcoat and risk scratching it. You can lengthen the adjustable handle to reach between the trailer and hull without crawling underneath it, and you can shorten the handle for cleaning the inside of the boat without bumping into things.

- ✔ **Bucket:** A five-gallon bucket is practically indispensible for boat cleaning and rinsing. Some boats even include racks to hold such a bucket. If you'd rather not buy a bucket from a marine-supply store, rinse the paint from an empty five-gallon paint bucket — you can usually mooch one from a friendly contractor.

✔ **Microfiber towels:** Use microfiber towels to get into the tight spots your brush won't reach. Microfiber towels are made of fibers so fine that they're touted to get under grit and lift it away, whereas a rag or sponge may rub grit in, causing fine scratches. I can't scientifically back the claim, but I use microfiber towels on my boat and believe they work.

✔ **Silicone squeegee:** A silicone squeegee is the simplest way to slap water off the hull and upholstery. It's also a handy tool early in the morning to squeegee dew from the windshield without leaving smears or dirty streaks.

✔ **Synthetic chamois:** You can wipe every little smidge of water off your boat with a synthetic chamois. And it will take only one chamois because you can wring it almost dry and wipe some more.

Avoid using a natural chamois on your boat. Synthetics are best because they have antimicrobial treatment to prevent mildew, something you're always fighting around a boat.

Using the right soaps and waxes for boats

Marine soaps and waxes are often formulated in consultation with the manufacturers of gelcoat and marine vinyl to ensure the formulations will protect and not harm the surfaces. The soaps and waxes cost more than automobile or household cleaning products mostly because they're manufactured and sold on a smaller scale and sometimes because the ingredients cost more.

Don't be tempted to use car care products on your boat because they're less expensive. You may save money in the short run, but over the years you'll see what happens when you don't go with the boat soap and wax: Your gelcoat fades and cracks, and your prize boat begins to look like a derelict.

You may as well stock up on a supply of the following products now because you'll need them off and on all summer long. You really don't need me to tell you how to use them, I think, because — well, you use them like most other soaps and waxes, and each product comes with its own instructions. The following items are in order of recommended importance:

✔ **Boat wax:** Boat waxes are designed to rub into gelcoats easily and provide a strong UV protection layer along with the gloss.

You should wax your boat twice a year if it's white and four times a year if it has a colored gelcoat. Colors absorb more ultraviolet (UV) light, which causes them to grow hazy faster than white gelcoats. If you don't wax regularly, the shine dulls and the color fades to a chalky finish.

Going green with approved boat-care products

There's a new movement among boaters toward green, earth-friendly cleaning products. Everything you do to your boat impacts the water, and the products you use to clean and wax it are no exception.

The Environmental Protection Agency (EPA) has established a department called Design for the Environment to help you know if a product is really green. The EPA's enormous database of chemicals and their properties allows the agency to analyze the ingredient list in products and compare it to their high standards for earth-friendly products. Manufacturers who participate in the process and show they have chosen green ingredients get to use the Design for the Environment logo seen here on their product's label. Yep, these products cost more, but they work without polluting boating waters.

- ✔ **Boat-washing soap:** Boat-washing soap comes in many colors and aromas. Using one that lacks dyes and aromas is considered better for the environment. (I explain more on this in the sidebar "Going green with approved boat-care products.") And don't pay extra for soap that touts wax as an additional ingredient; it doesn't substitute for actually waxing your boat with boat wax.

- ✔ **Non-skid deck cleaner:** Non-skid deck cleaner is mandatory for cleaning a textured deck and *sole* (the floor of the cockpit and bow seating area, which most people mistakenly call the "deck"), and it's the only cleaner that can remove black shoe or grease marks.

- ✔ **Black streak remover:** Black streak remover is for the outside of your boat, mostly. These marks develop on your boat when it rubs against docks, your trailer, or other boats. With a little elbow grease, most black marks come off with boat soap or wax, but some are stubborn; because streak remover does the job quicker and easier and doesn't use up your boat soap and wax, it's a good addition to the cleaning kit.

- ✔ **Spray wash-and-wax:** Spray wash-and-wax is handy for an afternoon touch-up on the boat. It comes in a pump-spray bottle, so you spray it on and wipe it off. Spray wash-and-wax gives an awesome final clean touch to the boat in a hurry, and unlike boat soap, it has a meaningful concentration of wax to help repel dirt and water.

✔ **Upholstery cleaners:** Upholstery cleaners for boats are formulated to clean many stains. Some also contain vinyl conditioners and UV shield.

✔ **UV inhibitor for vinyl:** UV inhibitor for your vinyl upholstery is imperative, even if your upholstery cleaner already contains some UV shield. Without UV inhibitor, your vinyl will stiffen and crack in just a couple of years. You should take a few minutes to wipe on some UV inhibitor every time you bring your boat home or prepare it for storage after a day on the way.

Chapter 14

Getting Your Boat Ready for Winter and Spring

*T*he last boat trip out for me is the saddest of the year. It's the end of the season and the beginning of that dreary time when the boat is tucked away in storage, hibernating. You may be surprised to know that your boat's engine can suffer some of the worst damage possible when your boat is stowed away for weeks or months. It makes little difference whether you store the boat for the winter or just don't use it for several months in the summer — things can go wrong inside your boat's engine if you don't prepare.

When your boat goes unused, fuel can decay and turn to varnish, coating your fuel tank, fuel lines, and especially your carburetor, with gum and sludge that will slough off and clog your engine. Oil that normally circulates throughout your engine when you run it no longer circulates, and after a few weeks, the inside of the engine is exposed to corrosion as the oil drains to the oil pan at the bottom of the engine. Worst of all, the water that inboard engines and sterndrive engines hold in their cooling channels, water pump, and exhaust manifold may freeze inside the engine; when that water freezes, it expands and breaks apart the heavy-cast steel, completely destroying the engine.

Those things never have to happen to your engine. This chapter is all about how to prevent damage to your engine during storage by treating the gas so it doesn't degrade, fogging the engine so it doesn't rust, and draining the water so it doesn't freeze and break your motor.

When you get the boat ready to go in the spring — boaters call it *re-commissioning* — you want to double-check that the preventive measures you took in the fall left your engine and boat ready for the summer. The treated fuel will be just fine, but your boat may be sluggish to start anyway. At the end of this chapter, I give you some tips to get it going again.

You'll often hear the term "winterize" used for the process of preparing your boat for winter storage. But the truth is, any time your boat sits unused for more than a few weeks, you should follow all the steps in this chapter for storing your engine — except maybe draining water from the engine, which isn't necessary in the summer. Just don't forget to drain the water before the first freeze!

Preserving Your Fuel and Engine

Each engine type requires that you take unique steps to protect it from the elements during storage. Only two steps are common to all kinds of engines: stabilizing the fuel to prevent fuel spoilage and varnishing, and fogging the cylinders to prevent corrosion. These are easiest to do while your boat is on the trailer and in the water on a ramp. Try to do these tasks at a time when other boaters aren't waiting on the ramp, or do them at a ramp with many lanes so boaters can work around you. (If performing these tasks while your boat's in the water isn't practical, see the Tip later in this section for a trick for doing them on dry land.)

Follow these steps to stabilize the fuel and then fog the cylinders:

1. **Determine the capacity of your fuel tank.**

2. **Before you load the boat onto the trailer after its last run of the season, add a fuel stabilizer to the tank in an amount sufficient to treat the fuel capacity. Then, if your tank isn't full, gas up all the way.**

3. **Drive your boat around the lake for at least five minutes to mix the stabilizer into the fuel.**

4. **Load your boat on the trailer, but leave it running in the water for the next steps.**

5. **In a sterndrive, inboard, or jet boat, open the engine hatch and remove the plastic cowl by turning the screws until loose.**

   Some engines have plastic fasteners you simply twist with your fingers.

   On an outboard, locate the latches and remove the plastic throttle body cover on the front of the engine.

6. **In a sterndrive, inboard, or jet boat, remove the flame arrestor on top of the engine.**

It looks like an air filter and has a wing nut on top. Unscrew and remove it. Underneath is the throttle body or carburetor.

In an outboard, a plastic throttle body cover is usually on the side of the engine facing the boat. Loosen the screws or fasteners to reveal the carburetors or the throttle body air intakes, depending on the type of engine.

7. **Spray an entire can of fogging solution (available at any marine store or in most marine departments of discount stores) into the engine's carburetor or throttle body until it smokes heavily, stalls, and dies.**

On an outboard, you may have more than one carburetor or throttle body intake. Alternate between them, spraying the can inside them. Sometimes you'll run out of fogging spray before the engine stalls. Just shut the engine off when the spray can is empty — you've still done a great job!

If your boat is on dry land, fogging your cylinders is easy if you get a pair of what mechanics call *ear muffs*. You can find them in any marine department of a discount store or a marine retailer. Attach a garden hose to the ear muffs and fit them over the water intake ports on the gear case. Turn on the water, and the muffs supply cooling water to the water pump and engine so you can run it in the driveway. Then follow the preceding steps for fogging your engine.

Changing Your Oil for Long-term Storage

Some mechanics suggest you change the oil before you store your boat, and some suggest you change the oil after you take it out of storage. Others suggest you do it both before and after, eliminating the bad oil before storage and eliminating the possibility of oil contamination after storage.

I checked with some engine manufacturers, and their recommendation is to change the oil once a year — before you store the boat. (However, your engine owner's manual may also instruct you to change the oil "every X hours of operation," meaning that you change the oil more than once a year; be sure to consult the manual for clarification.) Moisture in the oil occurs as the engine heats up and cools down repeatedly from use, a condition that won't occur when the engine and boat are in storage. So save yourself an extra oil change and the headache that contaminated oil causes. Change your oil *before* you store your boat, and it will be ready for boating when you want it.

To change the oil for long-term storage, follow the same steps for changing the oil I explain in Chapter 13.

Preventing Your Engine from Freezing Up

Your marine engine uses the same water you boat in to cool itself off. Whenever you load the boat on the trailer and turn it off, some of this water stays in the engine. Before storing your boat for the winter, you have to drain out this water, because freezing water expands with so much force that it can crack and ruin your engine. Here are the steps to follow for draining the water from your engine:

1. **When the boat is on the trailer and on flat ground, find the engine drain plugs or petcocks — which are like small faucets — that keep the water in your engine. Open them to drain the water.**

   Your boat may have both or either — and it will have several of them (check your owner's manual). You can remove drain plugs with an adjustable wrench and twist open petcocks with your hands.

2. **Find the manifolds that carry the exhaust away from your engine, and open or remove their drain plugs or petcocks to allow the water to drain.**

   The *manifolds* are the large pipes on either side of the engine that contain cooling water.

3. **Drain water-pump hoses and the water pump on the front of the engine if necessary.**

   To drain these hoses, it's best to use a screwdriver to loosen the hose clamps around the lowest ends of the hoses and remove the hoses to let the water in them drain out. There's no need to remove both ends of the hoses.

4. **Sterndrives have a rubber bellows at the back of the engine near the transom. It's a difficult spot to get to, but it's a good idea to open that hose clamp as well to make sure no water remains there.**

Every engine has a slightly different configuration of drain plugs and petcocks. It's essential that you consult your owner's manual to determine the number and location of these draining points. Miss just one this winter and let it freeze, and you'll be forced to buy a new engine in the spring — for $7,000 to $25,000 or more, depending on the engine!

One thing that makes outboards popular is that they automatically drain without any effort, giving you the option of getting the boat out of hibernation for an unseasonably warm winter day and taking a quick ride.

Keeping Your Battery in Shape for Spring

Boat batteries suffer from long periods of storage. As yours loses its charge and stays that way for weeks, metal plates in it degrade, reducing or even ending the battery's ability to take a charge next time you want it to work.

Proper care can prevent that, though. Here are my suggestions for keeping your battery ready for the next trip:

✔ Turn off the boat's battery switches so nothing inadvertently left on can run and overheat, not to mention discharge your batteries.

✔ Purchase an automated battery maintenance charger, and connect it to your battery. The chargers will constantly monitor your battery and send charging current only when it shows a decline in charge. You have several types of chargers to consider; here are some of my suggestions:

- Xtreme Charge battery chargers have a feature called "pulse tech" that sends a power pulse to the battery and causes sulfation on the plates to dissolve. *Sulfation* is a chemical process that degrades a battery's ability to take a charge.

- Built-in automatic chargers are handy and come with connectors for multiple battery systems of up to three batteries. Chargers from Minnkota, Pro Mariner, and Guest are all waterproof and can be permanently installed on the boat. When plugged in, they keep your batteries at peak performance. If, during use, a battery goes dead for any reason, all you need is an extension cord to get the charge going. These chargers often keep boaters happily playing stereos and running TVs and 12-volt appliances at the dock as well.

How to Freeze-proof Your Plumbing

Many boats have plumbing systems for *heads* (that's boat-speak for bathroom and toilet), freshwater sinks, showers, or galleys. These fixtures can be in the cockpit seating area or in the cuddy cabin. Swimmers and skiers often enjoy showers on the swim platform on the *transom* (back of the boat). In addition, storage compartments in all boats and livewells and livewell plumbing used in fishing boats to keep fish or bait alive also can hold water.

All this plumbing must be drained of water before storage so that it doesn't freeze and break pipes or fittings during cold-weather storage.

Freshwater systems

If you have a transom shower, galley, or head with plumbing, do the following to make sure they're fit and ready for the next time you boat:

1. **Locate the water tank in your boat.**

   Most are in the bilge area, near the engine. You'll be able to tell how much water it holds by looking at the translucent tank and noting the water line.

2. **Drain all the water from this tank.**

   You can do this by running the sink or shower until the tank is empty, or if the tank has a drain plug you can access, open or unscrew that and let it drain to the bilge. You should already have the drain plug out if your boat is on the trailer, and the water will drain right out on the ground.

3. **Pour a gallon or two of nontoxic RV antifreeze into your water tank.**

   This fluid is red, not green like very toxic automotive antifreeze.

4. **Pump the antifreeze through your system by opening faucets and letting them run until the antifreeze comes through.**

   Run each sink faucet until a few ounces of antifreeze go down the drain to replace any water in the sink traps (if your boat has traps; don't worry if you don't know about sink traps — just run the fluid down the drain).

Locker drains and other plumbing

Your boat has various drains in it that empty the livewell and storage lockers under the deck of your boat. Here's how to insure they stay free of freezing water for the winter:

1. **Remove any debris, leaves, trash, or other items from the livewells and other lockers so that if water enters during the storage period, it can drain away.**

2. **Inspect the livewells and lockers to make sure they're drained.**

   Most livewells and lockers drain completely when the boat is sitting level on a trailer or in a storage rack, but checking them is the best way to be safe.

3. **If you see any water standing in the bottom of the compartments or even a small amount in the drain, pour in some nontoxic RV antifreeze to prevent the water from freezing.**

The bilge

Even when you cover your boat, water can get inside, either by seepage through the cover fabric or by condensation that can form on the inside of the cover. Follow these steps to ensure that this moisture can escape through the bilge:

1. **Double-check to be sure the drain plug is out.**

   Store this plug in a place where you'll easily find it the next time you boat.

2. **Look inside the bilge and remove any dirt or debris that may work its way to the drain and interfere with drainage.**

   Allowing even a small volume of water to sit in the bilge all winter because of a blocked drain could have bad consequences.

Covering the Boat Lengthens Its Life

A taught, water-tight mooring cover is absolutely essential to the long life of your boat. Letting rain and snow and ice collect in your boat over the storage season can result in cracked through-hull fittings and loosened deck fittings, such as hinges, as the moisture thaws and freezes repeatedly. At best, your upholstery's padding will be waterlogged, staples holding it in place will corrode and come apart, and mildew will set in when the temperature warms.

Here's what to look for in a boat cover:

✔ The cover needs to be snug and taught so precipitation runs off or, in the case of snow, slides off.

✔ The fabric needs to be waterproof so precipitation doesn't penetrate. Seams should be double-stitched to strengthen them and minimize moisture intrusion through stitches.

✔ Tie-downs around the edges of the fabric should be sturdy and long enough to securely attach to the trailer to maintain the cover's tension.

✔ Broad areas of canvas should be supported with adjustable tent poles that increase the cover's ability to slough off precipitation.

The poles should come with a custom cover. If you buy a mass-produced, generic cover, you need to buy the poles separately.

✔ Air vents should be placed in the cover to allow air flow in and out of the boat, and the vents should be designed to prevent water from running inside.

Some boaters cover their mooring covers with inexpensive plastic tarps to extend the lives of their covers. Because the plastic is slick, snow and ice slip off more easily. I don't see anything wrong with this unless you block the vents of your cover, preventing air exchange and causing moisture build-up inside.

How to Get Your Boat Ready in the Spring

When the long winter is over and warm weather is again approaching, you'll likely be more than ready to get your boat back out and have some fun. If you winterized your boat properly, getting the boat ready for springtime boating is a snap. Here's all there is to it:

1. **Double-check the battery charge and connect a charger if needed.**

2. **Close all the engine drain plugs and/or petcocks you opened to drain.**

3. **Double-check the oil and fluid levels to make sure none leaked out during storage.**

   If there's a sign of leakage, consult a mechanic to make sure service isn't necessary.

4. **Launch the boat and crank it up.**

   If your boat is an outboard, you need to squeeze the fuel priming bulb on your fuel tank. If the motor is over 90 horsepower, you may also have an oil-priming bulb on your oil tank that needs squeezed. (You'll find the oil tank under a hatch near the motor.)

   If your boat is an inboard, sterndrive, or jet drive, prime the fuel system by pressing the throttle forward three or four times before turning the key. Press the shift-release button at the center of the shift/throttle handle to prevent the engine from going in gear, and then crank it up!

Chapter 15

Repairing Leaks and Other Damage to Your Boat

. . . .

In This Chapter

▶ Preventing major damage with some quick repairs

▶ Checking and repairing belts

▶ Repairing or replacing a damaged propeller

▶ Finding and fixing electrical malfunctions

. . . .

*B*oats operate in a harsh environment. Motorists are apt to complain about the occasional pothole in an otherwise smooth road, but boats bash over much bigger "potholes" in the form of waves all day long, all season long. Naturally, things loosen up under this torture.

It pays to keep an eagle eye out for little loose screws, rattling hinges, and other things that wear out from the constant motion and to repair them as they crop up. A great deal of major repairs to boats are necessary not because of accidents or defective equipment but because their owners failed to stay on top of fixing the little things in a boat as soon as they cropped up.

This chapter shows you why you need to keep on top of loose screws and fittings, defective engine belts, and loose wiring. It also tells you a good deal about what you can do yourself, in your spare time, to keep your boat working beautifully with minimum downtime because of avoidable damage and repairs.

Whenever you invite guests on your boat, show them how all the things they may have to operate work. Teach them how to open the hatches and relatch them and how to deploy the boarding ladder and return it to position. If seats recline or adjust, show them how to accomplish that. Their boating experience will be better and so will yours, because they'll be less likely to break things!

Doing Quick Repairs to Keep Things from Getting Worse

Around your house, you may ignore or work around little problems like a sticky door latch, loose cabinet hinge, or leaky faucet. It's easy to do; everything still seems to stay put, and life goes on thanks to new and automatic reflexes to handle the latch, hinge, or faucet more carefully. In a boat, though, with constant motion and pounding on the waves, loose things break and little leaks can become catastrophic.

Because small inconveniences can quickly and easily become big problems when it comes to your boat, I give you some advice on what to tighten and seal up.

Fix leaks

I probably don't need to tell you a boat works by keeping water out and not letting it in. But water, being what it is, wants to be where it isn't wanted. Just ask the folks living along the Mississippi River any given spring season as the water level creeps higher and higher, and they'll concur.

If your crew is hangin' out on the hook (that's boat-speak for goofing off while at anchor), swimming, or getting in and out of the boat for various water-sports activities, they'll drag water into the boat with them. Small amounts of water in a boat are normal at all times, and a little water on deck is nothing to worry about.

If your boat is built to the best standards of the National Marine Manufacturers Association (NMMA), it will have a bilge pump that automatically detects water in the bilge and pumps it out. (The *bilge* is the area that holds the engine in an inboard. You still have a bilge in an outboard, but the engine isn't in it — it's on the outside.) If you see or hear your bilge pump jump into action every few minutes or so, then you have a leak you need to address.

 A leak that keeps triggering your bilge pump doesn't have to immediately end your day, but you have to keep track of your battery levels, because the bilge pump could gradually drain your battery. Keep an eye on the voltage gauge, and if needed, clear everyone away from the propeller and start the motor periodically to recharge the battery.

In the long run, the annoying leak will get worse, so here are some considerations for finding and fixing leaks:

✔ **Visually inspect every through-hull fitting and watch for a telltale drip or a small rivulet (or a large, obvious leak) running down the inside of the hull from any fitting. Tighten the clamp with a screwdriver — the repair is often as simple as that.** If the leak is between the fitting and the hull, you have to fix it when the boat is on the trailer after things dry out. Follow these basic steps for fixing leaks in through-hull fittings:

1. **Loosen the locking nut on the inside of the hull, and push the fitting outside the hull so you can work on it from outside the boat. You can leave the hose attached for this.**

2. **Clean the hull area around the hole, apply marine sealant (clear sealant for a colored hull, white sealant for a white hull) around the fitting, and put it back in the hole.**

3. **Have someone else tighten the locking nut from the inside — not too tight or you'll break it or damage the hull core. Just make it snug.**

4. **Let the sealant cure according to the directions on the sealant packaging.**

✔ **Check every fitting screwed onto the hull below the waterline.** You can look for these leaks while the boat is in the water. You may find loose screws holding a depth-finder transducer on the transom or a water-temperature sensor, boarding ladder brackets, or a trim tab onto the hull. (*Trim tabs* are the adjustable metal tabs on the back of the boat.) Follow these steps for fixing screw hole leaks:

1. **Remove the screw.**

2. **Squeeze some sealant into the hole.**

3. **Replace the screw.**

If you think the screws on a trim tab are the culprits, follow the steps one screw at a time, letting the other screws hold the tab in place until you've resealed each screw.

✔ **You didn't leave the bilge drain plug out when you launched, did you?!** If you left the drain plug out, join the club! Everybody's done it once, at least. Put the plug into that tiny little hole under the motor, and then let the bilge pump run to pump the water back out.

Tighten or replace bolts and screws

Keep both a standard screwdriver and a Phillips screwdriver handy on your boat to double-check suspicious screws immediately. If you don't tighten or replace them when they need it, they'll only get worse.

I have a boat with a hard top bolted to a tubular frame. One bolt came out last summer and, because the top was still secure, I didn't rush to fix it. When

I ran the boat one rainy day, I noticed water dripping out of a couple of light fixtures. Turns out the hole left by the missing bolt allowed water to enter into the hard top, and the water shorted out an important light. It took about three minutes to replace the bolt with a wrench and caulk it. It took hours and $60 to replace the light damaged by letting the missing bolt go unfixed *a little bit longer.*

Another boat I had kept filling up with water; it seemed to take on dozens of gallons in only an hour or two. When I took it out of the water to see why, I saw water squirting through a toothpick-sized screw hole on a fitting. I'd noticed the fitting was loose before I launched the boat, but I didn't realize it would turn into such a major leak when the boat was in the water. It appeared to be a hole, but it could have resulted in a fully swamped boat had I left it at the dock overnight.

Both situations were annoying and completely avoidable. I consider that a good lesson learned.

Check and tighten hose clamps

Your boat has hoses mostly to let liquid move around safely without flooding the boat. Some hoses are conduits for water and some are for fuel. Odds are if your boat is taking on water, a loose hose or damaged fitting is to blame.

If your boat is well built, every hose fitting through the hull of the boat has two stainless-steel hose clamps on it, compressing the hose to the fitting that goes through the hull. A *through-hull fitting* is a fancy pipe that goes through the hull and fastens tight on both sides of the fiberglass — a flange on the outside and a threaded nut on the inside. The hose clamps look just like the ones on the hoses under your car's hood. On newer boats, the metal clamps seem to loosen a bit over time, and sometimes the hose on the fittings compresses over time, also loosening the clamp. You can easily tighten hose clamps with a screwdriver and stop the leak. It pays to poke your head in the bilge or anywhere else you're apt to find hose fittings and test them for tightness by putting a half-turn on them with a screwdriver.

Don't white knuckle your screwdriver when you tighten a hose clamp or you risk breaking it. Instead, use about the same force you'd use to turn off an outside hose faucet on your house.

Any leak found between a hose and the fitting it's clamped onto can usually be repaired simply by tightening the clamp. But if there's much of a leak — say, a steady drip instead of an occasional drip — it's a good idea to follow these steps:

1. **Remove the hose and clamp.**

2. **Put a marine sealer on the fitting.**

You can get a tube of sealant at any marine dealer. Keep it on your boat for unplanned fitting maintenance.

3. **Slide the loosened clamp(s) up the hose before pushing the hose onto the fitting.**

4. **Tighten the clamp(s).**

Through-hull fittings are pretty easy to find inside by just walking around your boat and noting any fittings on the outside. Then lift the hatches inside your boat nearest the outer end of the fitting. Figure 15-1 shows a through-hull fitting not yet installed.

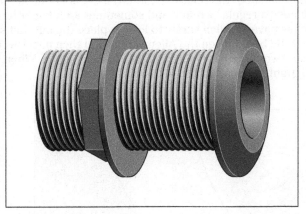

Figure 15-1: Check through-hull fittings periodically to catch leaks before they become serious.

Your inboard or sterndrive engine will have hose clamps to maintain, too. With the exception of one in the back of the engine that you can't easily access, the rest should be easy to spot and tighten using the same procedures you use for through-hull fittings — just skip the sealant step. As a rule, you don't need sealant on the engine hoses because the hoses are softer and easier to seal by tightening a clamp.

Tighten and repair hardware

Operating conditions for boats are rougher than most conditions for cars. The shock from waves is transmitted through the hull to every screw, hinge, and latch, and every brace, bracket, and bolt in the boat.

Things will loosen up over time, so here's a list of what to look for and what to do. This isn't an exhaustive list of dangling screws and other hardware, but it helps you know what to look for.

Hinges and latches

Hinges and latches on hatches need to be tightened periodically. When you find that the glove box or the anchor locker won't stay latched, take a closer look to find out what's loose or has worked out of alignment. Most of these mechanisms are so simple that you can see immediately what needs tightened and whether you need to do it with a screwdriver or a wrench. If you skip this maintenance step, you may find the gadget is soon broken beyond reasonable repair.

Lift latches are common for securing boat hatches (see Figure 15-2). To open one, you pull up a ring from the floor and twist it. Underneath, the bolt rotates to release the hatch. Slamming the hatch shut when the bolt is in the latch position (instead of the release position) inevitably bends the bolt. To adjust it, you need a regular wrench and sometimes an Allen or hex wrench. Some lift latches have an Allen screw to lock in place the nut that secures the bolt. To adjust the bolt, loosen the Allen screw, and then unscrew the nut and bolt one or two turns to give it clearance to latch again. When the adjustment is good, tighten the Allen screw to lock it in place.

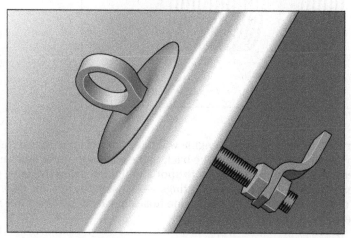

Figure 15-2:
A common lift latch on many boats can be adjusted with an Allen wrench and an adjustable wrench.

Brackets and braces

If you let a windshield bracket remain loose, hitting a large wave may be all it takes to cause the glass to flex and shatter, creating a much more difficult and expensive repair. Check brackets and braces on seats, windshields, and boarding ladders for solid connections. Wiggle the components with your hand and look for movement between connecting points. If you see movement, tighten the screws and bolts.

Ignition switch and running lights

Tighten the ignition switch in the dash. I've tested literally hundreds of boats, and I can't count how many have ignition switches that slipped and turned in their mounting holes on the dashboards (salty boaters call them the *helm stations*), making them harder to use. Ignition switches have a large threaded fitting that goes through a matching hole in the dash. A nut threads onto the fitting from behind the dash, and only the friction of being tight, tight, tight holds it in place. The minute you detect any slippage when you turn the key, get a wrench and tighten that nut under the dash. If you don't, you could twist and break the ignition leads, requiring a more expensive and complicated repair.

Any time you work on electrical connections, make sure the battery switch is turned off — unless you need power to diagnose the condition of a specific circuit.

Running lights are always good candidates for examination. Pay particular attention to a white stern navigation light mounted on a long pole, if you have one. The leverage of the pole responding to the motion of the ocean (or any water body) can loosen the screws holding it in place.

Spotting and Fixing Loose or Damaged Belts

Serpentine belts snake from pulley to pulley on the front of your sterndrive or inboard engine in, well, a serpentine pattern.

What these belts do is use the energy of the engine to run an alternator, which charges your battery, and a water pump, which keeps cooling water running through the engine. Today's belts last a long time — several years, sometimes — but when they wear out, they have a knack for doing it at an inconvenient time. A belt that goes out when your boat is in a strong river current or tide can even be dangerous.

You don't need to fix a belt yourself. Just regularly examine the condition of your belts so you can get your boat to a mechanic before a belt fails, leaving you stranded or drifting off toward a movie-cliché waterfall.

Testing belt tension

The serpentine belt should be firmly tense when the engine isn't running. You can test this just by pressing down on it between pulleys. It shouldn't be rock hard, but if it sags more than about an inch when you press on it, it probably needs adjusting. A squeal from the engine can be another sign that the tension in the belt needs adjusting.

So, if the belt sags under pressure like a CPA at tax time or if it squeals like a pig, get it to your mechanic. If you don't get it adjusted, the belt could fail and the engine could overheat and be damaged, requiring thousands of dollars in repairs.

Knowing when a belt needs changing

Your engine's belt could also show other signs of wear. Cracks in the rubber mean it's about to break. Have your mechanic change it before it does. Think about this: What if it broke in the St. Lawrence Seaway — say, right above Niagara Falls? If it did, you'd sure want to throw out a good anchor on a strong rope, and then holler mayday on the VHF radio for all you're worth! (I discuss emergency situations in Chapter 12.)

Understanding Propeller Types and Repair

Most boat and motor manufacturers spend a great deal of time and effort testing every boat model and engine combination with many different propeller types and dimensions to settle on the combination with optimum performance and price. If you want to upgrade to a better-performing prop (boat-speak for propeller), or if you have to replace a prop, getting the right propeller is as important to your boat's good performance and your engine's longevity as any other proper maintenance step. Even if a prop seems to fit onto your boat, if the prop's dimensions are too big or too small, using it can damage the engine.

This section gives you some background information on boat propellers and tells you how to determine when your prop needs repair or replacement, when to do it yourself, and when to take it to a professional.

Getting propeller dimensions right

A prop's main dimensions are *pitch* and *diameter,* and these measurements are listed somewhere on all props (although they may be corroded and impossible to spot on older props). For example, "15 x 21" means the prop has a 15-inch diameter and 21-inch pitch.

- ✔ **Pitch** is the theoretical distance a prop would travel in one complete revolution, and it's determined by the angle of the blades. Typically, a prop reaches only 80 or 90 percent of that distance.

- ✔ **Diameter** of the prop is twice the radius. You can measure the radius with a tape measure by placing it at the center of the prop and extending it over the blade tip.

A prop with the wrong dimensions can spoil your boat's performance, cost excess fuel, and damage the engine.

More than one dimension can be acceptable for your motor, but keep in mind that different dimensions can offer different specific performance benefits. For instance, you may want your boat to accelerate very fast to pull a skier or wakeboard rider out of the water. If so, you want a shorter pitch prop that fits your engine. Or you may be most interested in going fast, not caring so much about acceleration. In that case, you need a longer pitch prop. Your boat manufacturer or dealer can help you with prop dimensions to replace a damaged prop or enhance performance of your boat by installing and testing props with different dimensions.

Having the right number of blades

Propellers come with two or more blades. Two-blade and five-blade props are rarely ever used. Three-blade props are most often used and give the best speed in most boats.

Four-blade props give better acceleration than two or three blades, and the extra blade surface tends to pull down on the prop, levering the bow out of the water for a softer ride. Four-blade propellers are best for boats with big loads, but the extra blade increases drag and reduces speed.

The only way to determine if you have the propeller and number of blades that works best for your boat and load is to find a prop dealer who will let you test different props. Many do that, charging a 10 or 15 percent restocking fee to change propellers until you find the one you like.

Knowing the differences in prop materials

Propellers are made of aluminum, stainless steel, or bronze.

Aluminum propellers

Most boats come standard with an aluminum prop. Correctly sized by the manufacturer, aluminum propellers offer a good combination of good performance and value for a low price. However, aluminum propellers are softer and tend to be more severely damaged by collision than props made of other materials. Still, by breaking easily, they tend to absorb the force of collision rather than transfer it to the engine, where it can do more harm. More easily repaired than other metals, aluminum propellers are an ideal choice for shallow rocky waters where collisions are nearly unavoidable.

Stainless-steel propellers

Stainless steel is a hard metal that allows propellers to be cast with thinner blades and still have incredible strength. The thinner the blades, the less drag created as they pass through the water, so the stainless-steel prop gives a boat a big boost in speed and acceleration. Naturally, these props are also more expensive than other types.

Because of decreased drag, your boat may perform better with a longer-pitch, stainless-steel propeller than an aluminum one. Here are characteristics of stainless-steel props to keep in mind:

- ✔ Speed and efficiency are the hallmark of a good stainless-steel prop. A boat can gain several miles per hour in top speed with the correctly sized stainless-steel prop as opposed to an aluminum prop of equal dimensions.

- ✔ Stainless-steel props don't break or bend easily. The durability gives you the ability to get home even if you strike an underwater object.

- ✔ Because of the unique characteristics of stainless steel, it doesn't lend itself to do-it-yourself repair for minor prop damage.

- ✔ A stainless-steel prop is more likely to transfer damaging impact force directly to the gear case because the prop doesn't give way. That can sometimes result in more expensive damage. So, in areas where striking rocky reefs is more normal than not, an aluminum prop may be a better choice.

Bronze propellers

Bronze props are rare except on inboard motors. Like aluminum, they're softer and damage more easily than stainless steel, and their advantages and disadvantages are similar to those of aluminum (refer to the "Aluminum propellers" section).

Determining if your prop is damaged

Propellers don't wear out, but they often need repair or replacement because of damage from collision or corrosion. Your first sign of propeller problems may be a vibration you feel throughout the boat. Or you may find that the boat fails to accelerate as you accelerate the engine. If you tilt the propeller out of the water by trimming the engine or outdrive all the way up (see Chapter 7 for more about trimming the engine), any damage is readily visible. If you trailer your boat, propeller inspection is easiest when the boat is on the trailer.

A damaged prop will show chips in the blades or even missing blades, depending on the severity of the impact that caused the damage. Less obvious to the eye is a bent blade. Running into something soft but large, like an underwater tree stump, can bend a blade without breaking it.

Sometimes a prop *spins a hub*. The *hub* is the center of the prop that slips over the shaft of the motor. A rubber or plastic bushing between the propeller blades and the hub cushions the motor from impact damage. Impact can damage the hub, or the hub may just wear out from use. If your engine accelerates properly but your boat doesn't accelerate with engine speed, chances are the damage is to the rubber or plastic bushing in the prop, which is easily replaced at a prop shop. Only a few props are made to allow you to change the hub. Most require special tools to do the job.

You may be tempted to ignore a piece of fishing line or nylon rope twisted around your prop, especially because it's not apt to noticeably reduce performance — in the beginning, anyway. But check carefully for these foulings and remove them immediately. If you don't, the nylon fibers can cut into the rubber seals of your gear case, damaging them and allowing water to get into the gears, ultimately destroying them.

Removing the propeller to replace or repair it

If your propeller needs to be repaired or replaced, there's a good chance the easiest way for you to get it done is to remove the prop yourself and take it to a shop. It's not a hard job to do in most cases, and this section tells you how to go about it.

Removing outboard and sterndrive props

Most outboards and sterndrives manufactured in the past 30 years were built with a splined prop shaft. *Splines* are grooves that run the length of the shaft. Inside the propeller's hub, matching splines fit against the shaft splines (see Figure 15-3). This arrangement lets the shaft turn the prop instead of just spinning inside it. Removing a prop from the shaft is easy, as is replacing it.

Figure 15-3:
A typical propeller configuration.

Here's how to remove an outboard or sterndrive propeller:

1. **Remove the cotter key.**

   The *cotter key* is a wire pin that looks like a hairpin. It passes through a hole on the shaft and is held there by bending the ends of it back against the shaft. In most cases the cotter key fits through slots in the prop nut as well (for a description of the prop nut, see the next step). To remove the cotter key, you need to straighten the ends again with needle-nose pliers before you can pull it out.

2. **Remove the prop nut.**

   The *prop nut* is just what it sounds like, and it's screwed onto the shaft and hand-tightened. You should be able to unscrew it by hand to remove it. (When replacing this nut, hand-tighten and then check to see if the cotter keyhole lines up with a slot in the nut. If not, unscrew the nut just enough to make the keyhole and nut slot line up.)

3. **Remove the washer under the prop nut, next to the propeller.**

4. **Slide the prop off.**

   If it sticks from corrosion, spray an aerosol lubricant on the hub and the end of the prop shaft and let it penetrate for a few minutes to loosen any corrosion between the shaft and prop.

5. **If the prop proves stubborn to remove, place a block of wood against the hub and strike the block with a hammer.**

Move the block to different blades until the prop loosens. When you're ready to replace the prop, apply some silicone grease to the shaft and it probably won't get stuck again.

Removing inboard props

Inboard props tend to stick to the shaft more than outboard props. Don't ask me why, but they do. Some inboard shafts are splined, but older ones have a slot-and-key connection. For the latter, you'll find a slot in the prop and a matching slot in the shaft.

To remove a slot-and-key prop, you follow essentially the same steps listed in the preceding section for removing outboard and sterndrive propellers. Be sure to save the key (a half moon-shaped piece of metal) between the shaft and prop, as you need it to replace the prop. The key keeps the shaft from spinning inside the prop.

Repairing different types of propellers

You can do only the most minor maintenance and repair to your propeller, such as filing off burrs and minor nicks. All else should be left to the pros in a prop shop because you can damage the prop by not using the proper tools. Nevertheless, you should get in the habit of inspecting your prop regularly for damage because sometimes damage will have occurred without your knowledge. For example, a bent or gouged blade can put your prop out of balance, making it wobble on the shaft. You can often feel that as vibration in the boat, and you should keep your ear and touch tuned for it.

A badly damaged prop isn't useless. File it as smooth as possible using a fine metal file, and throw it in a ski locker to keep as a spare. If you have a prop mishap while boating and need a temporary replacement, you can usually tilt the propeller high enough out of the water to make an emergency swap to get you home.

Repairing aluminum props

Aluminum props aren't as hard as stainless steel, but they are more brittle. Striking rocks or stumps is more likely to sheer off large chunks of metal or even one or more of the blades on an aluminum prop as opposed to a stainless-steel one.

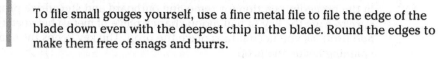

Here are some considerations for maintaining and repairing aluminum props:

- ✔ Aluminum propellers with missing blades or with gouges in the blade of 1 inch or more should be replaced. A good propeller repair shop can rebuild blades with gouges smaller than 1 inch, but if all three blades are badly damaged, a replacement prop may be more economical. Ask the shop manager for cost estimates of all your options.

- ✔ Gouges or chips in the blade under $1/16$ inch usually can be filed smooth on your work bench (if you have one), but if your boat is more high performance in nature, with horsepower exceeding 150, a professional repair will give a better result.

   To file small gouges yourself, use a fine metal file to file the edge of the blade down even with the deepest chip in the blade. Round the edges to make them free of snags and burrs.

Repairing stainless-steel props

Stainless-steel props can be repaired, but not usually by you. The hardness of the metal makes it difficult to hammer back into shape and file nicks smooth. The cost of a stainless-steel prop is in the neighborhood of $350 to $600, so the chance of doing more harm than good with a file or hammer and a do-it-yourself attitude is amplified.

One thing you can do to maintain a stainless-steel prop is to file off small nicks and burrs on the blade. This seemingly minor damage can reduce prop efficiency. If a nick is under $1/32$ inch in size, filing it smooth can be effective. The same goes for burrs that snag a cloth pulled lightly over the blades. Serious damage such as nicks more than $1/16$ inch deep need professional repair.

To file off very small nicks and burrs, follow the filing instructions in the preceding section.

Bent stainless-steel blades are best left to the professionals. If you notice a slight bend in a blade, you can try to bend it back into shape — but be careful, because it's easy to snap off the blade. If you don't detect any vibration or loss of power, don't worry about repairing a slightly bent blade until the end of the season.

I once hammered a bent stainless-steel blade tip back in place. It was a triangle on the tip about $1/2$ inch long and nearly 90 degrees out of whack. I bent it slowly with light taps over time. It worked, but I just as easily could have broken it off.

Repairing bronze props

Professional maintenance is often more important for bronze props than for aluminum. Bronze is easy to file, so removing small nicks and burrs is easy with a fine metal file. But bronze props tend to run at higher speeds or revolutions per minute (RPMs), making a small imbalance in weight between blades a bigger problem than in other props. So, if you file off a small nick on one blade, that one blade may weigh slightly less than the others and cause the prop to spin out of balance. And an out-of-balance prop can vibrate and cause damage to the engine.

Handling Electrical Problems

Nine out of ten times, if you have a problem with your boat, it's electrical. It may be as insignificant as hearing nothing from the left-rear stereo speaker or as critical as smelling hot wires and vinyl insulation burning. Shut off the battery switch if you catch a whiff of smoke.

In this section, I give you an overview of a boat's electrical system and tell you how to track down and fix bad connections.

What do those colored wires mean?

Wires in boats are color-coded to make it easier to determine which one in the bird's nest of wires goes to which thing onboard. Unsophisticated boat builders follow the beat of their own drummer, and the colors have little consistent meaning. Better boat builders follow certain industry standards that are much like building codes in your town.

Throughout this book, I mention NMMA certification of boats. I mention it again here, because nothing on your new boat has more potential for problems than wiring. If your boat is NMMA-certified, the National Marine Manufacturers Association has inspected the manufacturer's processes, including the wiring systems, and determined that they meet both the rudimentary United States Coast Guard requirements and the more stringent standards of the American Boat and Yacht Council (ABYC). The ABYC wiring standards cover 12-volt systems and, for cruising boats with onboard living facilities, 110-volt systems.

Part of the ABYC code requires certain colored wires for certain electrical functions onboard (for specifics on these wire colors, see Table 15-1). Should wiring issues crop up down the road — er, waterway — the color-coded wires will help you or your mechanic track down the problem more quickly, saving time and money. Wiring systems wired this way are safer for you and your crew, too.

Table 15-1	Color Code for Engine and Accessory Wires	
Color	**Item**	**Use**
Yellow with red stripe	Starting circuit	Starting switch to solenoid
Brown and yellow stripe (or just yellow — see note)	Bilge blowers	Fuse or switch to blowers
Dark gray	Navigation lights Tachometer	Fuse or switch to lights Tachometer sender to gauge
Brown	Generator armature Alternator charge light Pumps	Generator armature to regula-torGenerator Terminal/alternator Auxiliary terminal to light to regulator Fuse or switch to pumps
Orange	Accessory feed	Ammeter to alternator or generator output and accessory fuses or switches Distribution panel to accessory switch
Purple	Ignition Instrument feed	Ignition switch to coil and electrical instruments Distribution panel to electrical instruments
Dark blue	Cabin and instrument lights	Fuse or switch to lights
Light blue	Oil pressure	Oil pressure sender to gauge
Tan	Water temperature	Water temperature sender to gauge
Pink	Fuel gauge	Fuel gauge sender to gauge
Green stripe	Tilt down and/or trim in	Tilt and/or trim circuits
Blue stripe	Tilt up and/or trim out	Tilt and/or trim circuits
Green or green and yellow stripe		DC grounding conductors
Black or yellow (see note)		DC negative conductors
Red		DC positive conductors

Note: If a yellow wire is used for DC negative, a brown and yellow striped wire must be used for the blowers.

Working on a 12-volt battery system

Nearly all boats, their engines, and accessories run on a 12-volt battery system similar to what's in your car. In a boat, though, you can have more than one battery.

Different battery setups for different boats

Each engine should have its own 12-volt starting battery that's recharged by the engine's alternator. Most freshwater boats and some saltwater fishing boats have a trolling motor powered by one to three 12-volt, deep-cycle batteries. Each one needs to be recharged with a battery charger at the end of the day.

Many boats have one or more *house batteries* to run the many electronics and accessories onboard. Often the house battery is charged by the engine(s). If not, it needs to be connected to a charger after use. Your dealer will explain your boat's setup.

Cruisers and other boats with onboard living quarters have many house batteries, depending on the size of the boat and projected power needs of the crew. Some of these batteries are recharged by the engines, some by a generator, and some by a charger when the boat is connected to power onshore (such a charger taps into *shore power*).

Battery connections are black and red

Power comes from the positive side of a battery, which is always marked with a "+" and is always connected to the red wires in your system. Power flows out from the red wires on the positive terminal and back to the battery through the black wires on the negative terminal.

Boats made very recently follow new standards that require the ground wire to be yellow. To ease the explanation in this chapter, though, I refer to the ground wire as black.

It's impractical to take all the black and red wires to all the pumps, radios, lights, stereos, and GPS and depth finders in your boat's *aft* (toward the back or stern) and back to the battery. So instead, a single black wire and a single red wire are taken to the helm station and fastened each to its own terminal block (see Figure 15-4) underneath what you'll find yourself calling the dashboard. A *terminal block* is a plastic plate with metal terminals and screws to hold the wires in place.

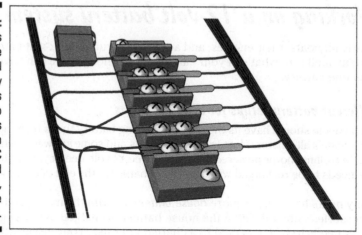

Figure 15-4:
Your boat's positive terminal has many devices wired to it. Colors match the ABYC codes, and as a bonus, they're labeled.

Each terminal block has a place to connect wires from several accessories. Using this system saves wire, eases the wiring job, reduces the risk of circuit failure, and optimizes power usage from the battery by eliminating long, power-sapping wire runs.

Resetting circuit breakers or replacing fuses

Occasionally, a stereo or pump malfunctions and overloads the circuit, thus overheating the wire. Overheating trips a circuit breaker (see Figure 15-5) or blows a fuse. Fewer boats today are built with fuses, but if you have one with fuses, the panel will look similar to the fuse panel in your car. (Sometimes fuses are contained in a holder on each individual wire, which isn't the easiest setup to work with.)

Sometimes the circuit breaker trips or a fuse blows for no apparent reason. If resetting the breaker or replacing the fuse solves the problem, move on. If it happens repeatedly, you need to have a marine mechanic or electrician find out why the breaker keeps tripping or the fuse keeps blowing.

Resetting breakers and replacing fuses are pretty common tasks in the boat, just like in the home. Checking for loose connections takes only a little more initiative, and if you're a little bit handy, doing it is worth your effort on 12-volt systems.

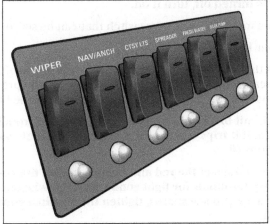

Figure 15-5:
Circuit
breakers
on a boat
save you the
trouble of
hunting for
a fuse panel
and burned-
out fuse.

Tampering with 110 volts is dangerous

If your boat has a sleeping berth and a microwave or a refrigerator, chances are it has wiring for 110-volt power. You may have a gasoline-powered or diesel-powered generator, and you'll definitely have a place where you can connect 110-volt shore power while your boat is docked.

I suggest that you not tamper with the wiring in a 110-volt system unless you're a certified marine electrician. Mistakes can be fatal! So if you have trouble with your wiring, take your boat to the shop.

Tracking down electrical problems

Electricity is like the wind: Its effects can be felt, but it can't be seen. In plumbing or tracking down a hull leak, it's easy to see the leak. But when you're dealing with a wiring problem, all you know is something doesn't work. In tracking down a short circuit — say the stereo doesn't work — you're left to spot the effects of electricity and find where those effects end.

The following is a handy strategy for finding problems in wiring. I use the stereo as an example. *Note:* As each progressive step fails to restore the device to operation, move on to the next one.

1. If the stereo is turned off, turn it on.

A stereo needs to be turned on at the stereo head unit and often at the accessory switch on the helm station (dashboard).

2. **If the battery is turned off, turn it on.**

   Remember, you may have a battery switch that can be set to "Off."

3. **Make sure your battery is charged.**

   If other things that rely on the battery, like the engine starter, work properly, you can eliminate the battery as a source of the problem. If other things that rely on the battery don't work, charge the battery.

4. **If the stereo circuit breaker is tripped and protruding from its socket, press it back in. If it trips again, or if it has a fuse that blows repeatedly, skip to Step 10.**

5. **Check the connections of the red and black wires on the positive and negative battery terminals for tight connections by wiggling them. If they seem loose or you see sparks, tighten the terminal connections with a wrench.**

   Be careful not to accidentally touch the wrench to the red and black terminals when tightening the terminal connections, as that may cause sparks.

6. **Look under the dashboard for the red positive wire that comes from the stereo, and make sure it's tightly fastened to the stereo.**

7. **Look under the dashboard for the usually black negative stereo wire, and make sure it's tightly fastened to the negative terminal block.**

   If the negative wire doesn't seem to be black, consult the owner's manual of the stereo for the actual color. Remember, newer boats often have yellow ground wires, also called *negative wires*. You're looking for the wire attached to the negative terminal block near the positive terminal block.

8. **If you haven't solved the problem yet, see if other things connected to the same positive and negative terminal blocks function properly. If they don't, check the terminal leads at the block and at the battery.**

9. **If none of the connections tested thus far seem faulty, it's time to assume the stereo doesn't work and replace it.**

10. **If a circuit breaker or a fuse repeatedly trips or blows, respectively, the stereo could be faulty. Your options are to replace it or visit your boat mechanic.**

    You may want to see the mechanic first because he or she could find that the problem is elsewhere in the wiring, saving you an unnecessary stereo replacement.

Using some helpful wiring tools

The tools of marine wiring are pretty simple and inexpensive to acquire. In fact, you probably already have many of them. This list has the makings of a pretty good do-it-yourself kit (see Figure 15-6):

- **A wire crimping and stripping tool** lets you strip wire ends to accept connectors and also crimp on the connectors. In addition, this tool has a wire cutter in it. It's the Swiss Army knife of wiring.

- **Needle-nose pliers** are helpful for fitting or gripping wires in tight places.

- **Various wire connectors** give you options for repairing systems and making them fit as well as possible.

- **Zip ties** are handy for bundling loose wires in a more organized manner or for holding wires along the path you want them to follow.

- **Electrical tape** can be handy for making a quick temporary repair to a bare wire, although it isn't used on boats as much as you may think.

- **Silicone spray lubricant** is helpful to protect circuits from corrosion.

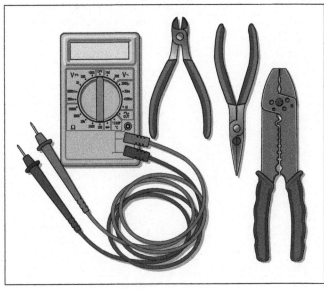

Figure 15-6: A wire-crimping tool, needle-nose pliers, wire cutter, and a few terminals are just a few of the basics of boat-wiring maintenance.

Part V
Enjoying Your Boat

The 5th Wave   By Rich Tennant

In this part . . .

If boating, docking, and hanging out aren't quite enough fun for you, you've come to the right part. I help you weigh the pros and cons of various boat-storage options, some of which come with some enjoyable amenities. I share advice for entertaining friends and family onboard by stocking and preparing boating-friendly drinks, snacks, and meals. I give tips for helping your friends learn to enjoy boating as much as you do, and I introduce you to the benefits and pitfalls of various kinds of boating clubs that you can join.

Chapter 16

Finding a Safe Harbor for Your Boat

*Y*ou have to keep your boat somewhere when you're not using it. Fortunately, you have several options. Keeping your boat on a trailer in the backyard is perfectly fine if it's properly protected. On the other hand, marina storage can add to the fun and camaraderie of boating — if you pick the right one. Marinas offer a variety of perks, and if you land in one that offers the right mix of practicality, cost, and social environment, sometimes just hangin' out in port is all you need for a weekend boating fix.

Storage facilities and their costs are different in different regions, partly because boating customs differ. Climate also impacts marine facility options and their costs. For instance, in year-round boating regions like Florida or Southern California, costs may be higher than in seasonal spots in Michigan or Missouri.

I can't predict where you'll boat or what kind of marina facilities or residential laws impacting boat storage you'll face, but I can help you know what questions to ask and how to sort through your options and weigh the costs and benefits to find boat storage that suits you best. So dig into this chapter, because I go over the costs and benefits of keeping your boat in a marina, dry-stacking it, and even keeping it at home on a trailer. I also give you some practical tips for keeping your boat safe and protected during storage.

First Things First: Make Sure You Have a Mooring Cover

Regardless of where you choose to store your boat, the first step is buying a good mooring cover for your boat if it didn't come with one. Even if you keep your boat in an enclosed garage, you should still put a cover on it for protection — and of course, you have to move it outside *sometime* if you ever want to use it. Some boats have factory-made covers as options or even standard equipment, but many others don't, leaving you with the task of getting one made to protect your boat. A good cover adds years to the beauty and enjoyment of your boat by protecting it from the elements.

When you keep your boat around water, it becomes a roosting magnet for waterfowl and other birds — and you know what they leave behind. Even in a relatively bird-free area, exposure to the sun is destructive; it gradually breaks down the ultraviolet-light barriers built into fabrics and vinyls, yellows the wax, and fades the fiberglass. Your boat's mooring cover should have these characteristics:

✓ **Waterproofing:** Waterproof fabric is essential. Whether you're storing your boat in the water or on dry land, you want to prevent rainwater from filling your bilge, which could wear down your battery by continually activating the bilge pump as water levels rise. (Most boats have an automatic bilge pump that senses a rising water level and starts pumping when it reaches a predetermined depth.)

Even with a waterproof mooring cover, if there's not enough slant to your boat's cover to shed water, you'll need to somehow prop it up in the middle for water to run off.

✓ **UV protection:** Fabrics protected from ultraviolet (UV) light are necessary because fabrics won't last long under the sun (almost) 24/7 unless they have UV inhibitors. UV-protected fabrics are more fade resistant, too. The most popular fabric for boat canvas is called Sunbrella (www. sunbrella.com/na/en/marine.pl). It's known for its ability to shed water and resist the effects of UV light.

Dark-colored sides on a boat are more vulnerable to UV light than lighter colored sides. If you have dark hull colors, protect that finish by having your cover designed to reach down beyond the color band.

✓ **A snug fit:** A proper fit is required to keep the cover weather-tight. Loose covers collect puddles on top, which eventually become enormous pots of water that stretch the cover and can even tear it by pulling it against structures of the boat.

✔ **An easy-to-install design:** If you store your boat on the water, the design of the cover should make it easy to install it from inside the boat, because you may not be able to reach all around the boat from the dock. Practical covers snap over the bow, the windshield, and the cockpit and usually end right at the edge of the deck. Such a cover should install easily from bow to stern, allowing you to retreat toward the dock as you snap it in place.

I find the hardest part of putting a cover on a boat is figuring out which side of the cover is the starboard (right) side and which is the port (left) side as I unroll it from the bundle. On my cover, I changed the tie-down ropes to help me out; I used green ropes on the starboard side to match the green navigation light on the starboard side. If you have a snap-on cover, you could use a little dab of green paint on the starboard snaps. That little trick saved me a lot of sweat and wrestling around with my cover.

Floating Your Boat in Wet Slip Storage

Ever hear the song "Sitting on the Dock of the Bay"? The easygoing, romantic atmosphere brought to mind by that song is often the first thought of new boaters as they imagine themselves immersed in their sport. The mind's eye pictures the boat gently tugging at its docklines as the sunset breeze pushes away the sun's sweltering heat. Dew drips from your tall glass of iced tea, and your favorite song is setting the tone over your stereo. . . . That can be reality, but dockside life isn't always as great as it's cracked up to be.

In fact, when you finish reading this section about the costs, pros and cons, and necessary preparations for wet slip storage (see Figure 16-1), you may decide it's not for you at all! Of all your storage options, this is the most expensive when you consider both the cost of the slip rental and the additional maintenance required when you leave your boat in the water all the time.

Getting what you want from a wet slip

Just any slip may seem fine until you actually begin to use it with your boat. You'll quickly discover some things you like and some things you really hate about it. This section has some insight on what to look for with regards to convenience and usability for your boat's proposed wet slip home.

Easy docking access

Easy docking access in a wet slip may be the most important thing to consider for a new boater. Docking will be daunting if you get stuck with the last slip wedged in near the shore between two giant boats, with several more boats on the next dock looming over your path to your slip.

Figure 16-1:
A boat in a wet slip is often a boater's dream, but beware the drawbacks.

If you choose to go with a wet slip, try to select a slip with the following characteristics:

- **An easy approach:** You want an entrance that's as straightforward as possible. Also look for the following:

  - A slip that isn't crowded between other boats.

  - A slip that doesn't require you to make a hard right or left turn to enter your slip.

  - A slip that doesn't have a strong current sweeping through it, either from the front or the side. Managing current while you dock is a tough battle to fight even for an experienced boater.

- **Easy boarding access:** Try to strike a balance between convenient access to the boat from the parking lot and to the open water once you're in the boat. Here are some boarding considerations:

  - Sometimes being closest to the parking lot is ideal. You'll frequently have tons of gear to take to the dock, and the farther you are from the parking lot, the longer and harder the haul.

  - Some boaters prefer an open-water feeling, with their boats moored only a hop, skip, and a jump from getting underway. If you choose a slip close to the open water, just be sure that the outer edges of the marina are adequately protected from seas and boat chop with sea walls or other wave-breaking devices.

- Climbing aboard the boat easily may be your priority. Floating docks offer the easiest access to boats — most of the time. When the water rises or falls because of seasons, rain, or tides, the boat goes right along with it, keeping the step from dock to boat consistent. Fixed docks built on pilings work out okay when the tides and other water fluctuations aren't too dramatic. Ask your marine operator (often called the *harbormaster)* what kind of water fluctuations to expect.

When mooring a boat on a dock built on pilings driven in the bottom, make sure you allow for water level changes. Naturally, coastal waters have tides, but some inland waters change with rain or when water is diverted for hydroelectric power. You need to leave enough slack to allow for water level changes, or your moorings (rope) might break as the boat drops down on the tide. Worse, I've seen boats held up by one or two lines on one side while the other side went down and under the water. Check with your harbormaster about water-level fluctuations and tides, and ask for advice on how best to allow for the changing water level given that your slip is in a dock on pilings.

Dockside amenities

When your boat is comfortably settled in a wet slip, you'll find you need amenities to support it, like electricity for battery charging, water for washing the boat, and a place to store your stuff. Here's the lowdown on such dockside amenities and what you're likely to need:

- **Shorepower station:** *Shorepower* is an electrical connection for boats that are equipped for it. Even some larger runabouts and a few pontoon boats have refrigerators, microwaves, blenders, and coffee makers that can operate on either 12-volt or 110-volt power. Shorepower is the most practical way to run these sorts of appliances while you're in port.

- **Connection for a battery charger:** Even if you don't need shorepower, you'll eventually need a battery charger. That makes at least a 110-volt electrical connection essential dockside.

- **Freshwater access:** Many runabouts and pontoons (as well as small cruisers) are equipped with freshwater tanks from which to draw for drinking water and showers. To fill the freshwater tanks — and wash your boat at the dock now and then — a dockside hose connection is a must.

- **Dockside storage:** You may have some items that you want to keep handy for the boat but not actually in it at all times. You need convenient storage for extra life jackets, tools, or a battery charger. If your slip doesn't come with a dockside locker, find out if you're allowed to install one. (You can get them from marine retailers.)

Preparing your boat for wet slip storage

If you plan to store your boat in the water, you need to do some things to make sure the boat can handle exposure to the weather, water, aquatic marine growth, and even wildlife, such as birds. This section highlights preparations to make.

Anti-fouling paint for your bottom

I mean your boat's bottom. *Anti-fouling paint,* often just called *bottom paint,* keeps algae, mollusks, and barnacles from growing on your hull. If you keep your boat in the water for long periods of time, marine growth collects quickly, adding fuel-robbing hull drag and even damaging the nice finish. No matter how much you clean it, once a hull has suffered the indignity of barnacles, algae, and calcium deposits, the finish will never have the same luster.

Unfortunately, there's one thing bottom paint can't prevent on boats that sit in the water: blisters. *Gelcoat,* the glossy white finish on your hull, is porous, so it absorbs water. Sometimes the gelcoat absorbs so much water that blisters appear — even on hulls carefully protected with anti-fouling paint. Most water-stored boats get at least a few blisters, and many get a lot. Repairing these blisters adds another expense to your maintenance regimen. For some boaters, this kind of marine fouling is the deal breaker that swings them over to dry storage, which I discuss later in this chapter, in the section "Stacking the Deck for Dry Storage."

Choose the right anti-fouling paint for your region. Appropriate paints differ by region because different marine life grows in different climates — and at different rates. Colder areas have different challenges than warmer areas. Confer with your marine serviceperson about the local flora and fauna. Ask what organisms are unique to your area and what paints do the best job of killing them or preventing them from getting a grip on your hull.

If you know from the day you select your boat that you plan to keep it in a slip, contract with the sales dealer to paint the bottom prior to taking delivery. Then your first paint job is behind you from the beginning!

Painting the bottom yourself

Do-it-yourself types frequently paint their own boat bottoms, but it isn't something you should do without considerable research. Unless you properly prepare the hull, the paint won't adhere to it and your effort will be wasted — along with hundreds of dollars of paint. Here are a few additional considerations:

- ✔ **Figure out where to paint.** Some marine operators won't let you paint in their marinas due partly to concern about environmental issues and partly to concern of paint getting on neighboring boats. Your harbormaster should be able to direct you to a marina where you can paint.

✔ **Fume-proof yourself.** If you paint your own boat bottom, safety precautions are necessary to protect yourself from fumes and chemicals in the paint. Anti-fouling paint contains *biocides,* poisons that kill plant and animal growth. As you may imagine, these biocides are also poisonous to humans. Wear protective clothing, goggles, a respirator, and any other safety gear recommended on the label of your paint.

✔ **Keep it green.** Not the paint, the environment. You can use any color of paint you want, but remember that the paint is poisonous, and it's important you get it only on the boat, not on the ground, on you, or on any wildlife. Anti-fouling paints have special directions about environmental concerns, and it's important you follow them.

Watching out for galvanic corrosion

When you keep your boat in the water, you must protect it against another risk that you can't see: galvanic corrosion.

In a marina, many boats with different power systems put varying degrees of very low electrical current into the water. As these currents pass by your boat, they leech metal from the part of your boat's propulsion system exposed to the water, especially the gear-case housing to which the propeller is attached. Also at risk are the trim tabs (if you have them), the metal through-hull fittings, and any other metal parts exposed to the water. The resulting damage is caused *galvanic corrosion.*

Here's the rundown on how to protect your boat from galvanic corrosion:

✔ **Bottom paint** is pretty low on the protection scale, but it does afford some protection. Boaters who use aluminum boats, like pontoons, in the sea find that bottom paint does a good job of warding off the worst corrosion.

✔ **Zincs** are small metal parts that are usually factory-installed on your boat and engine parts exposed to the water. Zincs dissolve more quickly than aluminum, bronze, and other metals on your boat, and they serve as sort of a lightning rod for your boat, drawing the current and its effects to themselves. The zincs dissolve, sacrificing themselves to protect other metals — that's why they're often called *sacrificial anodes.*

It's essential that you inspect zinc anodes regularly to monitor the level of corrosion and replace them when they lose half of their original surface area or are at risk of coming unfastened due to corrosion. Purchase new zincs from your local marine dealer or online at www.westmarine.com.

✔ **Galvanic isolators** are optional systems you have to have installed in your own boat. This gadget puts out a protective charge around your boat, warding off the effects of harmful stray currents from other sources in the marina and minimizing galvanic corrosion. Galvanic isolators need to be professionally installed, so contact your service technician for advice.

Another alternative: Hoisting your boat

If you're a lucky owner of a cabin at the lake or bungalow by the sea and you have a dock, hoisting your boat in the dock is a great idea. It's a really handy compromise between keeping your boat in the water and keeping it in dry storage on a rack or on the trailer, as I discuss later in this chapter.

Boat hoists fit into wet slips, submerged in the water. After you've driven your boat over a hoist, you raise it up, lifting your boat high and dry. Hoists afford complete protection against galvanic corrosion, eliminate the need for bottom paint, and minimize the risk of sinking or damage from boat wakes or wind chop. Most marinas allow tenants to install hoists, but make sure you're allowed to uninstall it if you move your boat elsewhere.

A hoist can eventually pay for itself by saving you money on the maintenance needed when you keep your boat down in the water.

Hoists come in several designs for various conditions. Here's a quick reference list:

- **Floating hoists** are made of molded polyethylene. Marine growth forms on the bottom of this hoist, but the hoist is unharmed by it.

  - **How it works:** This hoist remains floating, and you load your boat onto it by nudging the bow against the hoist's loading tracks or rollers and adding throttle until the boat has enough power to climb onto the hoist. Usually boats are easily pushed off this hoist by one or two boaters, but sometimes a winch is needed to relaunch the boat.

  - **Advantages:** The boat is held high and dry, safe from drifting debris, galvanic corrosion, and marine growth. A floating hoist is impervious to salt and galvanic corrosion.

  - **Reliability:** Few working parts means there's little to break.

  - **Application:** Best for boats under 25 feet in length.

  - **Disadvantages:** Polyethylene is affected by UV rays, and a floating hoist can degrade over time from sun exposure.

- **Displacement hoists** are made of galvanized steel, which is sturdy but doesn't hold up well to saltwater exposure, making them best suited to freshwater slips.

  - **How it works:** This style of hoist has tanks and an air pump. To load your boat on the hoist, you drive in so that your boat is positioned above the hoist, close the valves on the tanks, and turn on the pump to force air into the tanks and displace the water so they float, raising the boat. To launch the boat, you open a valve and allow the air to leave the tanks, which in turn allows the tanks to flood and sink, lowering the boat.

- **Advantages:** The boat is held high and dry, and you don't have to power onto the hoist — you just drive into the slip normally.

- **Reliability:** These hoists are sturdy in the face of chop.

- **Application:** Best for freshwater slips. I've seen them used for boats up to 45 feet in length.

- **Disadvantages:** Corrosion can take its toll on a displacement hoist, and the electric pump can be affected by moisture from humidity or rain.

✔ **Electric hoists** use powerful electric winches, cables, and pulleys to raise and lower an aluminum or galvanized cradle for your boat.

- **How it works:** Winches are set on two of a set of four pilings. Cables are fastened to a cradle, which is suspended on the cables between the pilings. When the cradle is lowered into the water, you can drive your boat into it, step out, and activate the winches to raise the boat.

- **Advantages:** None of the hardware of a winch hoist remains under water for long, so it doesn't collect marine growth or suffer from saltwater or galvanic corrosion.

- **Reliability:** It's as reliable as your electricity!

- **Application:** Best for shallow water where dock pilings are practical and water levels fluctuate less than 5 feet, and for boats up to 45 feet in length.

- **Disadvantages:** These hoists are dependent on electricity for launching your boat and aren't as convenient as other hoists when it comes to entering your boat while it's hoisted.

Carpeted bunks on hoists (and trailers) hold water, and if it's salty, it can't be rinsed away while a boat is sitting on it. That's no big deal for fiberglass boats, but if aluminum pontoons sit on these salty bunks, corrosion can quickly eat through the metal. When hoisting metal boats from salt water, use plastic bunk guards instead of carpet.

The cha-ching factor of wet slip storage

Wet slip storage for your boat may be the most romantically appealing thanks to the easy escape you can make by just starting the engine and untying the lines. But add to the liabilities and complications the costs I itemize for you in this section, and you'll see there's quite a price for romancing the seas from a wet slip.

✔ Renting slips by the foot is modus boaterandii for slip fees. Boat slips are usually rented by the length of the boat they can accommodate, not by the length of your boat. So if you have a 20-foot boat and the only slip available in town is for a 25-foot boat, guess how many feet you'll be paying for? Monthly rental fees for slips range in price from location to location.

✔ Water and electricity may or may not be included in your fees, so inquire about those amenities. (If you don't think you'll need them, refer to the earlier section, "Dockside amenities.")

✔ Your contract with the marina may impose minimum insurance levels for your boat. Boats can catch fire or slip their moorings — which is a boaty way of saying "come untied" — and bump into other boats, making you liable for damages. For these reasons, marina operators can require you to provide proof of certain insurance coverage.

✔ Fuel on the water costs more than fuel on the highway. If you have a trailerable boat, filling up a 100-gallon tank on the highway can save you $50 to $100 or more over the cost of buying gas at a marina.

✔ Marinas may prevent you from servicing your own boat or bringing in your own mechanic to service your boat. Such marinas provide all boat services and repairs themselves — and the rates may be less than competitive.

Weighing the pros and cons of floating your boat

If you're still deciding whether wet slip boat storage is right for you, here's a quick reference on the pros and cons of slipping your boat:

✔ **Pro:** A boat in a slip makes for a fun and convenient getaway because there's no major launching, no trailering, and no waiting for the dry-stack forklift to drop the boat in the water. Crank the engine, cast off the docklines, and hit the high seas — or inland waterways.

✔ **Pro:** It's romantic and pleasant. There's an entire community feeling to a wet slip marina that offers a pleasant lifestyle experience with fellow boaters, and I've never found experiences like it anywhere else.

✔ **Con:** Not only are monthly fees expensive, but storing your boat dockside dramatically increases maintenance costs for your boat. Taking care that corrosion doesn't compromise the engine and through-hull fittings and keeping the anti-fouling paint in good shape are expensive tasks.

Stacking the Deck for Dry Storage

Many people don't boat because of the inconvenience of trailering and the expense and maintenance of keeping a boat in a slip. How much easier would it be if you could treat your boat like a tennis racket — put it on the shelf when you're done playing and pick it up next time the urge to smash a few balls strikes? That's what dry storage does for your boat — except someone else picks it up, washes it, and puts it away for you (like your mother, only he or she won't scold you!).

Usually located at a marina, *dry-stack storage* — also called *racks* or just *dry stacks* — looks like a steel I-beam structure with boats nested in it like swallows under a barn roof (see Figure 16-2). Some dry stacks are fully enclosed like gargantuan barns, so your boat is completely protected from normal weather. If you're in a hurricane zone, the newer dry stacks are built to stricter standards so they can stand up to all but the most destructive hurricanes. You've probably seen one of these structures along a highway in your travels near a lake and thought little of it — except to wonder how they got a boat 40 feet in the air. (Hint: It involves a forklift.)

Figure 16-2:
Dry-stack storage may not be as glamorous as a wet slip, but it sure is a great value.

Photo by Randy Vance

Dry-stack storage may just be the most convenient storage method, but it still has its ups and downs (pardon the dry humor). In this section, I spell out these considerations and give you an idea of what you should expect to get for your money from a dry-stack storage service.

What you can expect from dry-stack storage

When you dry stack your boat, it rests as many as 40 feet overhead. The marina operator uses an enormous forklift to lift your boat from the water and set it high in its cradle on the rack — unless you get one of the lower racks, which is just fine. Whenever you want your boat, you call the marina and someone fires up the forklift to lift it down and have it waiting for you at the marina's dock. Dry-stack storage marinas have varying fees and services. Here are the most popular and useful amenities:

- Some marinas can forklift a boat as big as a 50-foot cruiser. Dry stacks with that capacity are more and more prevalent, increasing the options and convenience for cruising boaters. But many (if not most) marinas have a much smaller length limit. Check to see how big a boat your marina can hoist.

- Covered or uncovered dry-stack storage is a choice to consider. Some marinas offer both at varying costs. You can imagine the benefits of covered storage: protection from sun damage, rain, weather, and wild-life (although sparrows and swallows have a knack for finding their way inside, making individual boat covers important even in covered storage). For uncovered storage, you have to make certain your cover is supported and fastened in place firmly enough that water won't pool in it. In either kind of dry stack, it pays to visit your boat to check its condition and use it at least once during storage to exercise it and clean it.

- Weekends are usually the busiest time to launch your boat, so you should call a few days before your planned boating outing to ask the marina to pencil you into their dry-stack launching list. Tell them when you expect to arrive, and call again when you depart for the marina to remind them you're on the way. Chances are your boat could be launched just as you pull in the marina entrance.

- Weekday launching is often easier to do on the spur of the moment. It's not unusual for a boater to call 15 minutes before noon and find his or her boat ready for a noon picnic.

- Many marinas have no limitations on how many times you can launch your boat in a month. A few have a specified number of launchings in a month and charge a fee for additional launchings over the limit. Some limit you to one launch and load per day and charge extra for additional ones.

✔ Courtesy docks make it convenient for you to land the boat and leave it for a few hours while you enjoy dinner out or some waterside shopping. Some marinas are short on that amenity, but others are better prepared to let you take a break.

✔ I've checked into several marinas in my area, and a surprising number of them will wash a boat down and flush the engine for no extra fee before stacking it. (When boating in salt water, you always need to flush the engine before putting the boat in storage.) All you have to do is leave the keys with the marina operator and get out of the way.

Preparing your boat for dry storage

There's very little you have to do to prepare your boat for dry storage — that's the beauty of it. You don't have to bottom-paint your hull, buy and handle a boat trailer, or worry about galvanic corrosion, and most in-water risks just aren't a problem when you dry stack your boat. But there are a few things you or your marine operator will need to do to secure your boat for safe storage. Sorting out who will do what will take some coordination between you and the dock hands.

To make it easy to get a routine going, discuss the following issues about storing your boat with the dock crew to determine who's in the best position to handle them and when to perform the tasks:

✔ **Fuel it up.** It may seem weird to worry about fuel when you're done boating for the day, but filling the tank prevents damage to the fuel, the fuel system, and the engine from water condensation that can form inside a partially empty tank. And it makes your future return to the boat turnkey simple.

✔ **Stow away any loose items.** If for some reason you don't plan to cover the boat with its own cover, at least roll up the carpet and any snap-on cushions and stow them in a compartment. Even if you do cover your boat, it's best to stow any loose items in a compartment.

✔ **If you cover your boat, leave all storage hatches open.** You want a little air circulating under the cover to prevent mildew and promote faster evaporation of dampness.

✔ **Wash the boat to rinse out sand and grit, and wipe off water droplets.** If you forget to dry the boat, water spots can form calcium deposits that are not only hard to remove but sometimes actually mar the gloss of your boat's finish.

✔ **Flush the engines if you've been boating in salt water.** Because you'll likely be gone by the time the boat is hoisted, the dock crew should be responsible for this step.

✔ **Turn the battery switch to "Off" so the battery remains fresh for your return.** Discuss this with your marina operator. Someone may need to drive the boat to the forklift pickup, so you want to remind the operator that you'd like the battery turned off before the boat is hoisted.

✔ **Remove the drain plug so moisture can drain fully.** Your dock crew should definitely be responsible for this step.

Racking up the costs of stacking your boat

In some regions, dry-stack boat storage is inexpensive enough to approach the low cost of trailering your boat, especially if you take into consideration the excess fuel burned when pulling a full tow load. Even if dry storage costs more, the ease of having a home port where the hard part of boating is handled for you makes the storage fee pretty nominal.

Sizing up the costs and services of dry storage isn't too tough if you're willing to make a few phone calls. Here are some questions to ask regarding costs:

✔ **What's the cost of rack storage?** Like wet slips, rack storage is charged per foot of boat length the space can accommodate. The cost per foot of rack storage is 50 to 70 percent less than wet slip storage.

✔ **Is there a limit on how many times you can launch your boat, per day or per month?** If a limit exists, find out the charge for extra trips.

✔ **Is there an added charge for washing your boat and flushing the engines?** It's not hard to wash and flush your own boat, but saltwater flushing requires the boat to be out of the water. Some marinas charge extra for this service.

✔ **Does the marina have a battery booster, and is there a charge to use it?** Jump-starting your boat is something you'll face if you leave something turned on while the boat's in storage.

✔ **Are there any specific insurance requirements that you must meet to stack your boat?**

Weighing the pros and cons of racking up

You may detect a slight bias on my part toward dry-stack boat storage — and you would be right. Whether you live in a cold climate or tropical one, I think dry storage is far and away the best way to go for boaters who don't have their own home docks or who have to trailer their boats from home to distant waters. But I'll admit that I keep my boat on a trailer because I like it handy and close to home so I can add a little gadget, change a bad stereo speaker, or put in a new satellite radio receiver myself.

Evaluating marina amenities

Part of the fun of boating from any marina *is* the marina. Whether you want a dry-stack slot for your boat or a wet slip, you should take a much broader look at your proposed home marina beyond just the slips and electrical connections.

Some of the things you should expect from a marina are security, convenient parking, and clean restrooms with private showers. Following is an explanation of day-to-day services and conveniences like these and others that can make your marina experience more pleasurable:

✔ **Security:** A marina should provide video and live-personnel security for your boat 24/7. Thieves know how easy it is to heist $1,000 worth of stereo equipment or $10,000 worth of navigation electronics from any boat. It's less convenient for them to hit a boat in a dry stack, but if your boat's in a wet slip, they can easily sneak into the marina from the water, hotwire the boat, and drive it away. Boats don't have the same secure ignition systems and locks as automobiles.

✔ **Parking:** Parking your land vehicle at your busy marina can become a problem on weekends. Make sure you know where to park and that there are plenty of spaces. Some marinas offer reserved parking at an additional fee of hundreds of dollars a season.

✔ **Sewage pump-out station:** Even boats as small as 20 feet can have toilets on them. They're a great convenience on the water but a big inconvenience when they need to

be emptied. Make sure sanitary pump-out services are available conveniently and at a reasonable charge.

✔ **Ships' store:** Many marinas have found that a small convenience-style grocery store is a handy and profitable addition to a boat parts and accessories store. In addition to selling supplies like ice, soda, and snacks, such stores often offer concierge services you can arrange in advance for little or no charge — they'll make sure your boat's cooler is stocked before you even get to the marina!

✔ **Restaurants:** On-premise restaurants add to the convenience and community feel of a marina. It's pretty nice to be able to stop off at the grill for bacon and eggs or a carryout egg sandwich in the morning. It's a good time and place to chat with the local boaters and find out what fish are biting, where the water cops are hangin' out, and where the boaters are rafting up this weekend.

✔ **Shore-side bathrooms and showers:** Most marinas have private restrooms and showers for marina guests. Even boaters with full *heads* on their boats (that means a toilet, shower, and sink) use the shore-side facilities when possible so they can go longer between sewage holding-tank pump-outs and because the shore-side facilities are larger and easier to use. Make sure the marina you choose keeps them well maintained.

Storing a boat in a dry-stack cradle has its share of pros and cons.

✔ **Pro:** You'll never have to launch or load or tow your boat. All you have to do is enjoy handling it.

✔ **Pro:** If you're not tied to certain mechanics through a warranty, using the marina's mechanics because you're required to may be perfectly fine. You may be very happy with the marina's marine mechanics, and they'll be very handy to your boat whenever it needs attention.

✔ **Con:** You can't access your boat in a rack. So performing simple maintenance requires bringing it down from the rack and putting it in a cradle on the ground, for which there's often a charge. If your son or daughter left a favorite toy in the boat, it's likely going to stay there until you have the boat brought down next time.

✔ **Con:** You may be restricted to using the marina's mechanics. Even if you have a boat that's still under warranty but not bought from the marina's store, the marina operator probably won't allow the other dealer's mechanic to work on your boat on marina property. The logistics of moving the boat to the required mechanic can complicate minor and major repairs — unless you already have a trailer.

Buying into Convenient Moorings

The priciest of all the boat storage options may be worth it, if you can afford the bill. *Rackominiums* and *dockominiums* have cropped up in popular marine communities, and they've been very popular. Haven't heard those terms? I assume you've heard of an apartment complex going condo, forcing the tenants to buy or move. Many marinas are being redeveloped in a similar manner. Their superior amenities and ownership benefits — such as predictable service costs, yacht club atmosphere, and extremely clean and modern facilities — make them sell briskly in spite of the often-shocking price tags.

Sizing up the 'minium craze

Most of these new operations offer both wet slips and dry-stack racks for sale. In the many places where these operations have established themselves, individual slips or racks have generally increased in value, making them a potentially worthwhile investment.

Rackominiums

The term pretty much says what rackominiums are. Individual racks in a dry-stack building are given fee-simple titles that can be insured and transferred from individual to individual. Your boat is always stacked in its own little place, and if you ever want to trade up or sell out, the rack is a saleable piece of real estate in the same way a condominium is.

Dockominiums

Waterfront property that seemed outrageously priced ten years ago is astronomically higher today. Some owners of large yacht slips have reported sales prices of more than $1 million in popular urban boating regions. Just like a condo or racko, you get a title to your slip and you own it. And like I said, the dockos seem to increase in value.

Enjoying premium marina amenities

One of the greatest advantages to dockominums and rackominiums is the atmosphere and amenities. Like private clubs, these marina properties are well maintained and nicely landscaped. Amenities often exceed the number of those found in rental operations. Here are some of the top selling points of rackominiums and dockominiums:

- ✔ **Privacy:** These clubs are open only to owners, so everyone you'll meet has a stake in keeping the facilities clean and pleasant. It's one of the reasons they stay so well maintained.

- ✔ **Pools:** Many racko or docko properties have pools, giving you a great place to hang out when you want to be by the water but perhaps the water is too choppy to enjoy your boat.

- ✔ **Restaurants and shops:** Fine dining and snack bars — along with ship's store, grocery, and dockside concierge service to supply your galley or cooler — make the experience convenient and pleasant.

- ✔ **Fuel, service, and washing:** Exemplary services are reported in many dockominium operations, making your boating literally turnkey. Schedule a launching; request fuel, ice, and sodas; and stroke one check for the service at the end of the month. Launching is free, along with washing the boat and flushing the engines.

Using a Trailer for More Freedom and Frugality

While many boaters use marina-based storage options, many others don't, either because they don't like the cost or because marinas aren't convenient to the places where they most commonly boat. Trailering your boat offers so much freedom in where and when you use your boat that, in spite of the challenges of mastering trailering tactics (see Chapters 5 and 6 for more on trailering your boat), more than 75,000 new boat trailers are sold each year. That's equal to 25 to 30 percent of all new boats sold each year. For many, trailers are the most convenient way to store a boat.

Where to keep your trailered boat

A trailer gives you plenty of flexibility in storing your boat. Anyplace the trailer can be safely — and legally — parked becomes a storage option. This section covers a few common places to store a boat on a trailer.

Home storage

Home is where the heart is, and for many boaters, it's where the boat is, too. Most boats on trailers are stored in their owners' yards, driveways, or garages. If your trailered boat fits in your garage, all the better — it's like having your own covered dry storage. It's convenient, too, enabling you to clean, polish, and maintain your boat or add bling to it in the driveway while you sip a cold drink.

Many communities have ordinances against keeping a boat in the open on residential property. In fact, as I write this, painters are painting my carport, and my smaller boat has been moved to the driveway. Within 48 hours of moving the boat, I received a notice from the zoning enforcement officers of Winter Park, Florida, requesting that I move the boat in five days or pay a fine of $250 *per day*. I hope the painters are done soon.

Marina storage

Many marinas offer lot storage on their property where you can park your trailer with your boat on it, and for a fee, they'll launch your boat for you. It's a great compromise between free-style trailering and dry-stack storage, giving you the freedom to move your boat at your own discretion, change lakes, or haul your boat to your favorite service shop. These storage lots can cost half as much as dry-stack storage, although in urban settings where land is scarce there may be no savings at all.

Self-storage lots

You've probably seen storage lots in your community for things like RVs and boats. They offer gated security, allowing entrance only with valid security codes. These lots often provide video surveillance and sometimes on-premise personnel to make sure bad guys stay away from your boat. Parking slots are priced per foot, like dry storage or wet slips. The storage parking space for the larger of my two boats costs about one-fourth of what a dry-stack slip would cost, just to give you an idea of the savings.

Preparing your boat for open storage

Storing your boat on a trailer is practically as easy as falling out of the boat. But it doesn't mean there aren't some necessary preparations and precautions to take to keep the boat safe and clean for your next trip. This section covers security, protection, and maintenance precautions to consider when storing your boat.

Securing your boat

Boats are popular targets for thieves. The trailer that makes your boat so easy for you to transport does the same for criminals, too. A variety of locking devices makes it at least difficult for thieves to haul your boat and trailer away. Without one or more of these devices, your boat can be hitched up and driven into a portside shipping container while you take a shower. Here are some security considerations:

- Keeping your boat locked inside your garage (if it fits) is the easiest way to ward off thieves. "Out of sight, out of mind" applies here.

- You can slip a padlock through the tongue-locking lever of the trailer so the tongue won't fit over a trailer ball unless the lock is removed. Unfortunately, every thief worth his salt has a bolt cutter to quickly remove these. A better solution is a tongue lock available at marine stores or in the auto department of discount stores. These locks fit over the entire trailer tongue, preventing it from fitting onto a trailer ball. Some can still be ground away with a grinder, but not quickly, and the odds that someone will be noticed while doing this dirty work reduce the odds they'll try. You can find quite a variety of effective devices at marine retailers. I use one called a universal tongue lock I found at www.westmarine.com.

- Wheel locks rule. These are much like the boots the police use to prevent a ticketed car from disappearing before the owner pays the fine. A wheel lock prevents the wheel it's on from rolling, and the mechanism covers the lug nuts so the device can't be defeated by removing the wheel and replacing it. (Check out some options at www.carrythebig stick.com.)

- Some thieves target just an outboard motor or even the gear case of an outboard or the propeller. Special locking nuts are available to replace the standard nuts holding these components in place. They aren't impossible to defeat, but they sure are discouraging. Also, the damage caused by removing them leaves a recognizable mark that raises questions when the items are resold. (Check some out at www.mcgard.com.)

- Dash-mounted electronics brackets make depth finders and GPS units vulnerable. When leaving your boat unattended, it's best to remove these items and carry them inside in a gear bag. But if you prefer to leave them on the boat, locks to replace their mounting knobs can slow thieves down a bit (see www.durasafelocks.com).

- My favorite security device is cellphone based. It's called GPS Snitch and uses the innards of a cellphone coupled with a motion-sensitive device that turns on the phone if the boat moves unexpectedly. This gadget also has a perimeter sensor that can be set to turn on when the boat moves beyond a certain point. When triggered, this device calls you and sends you an e-mail and a text message. Hide this baby in the boat, and when you get the message that your boat's on the move, you can track it online and report its position to the authorities. (Find out more at www. blacklinegps.com.)

Protecting your boat from the elements

Shielding your boat from the elements isn't any different with a trailer than with dry-stack storage, except you won't have anyone else but yourself to blame if it doesn't get done! Covering your boat is essential. Even if you keep it in the garage, dirt and dust circulate and land more on your boat, it seems, than anywhere else. Here are a couple of tips to follow:

- ✔ Open your boat lockers to let them air out — unless you don't plan to cover the boat, for some reason. Then you're better off leaving the lockers closed and latched.

- ✔ Remove the drain plug, and make sure the bilge is free of debris that may block the drain. If you forget this one and your cover isn't totally watertight (most aren't), water can accumulate in the bilge, and the weight of this water could overload your trailer, causing it to break down.

Weighing the pros and cons of trailering

Trailers are popular for innumerable reasons, but here are some of the most prominent pros and cons:

- ✔ **Pro:** Freedom of where and when you boat is the key advantage. With a trailer, you're dependant on no one to haul your boat to the water and launch it, and you can trailer the rig to any water big enough to handle the boat.

- ✔ **Pro:** A trailer is convenient when it comes time to take your boat to a service shop, and it allows you to wax and otherwise care for your boat in your own driveway.

- ✔ **Pro:** Trailer storage is a low-cost way of storing your boat, especially if you can keep it in your garage, driveway, or yard.

- ✔ **Con:** The whole body of knowledge surrounding trailering a boat — such as how to back up the darn thing (see Chapter 5) — is something many boaters don't want to tangle with.

- ✔ **Con:** Trailering your boat can cut your fuel economy by more than half — especially if you're towing at or near the maximum of your vehicle's towing capacity. For example, my four-door V-8 pickup truck gets 17 miles per gallon on the highway without a load. It gets 7 to 8 miles per gallon when pulling my 5,500-pound boat and trailer. That's not so painful on a 20-mile run to the water, but it's often a deal breaker for a 100-mile run. The cost of fuel for towing makes rack storage economical.

Chapter 17

The Well-Fed Boater

*P*art of the fun of boating is having a picnic on the water, or even several of them if you plan to spend a weekend afloat on a larger boat. Almost all boats have built-in coolers or, even better, a dedicated storage spot that's a perfect fit for a cooler you pack at home and bring onboard. Your boat's galley may be as simple as an ice chest or as complete as a kitchen just like home. Even smaller cruisers are likely to have microwaves and coffee pots, making cool mornings on the water a new kind of pleasure. Eating well in compact kitchens and cooking onboard your boat require planning and special packing, but the effort is well worth it.

This chapter is all about keeping hydrated and preventing your stomach and those of your crew from growling by providing refreshments and snacks in style. I explain how to make the most of your cooler space and onboard refrigerator; how to prepare in advance for snack attacks, picnic meals, or outdoor barbecues; how to minimize the mess of food and drink onboard; and how to keep safe when enjoying alcoholic beverages onboard.

Navigating Your Galley

Your *galley* is your kitchen on the water. In a runabout, the galley is just whatever you bring along in a cooler and whatever you can cook on a grill if you bring one. But even small cuddy cabins and cruisers may be equipped with sinks, stoves, and refrigerators, and boats that break the 30-foot mark often also have a sink and a grill installed in the cockpit — that fun open-seating area where you drive and all your adorers hang out and worship you for taking them boating.

Refrigerators and coolers

Coolers are the main mode of keeping things cold on boats, but many boats you'd swear were too small to have a refrigerator actually have one that runs on both 110-volt power from the shore and 12-volt power from the boat's battery. I've seen refrigerators on a lot of little cuddies and even some runabouts between 23 and 27 feet long.

Using onboard fridges

If you get a 110/12-volt refrigerator on your boat, expect it to be about the size of the beer-filled box you had in your college dorm (you rulebreaker, you). It works great to *keep* things cool, but it's slow to *make* things cool in the first place. In fact, it may never make things cool if you put them in warm and try to run the fridge on your boat's battery.

Here are some tips for using an onboard fridge:

- Pre-chill all the drinks and food you plan to put in it. You may prefer to put only chilled food in the fridge rather than drinks. You need to get drinks more often than food, so keeping drinks in a cooler increases the efficiency of the fridge because you open it less often.

- Whenever you're in port with the boat, connect it to the onshore electrical power to preserve battery power.

- When running the fridge on 12-volt battery power, keep a close eye on the voltage indicator on the fuse panel in the cabin — if the gauge indicates voltage below 12 volts, run the motor to recharge the battery.

- Open the fridge as infrequently as possible so it runs less and keeps cool with less power.

Making the most of built-in coolers and cooler spaces

These containers do the heavy lifting of keeping things cold on a boat — even if there's a refrigerator. In fact, most boats are equipped with built-in coolers or compartments made to fit coolers and keep them secure yet accessible.

I prefer hard coolers to soft coolers because soft coolers often develop leaks. My wife, on the other hand, prefers soft coolers because they tend to fit more easily in various compartments, making them easier to stow.

She gave me some tips for keeping the contents of both kinds cold:

- If you're taking food along, pack it in a cooler separate from the one holding drinks. Stow the food cooler safely out of the sun and away from prying little fingers. It will stay cold longer if you open it as infrequently as possible.

✔ Choose a cooler size that fits the day and the work it has to do, and fill it to the top with ice, eliminating air space so the ice thaws more slowly.

✔ Open the drain on your cooler so melting ice water can drain out to the bilge. Many people mistakenly believe that retaining the cold water retains the chill on the cooler contents. However, studies by the folks at Coleman, a major manufacturer of coolers and camping gear, say just the opposite is true.

The more you open coolers, the faster they warm up and the ice in them thaws. Open your coolers as infrequently as possible.

Appliances that bring the heat

Small cuddies and cruisers, the size of boat you can easily trailer from lake to lake, often come equipped with alcohol or propane stoves and sometimes with electric stoves. Microwaves and coffee makers also are increasingly popular. Here's how these items may fit into your boating cuisine routine:

✔ **Electric stoves:** These run on 110-volt power, so you need to either be connected to 110-volt shore power or run a generator (also called a *genset*) onboard. Unless you use a genset to run air conditioning, too, generating your own power is an expensive way to cook.

✔ **Built-in gas or alcohol stoves:** Gas or alcohol stoves heat things up safely and quickly with a minimum amount of fuel and no battery drain or need for a genset. If you plan to cook much using your stove, opt for one of these.

✔ **Portable gas stoves:** As opposed to a built-in gas stove, there are a variety of gas stoves available at camping and marine stores that make short work of cooking onboard and stow away safely when you're done.

✔ **Coffee makers:** On boats, these usually run on 12-volt battery power. Be sure you have a full battery before you run a coffee maker, or start the motor and let it run a little while — maybe five minutes — to bring the battery back up to snuff.

Grilling onboard is becoming one of the most popular ways to dine while boating. Many stainless-steel marine grills from well-known companies like Coleman and Magma are specially designed for boats. Here are some details on how they work:

✔ You can mount a boat-friendly grill safely on a stainless-steel boat rail or on a special rack that fits into rod holders in the *gunwale* (the top of the side of the boat). When the cooking is done and the grill is cool, you can just stow it away.

✔ Some grills require a small canister of propane that you screw into the gas regulator on the side of the grill. Charcoal grills are also available and usually cost the same as or more than propane grills. Some boaters prefer the taste real charcoal smoke puts to the food.

✔ Most boat grills have piezo starters that ignite them at the touch of a button.

I recommend that you only use a designated boat grill for grilling onboard, and most I've seen are fueled by propane tanks, although you can find a charcoal marine grill here and there. They need to be mounted on rails or mounts that fit in fishing rod holders. Any other kind of grill is apt to be dangerous and require you to revisit my discussion of what to do in case of a fire in Chapter 12.

Civilized eating: Tools and utensils

What's civilized at home may be overkill on a boat. In a day boat, a roll of paper towels and *maybe* some plastic utensils are fine for so-called elegant galley cuisine. Of course, the more elaborate your galley, the more refined your food prep skills, and the more tools and utensils you'll find you *need* to make a happy meal. In this chapter, I assume that you only need the bare essentials — say maybe a boat grill and a microwave.

The following points address items to consider bringing onboard for mealtimes; you can take or leave my advice:

✔ Say what you want about being green — there's nothing green about dirty dishes on a boat. Take along paper or Styrofoam plates and plastic cups or drinks in individual containers to cut back on the mess that you have to carry back to port.

✔ Foil is the ideal accessory to make a disposable vegetable steaming tray or to line the grill with to keep it clean.

✔ Resealable bags are the best containers on boats. From plastic utensils to fresh vegetables to filleted fish from the day's catch — they all fit in resealable bags and take up the least amount of storage space.

✔ Plastic utensils are nice if you absolutely can't eat corn on the cob and barbecue chicken with your fingers.

✔ You'll likely need a sharp knife. I keep a couple filet knives onboard, and that suffices for most things. Remember, less is more on a boat.

✔ Trash bags are essential. Keep one handy to collect empty soda cans for recycling, and use another for disposable plates, utensils, and garbage. Twist the ends between uses, and then use twist-ties to tightly seal the bags when full.

Planning to Eat, Drink, and Be Merry

The key to fun, food, and drinks onboard is advance planning. Stopping by the grocery store on your way to the lake to pick up a case of shelf-temperature soda and a bag of ice will leave you sipping warm sodas in an hour. Improperly handled food could leave you with another problem altogether.

This section contains tips for making ice, chilling drinks, and setting up meals in trouble-free packaging. For the best results, you have to accept the fact that preparation takes a little more time than just slipping something out of the package and slapping it on the grill.

Keeping your stuff cold: You gotta pre-chill

Early in my career, I ran a resort and a small rental marina. On weekends, we couldn't stock enough bagged ice to keep the boaters happy. And we couldn't make them understand that four cases of warm beer stuck in a small onboard refrigerator take about three days to cool down. That was simply too much volume of warm matter for a fridge to make cold. Sometimes our refrigerators died trying to do it.

Ice may be the answer, but the question is, "Did you pre-chill your drinks?" Here are some tips for getting things chilled and keeping them that way:

- **Drinks:** Either buy your drinks cold on the day you depart with the boat, or chill them at home over time and keep them that way until you load them into coolers. Putting more than a case of warm drinks in a boat fridge takes too long to chill and burns too much power. Plan ahead and add your drinks to your home refrigerator 12 at a time so you have what you want already cold when you're ready to go.

- **Ice-to-drink ratio:** Pack your cooler full of cold drinks then add ice. Half the volume of your cooler should be ice, and the other half drinks.

- **Bottled water:** If you plan to take bottled water, freeze the bottles a few days before you go. You can put them between other drinks for chillin' power and even add them on top. As they thaw, they also provide plenty of thirst-quenching power.

- **Extra ice:** Make slabs of ice by filling zippered freezer bags with water and laying them in the freezer. When frozen, you can stack them along the sides of your cooler, forming a wall of ice to keep the inside cool. Also, 2-liter soda bottles filled with water and then frozen make perfect ice packs to lay in large coolers or in the fish boxes of fishing boats to keep your catch cool.

✔ **Block ice over bagged:** For large containers and especially food containers, if you buy ice, buy block ice. It thaws more slowly than bagged, often taking days instead of hours, which helps preserve food on long trips. But if bagged ice is all you have access to, get the most your coolers can hold.

✔ **Freezer packs:** These are the things — often filled with blue goo — that you freeze and then put in your cooler for cooling. They work fine, but they take up space that could be devoted to frozen drink bottles, which provide something to drink as they melt. Still, freezer packs work well in food coolers because they don't thaw and drip on food, making it soggy.

Having plenty of drinks on the drink

Water, water, everywhere . . . and not a drop to drink. That's the lament in *The Rime of the Ancient Mariner.* It's no less true today, even in fresh water because practically no untreated water is safe to drink anymore. What's more, the refreshing feel of fresh water on your body is apt to make you fail to notice your thirst. And by the time you feel thirsty, medical experts agree, you're well on the way to dehydration.

To keep your crew refreshed, alert, and chillin', consider these guidelines regarding your beverage options:

✔ **Water:** Water is the best hydrator. It may be hard to get kids to drink it, but water quenches thirst better than sugared sodas and even juice, although juice boxes are a good second choice for the most stubborn little boaters.

✔ **Sodas:** Soda isn't the best hydrator, but it still does the job, and nothing beats the fizz and flavor. Adults can regulate their intake, keeping their hydration needs in mind, but kids are a different matter. I take sodas onboard my boat and let my kids drink them only if they alternate each soda with a bottle of water.

✔ **Sports drinks:** Sports drinks are designed to replace the electrolytes your body uses or loses when it sweats. There seems to be enough science around their effectiveness that I'm a proponent of drinking one or two on a really hot day on the water.

✔ **Single-serving drink mixes:** One of the handiest things I've found for boating are individual powdered drink mixes that come in little single-serving packets. You simply add them to a bottle of water, shake it up to dissolve, and enjoy. I keep some onboard my boat at all times. They offer great variety for a big crew: Popular sports drinks, iced tea, and even energy drinks come in these little packets.

✔ **Coffee or tea bags:** I can't go out without my morning coffee. Just forget it. But it's also a pain to make coffee onboard, sometimes even with a coffee maker. Coffee bags, like tea bags, make an individual cup, and unless your pipes are used to being burnished daily by the high-test coffee chain variety, you'll find that coffee bags make a fairly robust cup on a chilly morning. You can microwave the water in port, or heat it in a pot on your grill. Or, pack a thermos of hot water so you and your crew can choose between coffee, tea, or even hot cocoa.

A navy travels on its stomach

I think the old saying may have been "An army travels on its stomach," but you get the point, right? Keeping a mixed crew happy requires snacks, meals, and sweets. Keeping them fed without trashing the boat or loading it up with a supply train of gargantuan coolers and grocery bags adds to the challenge.

In this section, I explain some tips for stocking the galley that work for a day or a week. And they work with a minimum of your work done onboard, although you need to invest a little time at home.

Scaring up snacks for any time of day

Being out in the sun and the water takes a lot out of you, so it's a good idea to keep up your energy throughout the day with some healthy snacks — and okay, maybe some less healthy ones, too. Here are some recommendations:

✔ **Apples and grapes** make great snacks and come in their own all-natural wrappers. All you have to do is wash 'em, chill 'em, drop 'em in a cooler, and haul 'em out when the munchies get to you and your crew. They're no substitute for candy bars — at least not in my kids' eyes — but they offer a healthy option.

✔ **Baby carrots, broccoli and cauliflower florets, and celery sticks** chopped, bagged in zippered bags, chilled in advance, and packed along with a disposable container of dip makes for great snacking for the nutrition-minded.

✔ **Nuts, granola, raisins, and trail mix** don't have to be chilled and offer strong doses of fruit, fiber, and protein.

✔ **Candy** isn't on the list of needs, but boating is a special event, and reserving special treats for special events makes everything even more fun. I buy the bite-size candy bars, freeze them, and drop them in the cooler. Dole them out one at a time so you don't end up with candy sticking to the boat or the snack eaters.

Gearing up for breakfast

Some boaters just use snacks for breakfast, but a real breakfast can be a nice touch onboard. I've had good experiences with cooking an egg casserole in advance and warming it up onboard. That led to a few other ideas:

- ✔ Buy a premade piecrust at the grocery store — even better is one that comes in its own disposable pie pan. Scramble about six eggs and pour them into it, add three or four chopped sausage links, and layer on some grated cheese — whatever kind you like. Bake it in the oven for 35 minutes at 350 degrees. Let it cool, and then freeze it for packing in the cooler. Chances are that after a night onboard it will be thawed and you can heat it up on a grill or galley stove. If you're in port, slice it onto plastic plates and microwave it.

- ✔ Scramble eggs together with diced cooked ham, and freeze the mix in a disposable container. At breakfast, lay out flour tortillas and spoon on the eggs and ham. Sprinkle on grated cheese, roll it up, and lay it on a sheet of foil on the grill for warming. Add a little salsa for some zip if you please!

- ✔ Single-serving cups of yogurt, half-pints of milk, single-serving cereal boxes, and granola provide the makings of a grab-bag breakfast that's quick, disposable, and likely to please most tastes.

Scrambled eggs are easy to prepare and eat onboard, and unlike fried eggs, practically anyone who likes eggs at all can enjoy scrambled eggs. To eliminate the issues of handling fragile eggs, crack and scramble all you need for a trip and put them in an airtight disposable storage container. There's no breakage and no egg shells to handle onboard, and you save a ton of space in the fridge.

Laying out lazy lunches

In this section I lay down some no-cook lunch options because on a hot day, cool food cools you off and hot food isn't as appealing — save that for the evening when the sun rolls low in the sky.

- ✔ **Sandwiches:** Get bags of sliced cheese, deli meat, and mixed salad greens from the produce department. Chill the salad with the meat and cheese, and stow the bread anywhere it won't get crushed. Make sandwiches onboard when stomachs start to grumble.

- ✔ **Wraps:** Soft tortilla wraps are easier to eat onboard than sandwiches because everything is self-contained. The wraps themselves can't get crushed under a bag of beach towels, either. Simply lay your favorite sandwich stuffing on a tortilla, and roll it up.

- ✔ **Canned/packaged meats:** Tuna, chicken, and — oh, I may as well mention it — Spam don't need refrigeration until they're opened, which makes them handy for boating. With the tuna or chicken, you can flake it onto a bed of bagged salad greens in a disposable bowl for a pretty classy-looking salad.

Save those leftover mayo and ketchup packets from your last fast-food stop — they come in very handy onboard. Otherwise, buy smaller containers of condiments that fit easily in the cooler.

Digging into dinner

In my opinion, dinner should be hot even onboard a boat, so I assume you have one of those handy grills I mention earlier (refer to the section "Appliances that bring the heat") or you have a gas or alcohol stove (either built-in or portable). Obviously, dinner possibilities are endless, but to spark your imagination, the following list includes some handy ways my family gets a hot onboard meal that tastes pretty close to home cooked — or better. You can substitute marinades or seasonings and even meats and vegetables as you please, and the cooking techniques are a breeze. What's even better is that most of these meals can be prepared at home in individual portions just perfect for slapping on the grill.

- ✔ Boy scout stew is something I picked up as a kid. We laid out a sheet of foil and piled in slices of potato, a slice of onion, carrots, and a hamburger patty. Then we folded the foil over and crimped the edges to make it nearly watertight and threw it on the grill. Thirty minutes later we had a pretty darn good hot meal. Do the same with 4- to 6-ounce pieces of chicken or beef and add the vegetables you prefer. Sprinkle with seasonings, and drizzle on some olive oil before sealing the packet.

- ✔ Any type of grilled meat is a favorite of mine onboard. Steaks take only about ten minutes on hot marine grills, and chicken breasts only take a few minutes longer to get safely cooked through. Accompanying veggies may take longer, so close them up in foil packets and give them a head start on the grill.

- ✔ Kabobs make you look like a great cook because they're packed with tasty bites and are somewhat out of the ordinary. Prepare them in advance, wrap them individually, and just lay them on the grill as needed. Soak bamboo skewers in water (to make them resistant to the heat of the grill) while you quarter tomatoes, onions, bell peppers, and portabella mushrooms. Cube your meat, and then alternate between items, skewering them on the bamboo skewers. Wrap them in foil, and throw them on the grill. The great thing about kabobs is that there are so many different items to choose from that everyone ends up happy.

Planning your weekend meals

Planning food for a whole weekend really only requires penciling up a menu and getting the portions prepared. The trick is packing them in the cooler so you can find each item when you need it. If you follow these tips, you'll be able to get what you want out of the cooler without too much guesswork or digging around:

- ✔ At least two days before your boating trip, wrap individual meals in foil, mark the contents, and put them in the freezer.

✔ Follow your menu plan in reverse when you pack the cooler and put your last meal of the trip in the cooler first. If it's dinner on Sunday, add Sunday lunch on top of it. Then add Saturday dinner and Saturday lunch on top of that.

✔ Lay frozen water bottles or frozen flat zippered bags of ice in between servings to keep the food cold. As you work your way through the menu while you're boating, feel free to drink the bottled water as it thaws.

A word about alcohol

As a refreshment onboard, perhaps few beverages are more popular than a couple of cold beers. But when boating accidents are analyzed, investigators find that more often than not, alcohol was involved. That's not saying the boaters were drunk — but they often had "a beer or two," as the saying goes.

While you're boating, the wind, the sun, the body's propensity for dehydration, and the motion of the ocean (or lake) all combine to increase the impact of alcohol on your balance, judgment, and coordination. One beer at sea can equal a landlubber's two or three.

Still, it's not illegal to drink while boating in many states. However, in all states it is illegal to drive a boat while under the influence. Many states apply boating alcohol offenses against your driver's license, too. And many states have a strict blood alcohol content limit of .08. At that level, it usually takes less than two 12-ounce beers for most people to hit the uh-oh mark.

Drinking onboard isn't just about the captain's coordination, either. A crewmember approaching the blood alcohol limit is more apt to have an accident onboard that could end the day — or worse.

I'm not a teetotaler and don't expect my crew to be, but if I'm boating in a state where it isn't illegal altogether, I take precautions by loading no more beers on my boat than two per legal-aged drinker. Also, rarely do I drink more than half of one beer with lunch. Usually I save my two until the boat is in the driveway and I'm washing it up — it sure is nice to have 'em then!

I find that when I don't drink, my crew drinks sparingly with little discussion about the issue. We come in happy and have the party in the driveway while we hose down the boat.

Chapter 18

Getting Your Feet Wet with Boat Clubs

In This Chapter

▶ Giving boating a try by way of fishing clubs

▶ Joining in clubs and events centered around specific boat brands

▶ Coasting into boating with the U.S. Coast Guard Auxiliary

▶ Sharing the cost of boat ownership with timeshare-like clubs

*B*oat clubs provide a great way to build a social circle around the sport and get some hands-on experience before taking the ownership experience by the horns. In this chapter, I explain how to locate different types of clubs in your area, get yourself in the door, and maybe even get a taste of boating before you ever plunk down a down payment. Beware, though — after you connect with some new, enthusiastic boating friends, you may get hooked!

Getting Hooked on Fishing Clubs

Fishing clubs are a great way to gain some experience in boating and fishing, and you don't necessarily have to own a boat to join in the fun. For small monthly dues, you can socialize with other boaters and get a leg up on fishing tactics. Clubs often conduct fishing tournaments and give non-boating anglers a chance to fish with and learn from experienced boating anglers in exchange for sharing the cost of gas. And the awards in tournaments may be trophies or cash prizes.

In this section, I explain how fishing clubs can help you become a better boater and angler and what you can expect when you join one. I also kick-start your search for a local fishing club.

If you join a fishing club as a prospective boater, make sure your new friends know that you want to learn the game. Tell them that you'd like to help with mooring, tying lines, setting the anchor, and other boat tasks. Stating your interest upfront ensures that you'll be treated more like a boating partner than a guest, which is a better way to learn.

What fishing clubs have to offer

Fishing clubs conduct many fun and engaging activities: Tournaments, barbecues, seminars on fishing tactics and boating safety, and organized trips to various lakes and streams are all part of the mix. Following are some of the benefits you can expect from fishing clubs and their regular activities:

- ✔ **Hone your fishing skills:** Reading about fishing tactics, lures, and places is a good beginning for building a framework of fishing knowledge. But nothing puts the art of fishing into perspective like hands-on training. In fishing clubs, you can connect with many different anglers, probably catch a boat ride with them, and get some on-the-job training for being an effective boater and angler.

- ✔ **Compete in fishing tournaments:** Fishing tournaments bring anglers together in competitions that can be casual, with white elephant awards for winners, or serious, with awards in the thousands of dollars. Bigger entry fees go with bigger awards, so when real prize money is at stake, you should pony up part of your host boat's entry fee as well as part of the gas cost, and you also should take the angling as seriously as your host does. Personally, I prefer the more casual tournaments, but as with golf, the game can be more fun with big stakes.

Finding the right fishing club for your interests

Species-specific fishing clubs exist for practically every enthusiast. Some clubs are more regional in nature and seek only to bring other anglers together for the common cause of having fun and learning more about fishing. On the other hand, finding competitive clubs is pretty easy, too. In this section, I give you some leads for tracking down the fishing groups near you, and I also list a sampling of clubs that specialize in the pursuit of freshwater species.

Bass clubs

The black bass is the most abundant game-fish species in North America. I'd be willing to bet that the lion's share of fishing clubs are bass clubs that promote bass fishing. Here are some national bass-fishing groups that may very well have a chapter in your area:

✔ **Bass Anglers Sportsman Society** (BASS) is a nationally renowned club for serious bass anglers. Local chapters of BASS called Federation Nation clubs conduct tournaments that begin the qualifying process for hopeful professional anglers who want to fish for hundreds of thousands of dollars in prize money. Find out more about this organization and locate a club in your area by visiting sports.espn.go.com/outdoors/ bassmaster/federation/index.

✔ **FLW Outdoors** is a group formed by the parent company of Ranger Boats. This national tournament-fishing organization has local chapters that can be casual or very hard-core, and competitors from local tournaments can progress through the fishing circuit and eventually compete in top FLW tournaments for the ultimate cash prize, $1 million. Find out more at www.flwoutdoors.com.

✔ **Unaffiliated clubs** are local clubs that stay out of the national limelight of BASS and FLW but still have a central organization and a free membership magazine called *Bass Club Digest*. Members enjoy these clubs because they don't require membership in the national umbrella clubs. You can find a local club by visiting www.bassclubdigest.org/ find_bass_club.htm.

Walleye clubs

Walleye clubs are most popular in the northern Midwest where walleye are most abundant. The season is short for catching this cold-country species, but the anglers who pursue them are relentless, systematic, and often eager to embrace people who want to learn how to fish for walleye.

Here's the scoop on some walleye club options:

✔ **In-Fisherman Professional Walleye Trail** is similar to BASS and FLW (refer to the previous section on bass fishing clubs) but doesn't coordinate local clubs, although it does coordinate local tournaments. Often these tournaments are buddy tournaments, so anglers with boats are looking for anglers without boats to fish together and share expenses. You can discover more about these tournaments by visiting www.in-fisherman.com/pwt.

✔ **Local walleye clubs** are available in many areas, but finding them through a national organization isn't as easy as finding most bass clubs. Nevertheless, I located several simply by typing "local walleye fishing clubs" into my favorite Internet search engine. You also can turn to local tackle stores, which often post meeting announcements and can help you find local club contacts.

Other club opportunities

Beyond the tournament fishing craze, other fishing clubs exist with the primary goal of conservation, not competition. Following are two options:

✔ **Muskie clubs** (many of which are located in the Midwest) serve anglers addicted to muskellunge, as this kind of fish is formally called. The Latin name means *wolf*, and as a predator, few fish are more notorious for either ripping tackle apart in a fight or turning their noses up at an angler's bait just inches shy of the boat. The wolf fish grows to more than 4 feet long! Attend a meeting of a local muskie club and you're likely to be seduced by secret lures and the pursuit of the muskie with tales of success and failure. Muskie anglers fish for the glory of the catch and seldom keep their fish, releasing them as quickly as possible so the fish will live to fight again. (Enter "local muskie fishing clubs" into your favorite search engine to see what chapters exist in your area.)

✔ **The Coastal Conservation Association** (CCA) is more of a conservation club than a fishing club, but nearly all its members fish and prefer to do so in coastal waters. CCA members are concerned because fragile salt marshes, estuaries, and coastal flats are vulnerable to pollution, excessive commercial fishing, and even excessive recreational fishing. Local chapters of the CCA work to balance the fun of fishing with promoting safeguards to make the waters flourish. Find out more at www.joincca.org.

Joining Boat-Brand Clubs and Rendezvous

Some years ago, Jeep and Harley Davidson realized that people bought their brand of products because they identified with the brand and wanted to associate with other people who also liked it. Boat builders and many of their dealers quickly learned that the same was true of boat owners and began starting their own boat-brand clubs. They also began to organize national brand rendezvous that sometimes draw thousands of boaters sharing brand loyalty together.

It turns out that these brand-centered clubs and rendezvous help new and would-be boaters grow into the sport and give experienced boaters an exciting new social outlet to pursue with their boats.

Finding boat-brand clubs

It's not hard to find boat-brand clubs in your area. Boat dealers often organize them for the express purpose of capturing the imaginations and interest of new boaters and welcoming them into the sport — and especially to their own boat brands, of course. Here are some suggestions for making connections:

✓ **Visit a local boat dealer.** One of the best ways to find boat-brand clubs is to visit your local dealer. In my town, several dealers of various brands have clubs that conduct regular weekend rendezvous.

✓ **Do a Web search.** Finding most anything online today is pretty easy. Suppose you live in Topeka, Kansas, and you want to find an Aquasport club in your area. If one exists, chances are it will come up when you do a Web search of "Aquasport Topeka Kansas" at your favorite search engine.

Tapping in to rendezvous

Rendezvous are events for specific boat-brand owners, and boat builders usually conduct these fun events, with the help of their local dealers, to encourage people to consider their brand of boat. These rendezvous are thoroughly enjoyable events and put you squarely in the middle of like-minded boaters. For example, one of the most wildly successful boat rendezvous is Aquapalooza, a Sea Ray Boats event that the company moves around the country to various popular lakes. All the boat builder–sponsored events I've run into are family events and often have activities specifically organized for kids.

Manufacturers of fishing boats often conduct rendezvous as well, and their activities are often centered on fishing (big surprise). Rendezvous can be annual or even monthly events, and many times even boaters with a different brand of boat, or no boat at all, can wrangle an invitation.

You can find these events in much the same way as the local clubs:

✓ **Contact a local dealer.** As I said before, boat-brand makers' rendezvous are often affiliated with local dealers. Finding these events is usually pretty easy. In my community they are advertised in newspapers, and most boat dealers are aware of them and can give you a contact.

✓ **Check the manufacturers' Web sites.** Most boat brands that conduct rendezvous post details about them on their Web sites.

Joining a Watersports Club

Water-skiing and wakeboarding clubs exist to bring skiers and board riders together to learn from each other and become better skiers and riders. Many exist to train members for competitive ski and wakeboard tournaments, but many operate just for fun and practice as well.

Water-ski clubs tend to be rarer than fishing clubs, but if serious board sports are your passion, you should ask your boat dealer or check online for a local team. I found many ski clubs listed at aquaskier.com.

Clubs always have experts (and sometimes professional instructors) on hand to help tune up your ride. Often, your membership dues in a watersports club get you access to a club boat, complete with experienced drivers. You can hone your skiing or wakeboarding under the best possible circumstances and just hang up your ski or board when you're done.

Joining the U.S. Coast Guard Auxiliary

Perhaps the most prestigious boat club in the United States is the U.S. Coast Guard Auxiliary. This volunteer organization specializes in teaching its members the same skills taught to every Coast Guard cadet. Experienced auxiliary members work with the Coast Guard in search and rescue efforts and in conducting safety seminars and inspections of personal boats (see Figure 18-1).

If you're considering boating (and I assume you are simply because you've picked up this book), I encourage you to join a local Coast Guard Auxiliary branch. You'll receive training in boat skills and safety, enjoy the camaraderie of being around other boaters and water-lovers, and gain on-the-water experience in the many boats of your fellow auxiliary members.

As I said, the U.S. Coast Guard Auxiliary is a volunteer organization that works directly with the U.S Coast Guard. Here's how it works and some other pertinent info:

✓ **Who's qualified to volunteer:** Men and women over the age of 17 interested in assisting the Coasties in various safety and other volunteer missions may join the Auxiliary.

✓ **Duties:** Volunteers are trained in safe boat handling and boater safety, and sometimes they even assist in search and rescue missions. The Auxiliary is often referred to as the marine equivalent of the Civil Air Patrol.

✓ **No boat needed:** Auxiliary volunteers don't need their own boats to participate in water-based activities, but as your skills and commitment increase, you'll eventually want to acquire a uniform, which is pretty snazzy.

✓ **Finding a local flotilla:** Every state has an Auxiliary presence and may have many U.S. Coast Guard Auxiliary *flotillas*, which are like club chapters. To find a flotilla in your area, visit nws.cgaux.org/flotillafinder/index.html.

Figure 18-1: These U.S. Coast Guard Auxiliarists from the Juneau, Alaska, flotilla are on a safety instruction mission to Alaskan boaters.

Photo by Noreen Folkerts

Some Boat Clubs Are Like Timeshares

Ever been to Disneyland or some other popular tourist destination and been inundated with offers for free gifts, free tickets, or free lodging if you sign up for a tour of a timeshare condo project? In those properties, instead of paying for the whole condo, you pay a fractional price for the week or two that you get to use the condo every year.

A similar arrangement exists for boaters. These clubs go by many names, and they operate under a wide variety of arrangements. The label *fractional ownership boat club* fits some of these groups, but others don't really offer ownership of anything — your dues simply give you access to the fleet. In this section, I explain the benefits of club ownership — and a few of the liabilities as well.

Joining a fractional ownership boat club

Fractional ownership boat clubs are pretty cool, really. You buy in with an initiation fee — go ahead, call it a down payment — and you get a share of a boat or even a share of a fleet of boats. Your access is based on a reservation system and usually guarantees a minimum number of prime weekends or holidays, so you don't get stuck only with off-peak times you can't easily use.

Finding the clubs

To find fractional ownership clubs near you, enter "boat clubs" and the name of your state into your favorite search engine. Here are a few I've received some information about in the course of my work at *Boating Life* magazine:

- ✔ Freedomboatclub.com: Established in 1989, this club has locations in 12 states on the eastern seaboard. Its reservation system is accessible online and by phone.

- ✔ www.sailtime.com/member/power: SailTime offers training for wannabe boaters as well as access to a fleet of boats. The company has many operations in popular boating destinations.

- ✔ Allpointsboatingclub.com/boating.htm: Initiation fees and monthly dues in this boating club cover fractional use for three years. An online system handles reservations. All Points Boating Club only serves members in central Florida, but a quick Web search can reveal similar clubs in your area.

What you pay upfront

Most fractional ownership clubs collect a membership fee upfront. Different clubs use the funds in different ways and grant different privileges. Here are a couple of the possibilities:

- ✔ **Initiation fees:** Some clubs call their initial membership fee an *initiation fee.* Depending on the club and the boats it offers, that fee can be from $5,000 to $50,000 or more. That's a one-time charge to belong to the club. As with country clubs, some memberships can be resold under certain circumstances, and sometimes you forfeit the fee if you leave the club for any reason.

- ✔ **Ownership fees:** Other clubs operate on more of an ownership basis, similar to a timeshare. Although you don't actually own any one boat, you own a sort of stock in the club that entitles you to reserve any of its assets (boats) for use. This kind of membership can often, but not always, be transferred or resold.

Often your access to certain classes of boats is restricted by your fee. It would be nice if a $5,000 membership fee gave you access to a 45-foot cruiser, but chances are that a $5,000 membership limits you to boats of a certain size or class. You wouldn't expect to buy a cruiser for the price of a runabout, and likewise pricing for club memberships can come with some limitations that you can overcome only by paying a bigger membership fee.

Paying periodic and assessment fees

In addition to an initiation or ownership fee, many boat clubs charge recurring fees along with additional fees for extraordinary expenses.

✔ **Monthly or annual operations fees:** Most clubs levy monthly or annual fees to cover the cost of maintaining the boats. Oil changes, routine service, docking or storage fees, and insurance are some of the expenses these fees go toward. The beauty of such an arrangement is that the club monitors the bills, writes the checks, and handles the drudgery of the business of boating!

✔ **Assessments:** Sometimes unexpected losses occur within a boat ownership club. Perhaps a hurricane or a tornado strikes the storage or marine facilities, and damages result that aren't covered by insurance. In many cases, you must pay additional fees to maintain the club.

Incurring boating expenses

Anytime you boat, you incur boating expenses above and beyond the normal boat-maintenance costs, such as filling up with gas, adding oil, washing the boat, and paying launch fees. Your club handles those chores for you, but you still have to pay for them.

✔ **Fuel, oil, and launch fees:** The club incurs these fees when getting your reserved boat ready for the water. It passes the fees down to you in a monthly statement or asks you to pay up when you return for the day.

✔ **Concierge fees:** The fee for provisioning the boat is money well spent. With a call ahead, you can have your reserved boat stocked with drinks, ice, and snacks for the day. You save the shopping time, and the club bills you for the goodies.

Weighing benefits and liabilities

The most obvious benefit of fractional boat ownership clubs is boating as often as you want and, in some clubs, with as many different boats as you wish. This section reviews both the benefits you should expect to enjoy and the risks you should consider first.

Enjoying variety and convenience

Here's a rundown on the benefits of boat ownership clubs:

✔ **The ability to choose from among many boat types:** I've come across clubs that offer virtually all styles of boats to their members. You can cruise one weekend, overnighting in a port you've always wanted to visit, and when you come back, you can take out a speed boat for a brisk ride around your home turf. Pontoons, fishing boats, bay boats, and offshore boats are also commonly available in boat clubs like this.

✔ **The ability to easily reserve time on the water:** When you join a club, all you need to do to reserve a boat for a day or even a few days is either phone or, in some cases, log onto a Web reservation site and enter your reservation request.

✔ **No launching or loading:** Some clubs deliver a boat to your driveway for you to trailer to your destination, but many of the clubs have a home port that operates much like a dry-stack marina. You phone ahead for a launch appointment, and the boat is waiting at the waterfront for you when you arrive.

✔ **No fueling, washing, or checking the oil:** A big part of getting on the water and later stowing the boat is wrapped up in washing, waxing, gassing up, and checking fluids. When you're a member of a boat ownership club, those tasks are done for you — your job is simply to turn the ignition key.

Watching out for the downside

Boat ownership clubs aren't for everybody. The need for reservations limits the spontaneity that boaters often relish. And these clubs don't carry much pride of ownership, so if you're one of those folks who meticulously rubs out every smudge, scratch, or ding in the boat, you had better buy your own boat.

If I were contemplating joining a boat ownership club, I'd look for a trial membership and test it out for a few months before making a longer-term commitment. I'd also ask the following pointed questions of the sales representatives, and I recommend that you do the same:

✔ **Does the initiation fee — or whatever the club calls the upfront fee — get you an official title to a share of the boats or just the right to use them as long as the club is in business?**

✔ **Can you sell your membership if you later decide to buy your own boat and quit the club?**

✔ **Are there any penalties for cancelling your membership? Are there any residual obligations?**

✔ **On the topic of accidents and insurance, who's responsible for the deductible, and what levels of insurance are carried on the different boats?**

✔ **Are there any personal liabilities against which you should protect yourself in case of an accident?**

✔ **Who handles the cost of repairs in case of an accident?** Be certain you're comfortable with the limits of your liability to the club in case of damages.

Part VI
The Part of Tens

The 5th Wave   By Rich Tennant

"Very clever, but how much do you want for the boat without the bottle?"

In this part . . .

In this part, you pick up ten tips for boating like an expert, the ten most important things every boater should carry onboard, and ten (plus a couple extra) surefire ways to identify a bad boat before you buy it.

Chapter 19

Ten Tactics That Separate Pros from Amateurs

· ·

In This Chapter

▶ Keeping a crew and passengers aware and secure

▶ Practicing proper communication

▶ Using the proper gear and knots

· ·

*E*xperienced boaters adopt attitudes and know techniques that keep them and their passengers safer and make them look smoother at the helm and cleverer at the dock than newer boaters. I learned some of these things the hard way, but as a reader of this book, you don't have to! In this chapter, I present ten insights that will help you become a more professional boater in no time.

Know the Limits of Your Crew

The great mutinies in naval history weren't due to wealth, greed, or power. They mostly grew out of fear of and unfamiliarity with uncharted waters too far from home. Although your boating crew or passengers aren't likely to outright mutiny against you, you don't want to endanger their comfort or safety due to your inexperience or lack of wisdom as their captain.

Never plan an all-day cruise for friends new to boating if you're not sure they can handle the conditions. And by conditions I mean the rocking and rolling and exposure to the elements. Taking someone fishing offshore for eight hours is fun for them only if they don't begin hurling from seasickness two miles out of port. The elderly and frail may love a boat ride, but don't plan on ever reaching speeds high enough to put the boat up on plane. Just a few hours on the water can ruin the trip for fair-skinned people without sun protection, and while you're at the helm, you're the one in control of their exposure to the sun.

Take your responsibility to your passengers and crew seriously. For more details on keeping your passengers safe and how to both prevent and handle emergencies, turn to Chapter 12.

Give Fair Warning for Any Maneuvers

In a car, passengers have seatbelts, doors, and bucket seats to hold them in place. They can see the lines on the road and many other cues that let them know exactly which way the car will turn or whether it will go up or down a hill or suddenly accelerate or stop. In contrast, boating seldom offers such cues — unless the captain at the helm shouts them out, which can help keep a passenger from taking an unexpected swim.

For example, if you see the need to suddenly veer to the port side, shout it out so your crew can adjust themselves for the turn. The correct vernacular for a left turn is "Turn to port," but you may want to call "Left turn!" to be crystal clear for those who don't remember what "port" means. Add "Turning to port!" afterward so they can learn the lingo.

Also, if you see large wakes that you expect to shake up the boat, warn your crew. I just tell mine that there are "big bumps ahead." I'd rather not sort out who knows the jargon and who doesn't.

Prepare Your Crew for Docking and Disembarking

You wanna see something painfully funny? Go to www.youtube.com and type "love boat bloopers" in the search box. After watching the resulting short clip of boating mishaps set to the theme song from the old *Love Boat* TV show, you'll understand why boating's most dangerous moment is getting from boat to dock or dock to boat. What the video montage doesn't show is how many people had to go to the emergency room for stitches or to have broken bones set afterward!

When you're docking, prepare your crew for the process. Make sure your crew members know that, when docking your boat, you don't need them to be human brakes or fenders and you don't want them to try to guide the boat by hand or stop it by trying to grab the dock. Explain to them that docking works best if you, the captain, do it with the motor while everyone remains with butts firmly planted in their seats. Ask them to remain that way until you tell them, "You're clear to go."

If you need help, assign each person to a task and be very specific about it. Be friendly, and most of all, make sure everyone understands their roles, whether it be to sit tight or tighten the bowline.

Imagine trying to dock while kids are scrambling prematurely onto the dock. If you didn't see them and you overshot your approach and popped the shift into reverse, they could be thrown in the water and sucked in the prop blades. I've seen it almost happen — with my own crew.

Yell to Be Heard, Not to Offend

When you're maneuvering a boat, you have to contend with engine noise, the rushing of the wind, and the sloshing of the water. At the dock or launch ramp, you also may encounter other boats making the same noises and people yelling the same commands as you.

Yelling to be heard is common in boating, but be careful that it doesn't cross the line into yelling out of irritation or anger — or that your crew members don't interpret it that way.

The best way to avoid potentially volatile communications in the heat of the moment is to discuss the boating process beforehand.

Resist the Temptation to Hot-Dog

As a kid, I worked a boat rental dock in Lake of the Ozarks, Missouri. There's probably still a water patrolman around there somewhere who remembers giving me an undeservedly friendly warning to slow down as I returned my rental boats to the dock after taking a test drive to make sure the renters didn't break them.

As a stupid kid, I used to charge the dock at full speed and chop the throttle at the last second, jam the boat into reverse, and stop the boat in the nick of time. It was fun, but if the engine died during shifting, as engines often do, I would have coasted hard into the dock. I've since learned that it's always more impressive to watch a guy dock a boat precisely, quietly, and without theatrics.

A professional boater never uses more throttle than needed to maneuver the boat, especially when docking. I see hot-dogs all the time who never learned that lesson. I was lucky to have learned it before the inevitable ever happened.

The better you get at boating, the greater the temptation to hot-dog. A serious boater never shows off — at least not at the helm. You know what the last thing a hot-dog says before taking his boat to the fiberglass repair shop? "Watch this."

Be Clear about Who Has the Helm

If you plan to let others drive — ahem, *pilot* — the boat, be sure they know what their responsibility is. Make sure you communicate clearly at all times with your crew, and don't give the helm to others unless you're sure they know what they're doing.

I once boated with a friend who asked me to take the helm for him while he tidied up the boat after fishing. Moments later, he returned and asked for the helm. I was happy to relinquish it and went back to enjoying the scenery. He walked away from the helm without asking me to take over again. I was looking away, so nobody noticed as we eased out of the channel and ran up on rocks, crushing a $1,000 set of props and a $4,000 drive unit. I felt bad about it, thinking that I should have read his mind or understood that he wanted me to take the helm again. But the rest of the crew agreed that he had the helm at the time and was at fault.

Use Proper Docklines

I've spent more than 25 summers on or around boat docks, and I always find it amazing how many boaters buy a new boat with life jackets, fire extinguishers, skis, and wakeboards and then tie their boats to the dock with scraps of rope they cobble together from dog leashes, clotheslines, and whatever they find on the dock.

Want to look like a pro? When you pull into the slip with your shiny new boat (or pre-owned one, for that matter), reach into a locker and pull out at least four spiffy new nylon docklines with a loop already woven into one end (you can buy them like this; see Chapter 4 for more information).

Docklines shouldn't be an afterthought. They're as important to the safety of your boat as the drain plug. The lines should match in length so you don't have to sort them to use them, and they should all be of the same diameter and strength. Your boat is only as secure as the weakest line on the dock.

Avoid the Tangled Mess of Lines

You can tell a captain knows his or her stuff when he or she glides into a slip and pulls out well-kept, unknotted docklines neatly coiled and ready for use.

If you don't spend the time coiling a line after use, much like you would an extension cord, the next time you need it, the line will be wrought with knots and tangles and you'll be forced to spend more time untangling and untying it than you would have spent coiling up the line in the first place.

Every unwanted knot left in a rope soon becomes as hard as a brick and impossible to get out, decreasing the line's usefulness and increasing the odds that the knot will break the line or chafe an ugly scab on your boat.

Tie a Bowline Knot

Boaters use many different kinds of knots for mooring their boats, towing other boats, or securing things in place.

If you learn to tie only one knot, it should be a bowline loop. This knot won't slip out, but no matter how tight it gets, you can always get it untied. You can use it to hitch to a cleat or tie it through a tow-eye when pulling a boat.

Here's a great way to master the bowline and remember how to tie it (I think I learned it in Boy Scouts). As you work this knot, say this: "The rabbit climbs out of the hole, runs around the tree, and then back down in the hole":

1. **For a 6-inch loop in a line, bend a small loop in the line (call it the "rabbit hole") 18 inches from the bitter end. To do it, fold the bitter end (the "rabbit") over the line (see Figure 19-1a and b). (If you want a smaller loop, say a 4-inch loop, use 12 inches of line.)**

2. **Bring the bitter end up through the rabbit hole (see illustrations c, d, and e of Figure 19-1). Pull enough of the rabbit through the rabbit hole to wrap around the long end of the line (the "tree").**

3. **Wrap the rabbit around the tree just above the rabbit hole, as shown in illustrations f, g, and h of Figure 19-1.**

4. **Take the rabbit in your right hand and bring it under and through the rabbit hole (see Figure 19-1i and j).**

5. **Tighten it up.**

   Double-check your knot against the one in Figure 19-1.

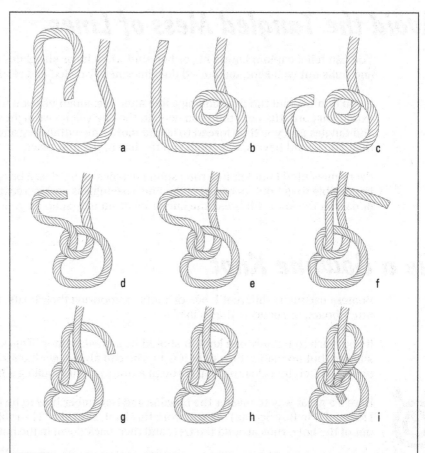

Figure 19-1:
Tying a
bowline
knot.

Go All the Way with a Half-Hitch Knot

If you master the bowline knot (refer to the previous section) and are up for another, I recommend you add the half-hitch to your knotting repertoire. Sometimes a loop is useless because there's nothing to hook it over, such as a cleat. For example, if you want to lash your boat to a thick piling, the bowline doesn't work well on the piling side of the equation.

In a case like that, the half-hitch is your knot. It's easy to tie, it's easy to get out, and it's the perfect solution for fastening lines to pilings when mooring your boat.

Follow these steps to tie a half-hitch knot on a piling, and refer to Figure 19-2:

1. Wrap the line twice around the piling, leaving 1 foot or so of the end of the line — called the bitter end — to work your knot (see Figure 19-2a and b).

2. Take the bitter end of the line over and around the line (see Figure 19-2c).

3. Grasp the line between your thumb and forefinger where it crosses the bitter end.

4. Fold the bitter end through the (sort of) triangular loop formed by the rope and the piling (see Figure 19-2d and e).

   That's your first half-hitch.

5. Wind the end around the back of the line again, making a second loop (your second half-hitch, as shown in Figure 19-2f).

   Two half-hitches don't make a whole hitch, but one half-hitch isn't much good without the second one.

6. Wind the line through that second loop (see Figure 19-2g).

7. Tighten the knot.

REMEMBER

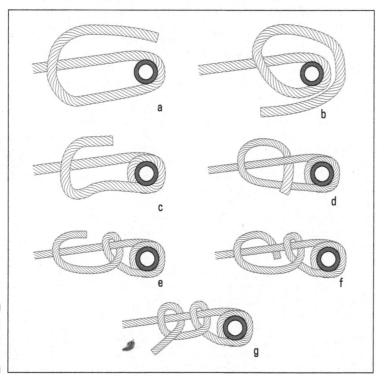

Figure 19-2:
Tying a
half-hitch.

a

b

c

d

e

f

g

If you're tying a half-hitch on a piling and you plan to take the other end to a cleat to moor your boat — a bowline works fine on the cleat side, by the way — put the half-hitch higher on the piling than the cleat. As the boat works against its lines, the line won't rub on the boat's fiberglass as much as it would if the half-hitch were lower on the piling.

Chapter 20

Ten Important Items to Keep Onboard

. . . .

. . . .

Keeping your ship shipshape means keeping your crew safely outfitted and carrying a certain amount of redundant gear onboard. Outfitting your boat with an extra propeller, the tools to change it, and spare equipment to replace what's most commonly used and frequently broken is the mark of a skillful boater. I discuss most of these things in detail throughout this book, and this chapter gathers ten of the most vital points into a quick-reference checklist.

Life Jackets

You (hopefully) already know your boat can't be legally operated without a life jacket available for every passenger onboard. Chances are, you bought one for every member of your family. But what about guests you may bring along on an upcoming trip? It's way too easy to assume that because you were properly equipped on the last trip out, you'll be good to go on the next one.

Life jackets not only have to be in adequate supply, with one for each passenger, but they have to *properly fit* the passengers, too. Keep an inventory list of life jackets onboard, along with their sizes. Store all the jackets in a duffel bag you can access conveniently before you depart from the dock.

Clean-Up Equipment

Some people have rules about eating or drinking in a car, but I can't imagine a boat's crew standing up under such mutiny-inducing restrictions. Snacks, sodas, and other beverages are a part of a fun, relaxing day on the water (refer to Chapter 17), so be prepared to quickly clean up spills before they become stains.

Keep the following cleaning items conveniently onboard:

- ✔ **Spray bottle of marine boat cleaner from a marine store.** Don't use household cleaners, because many have ammonia, which is bad for all parts of the boat.
- ✔ **Paper towels or clean rags.**
- ✔ **A synthetic chamois or large sponge for sopping up spilled drinks.**
- ✔ **A soft scrub brush for cleaning crumbs from carpet or non-skid deck treads.**

Extra Rope

Sooner or later, you'll have to pitch a line to a dock hand to get your boat under control in an unruly current or breeze. You may need to pitch a line to a disabled boat to help tow it ashore, or you may just want to tie an overly rambunctious rug rat to his seat to keep him from falling overboard (just kidding on that last one).

My point is that rope is never in adequate supply on most recreational boats. For the cost of a couple of waterfront hamburgers, you can have 100 feet of line stowed safely aboard. Coil it neatly, and then drop it in a locker. You'll be glad you did.

A Boat Hook

When people fall overboard on a boat, it's usually because they lean too far over the *gunwale* (the side of the boat) to reach a line or piling or even to rescue a hat blown into the water.

That 12-pack of beer you and your friends are going to drink at your driveway boat-wash party on Saturday evening costs more than a floating, adjustable, aluminum boat hook. Instead of leaning over the gunwale, you can use this hook to safely hand a mooring line to a dock hand or pull a Dale Earnhardt #3 hat from the water. Find one (a hook, not a hat) at www.westmarine.com, your local boat dealer, or a marine supply store.

A Backup Horn

Boat horns may be the most unreliable gizmos on boats. Few work for very long, and if you're inspected by the Coasties, one of the first things they'll nail you on is lacking a sound signal, thanks to a dysfunctional horn.

Attach a loud whistle to your ignition keys. It counts as a sound signal in a pinch and can save you from a ticket.

Spare Fuses

Find the fuse panel in your boat and determine the type of fuses it takes: cylindrical glass fuses or the spaded flat fuses popular in automobiles today. Skip your latte one morning and spend the money on two packages of spare fuses. Choose the variety packs with various amperages so you're sure to have what you need when you overheat the stereo with Pink Floyd and blow a fuse.

Four Key Tools

Many boaters aren't all that handy with tools, so I'm never surprised to see so few tool kits onboard pleasure boats. But a kit with just these four tools can save the day in most any boating outing:

- ✔ **Screwdriver with replaceable bits:** You've seen these screwdrivers at the cashier's counter of any hardware store. It's like a regular screwdriver, but in place of the blade, it has a socketed shaft that accepts a supply of various screwdriver and fastener bits. Use this tool to tighten any screw you see poking its head even a millimeter above its hole.

- ✔ **Pliers:** Pliers can help you tighten and adjust loose battery cables, which are the most common cause of battery failure and a boat that won't start. You'll also need pliers to change a propeller, because many props use a cotter key to hold on the prop nut, and the pliers let you bend the cotter key straight.

- ✔ **Adjustable wrench:** With an adjustable wrench that's large enough, you can skip bringing a propeller wrench, saving space onboard.

✔ **A sharp, serrated knife:** With ropes onboard, sooner or later you'll get a knot tied that you can't untie. Choose a serrated knife for cutting ropes. Nothing works better. Many popular brands like Gerber and Buck make folding knives of stainless steel so they don't rust in marine environments.

Spray Grease

Spray grease loosens rusted nuts, counteracts corrosion, and restores clean connections between wiring connections. Just spray it on and let it do its work.

To protect your tools from corrosion due to humid and salty air, lay them on a clean, old terry cloth towel and spray this grease liberally over them. Turn them over and spray the other side. Use the towel to rub it in, and then roll the tools in the rag to make sure they're covered.

Materials to Plug Leaks

One of these days it may happen to you: You'll notice something isn't quite right when the boat comes up on plane a little slower, when water comes out of hatches when you slow down, or when you find just the bow of the boat peeking above the water like a harbor seal. You've sprung a leak.

Old timers carried wooden plugs of various sizes and jammed them in broken and leaking through-hull fittings to stop leaks. Thankfully, leak-plugging has advanced somewhat and wooden plugs are no longer the only solution.

A friend of mine, the Alaskan Coast Guard Auxiliary commodore Michael Folkerts, offers this suggestion: Buy a couple of wax rings used to seal your bathroom toilet bowl to the plumbing. If you spring a leak, you can mold the wax to the exact shape needed to plug it up. Add a roll of duct tape to that short shopping list. You can use it in a pinch to temporarily slow the leaks in hoses or fittings.

Sun Protection

For your kids' sake (and your own!), leave the bimini top in place if you have one and get one if you don't. Keep a generously sized bottle of waterproof sunscreen onboard, too. Bullfrog is my favorite brand; it was made by water rats for water rats, and I haven't found a brand I like better.

Chapter 21

Ten (Plus Two) Mechanical Checks for Buying a Pre-Owned Boat

- -

In This Chapter

▶ Checking the state of engine oils and fluids

▶ Flipping switches to test engine devices and electrics

▶ Keeping an eye and ear out for structural weaknesses

▶ Double-checking trailer functions

- -

Some people believe that all boats are horribly unreliable and poorly made. In truth, their engines are often the same engines used in automobiles. I've actually looked inside a Yamaha F115 outboard and seen "FORD" stamped on certain internal engine parts because the engine block was once used in a compact car. General Motors is the chief supplier of engines to the marine industry. Even the drive systems added by marine manufacturers are precisely engineered and carefully designed to ease the routine maintenance requirements as much as possible.

Over the course of its life, your car engine will operate at an average of only about 2,000 revolutions per minute (RPMs) thanks to the laws of inertia, drag, and the car's ability to coast on level ground. But a boat never gets to coast downhill. When it reaches the intended speed, the engine must keep running at high RPMs to keep it there. To top it all off, much of a boat engine's drive system has to operate and often live *underwater*. It's not an easy place to live, and maintenance requirements are naturally higher.

The problem with boats is that boaters often see them as cars that run in water and overlook their special maintenance needs. That, in turn, means boats often become less reliable. This chapter focuses on some checks you can perform and a couple you should definitely have a mechanic perform before you buy a pre-owned boat. Part IV speaks in detail to many of these items.

Check All the Engine Fluids

When you go to the doctor for a physical, the staff takes a variety of your body fluids to check as indicators of how things are working. Similarly, engine fluids tell the story of a boat engine's health, and some problems can be diagnosed simply by looking at the oils and fluids. Chemical tests can reveal more hidden problems.

Following are the major engine oils and fluids to check and what you can determine from their conditions.

Engine oil

Oil in your new or pre-owned engine should be clear, not black. When you rub a drop of it between your fingers, it shouldn't leave a sooty smear — just an oily one. Here's some more detail about oil color and what the color you see may mean:

- **Black, opaque oil** may indicate that soot from the combustion of fuel in the engine is getting into the oil. This condition means the engine is extremely worn and ready for an overhaul.

- **Creamy or whitish oil** may be contaminated by moisture. This problem may be the result of improper boat winterization.

- **Clear, honey-colored oil** is what you want to see. But beware that the owner of a pre-owned boat could simply have changed the oil just before you arrived. An older engine is unlikely to have honey-clear oil unless it was recently changed, so don't assume that the engine is in good shape just because the oil is fresh and clear. If all else on the engine looks properly maintained, chances are the owner changed the oil out of habit, not to hide a fault.

At www.enginecheckup.com, you can purchase an engine oil analysis kit that helps you look for troubles in the engine. By placing a drop of oil on various chemically treated pads, you can analyze the oil for excessive engine wear, poor combustion, and other problems.

Gear case oil

Gear case failure is one of the most common and most expensive major engine failures. Outboards and sterndrives both have gear cases.

At the bottom of the gear case is a screw that accepts either a regular screwdriver or a hex wrench. Remove the bottom drain screw and let a drop or two of oil drip out onto your finger. Here's what to look for:

✔ The gear case oil should be honey-clear and free of grit. Milky oil likely means the seals leak and let water in, requiring a repair that will cost several hundred dollars. It could also mean there's major gear case damage, and the only way to check for that is to have a mechanic open up the gear case and examine it.

✔ The gear case drain screw plug is magnetic, and under normal use conditions, fine metal filings are likely to adhere to the screw. If there are problems with the gear case, the metal filings will be chunks ranging in size from gritty sand to small pebbles.

The first thing I recommend doing to a pre-owned boat is having a mechanic change the gear case seals and water pump impeller housed inside. The water pump impeller turns as the drive shaft turns and forces cooling water to the engine. It routinely needs changed every two years, so you may as well do it immediately when you get your boat. If you feel fairly certain the boat you're looking at is the one you want, plan to do this *before* you conclude your purchase. If the mechanic opens the gear case to change the seals and pump and finds signs of excessive wear, you can adjust the final price for the repairs. If all is well, you can boat with peace of mind that you've headed off one of the major causes of engine failure until the next time the seals need changing or checking in a couple of years.

Hydraulic drive trim fluid

On outboards and sterndrives, the gear case needs to be trimmed up or down to give the propeller the proper angle of action for a smooth, efficient ride. You control this trimming action through a hydraulic line that requires adequate hydraulic fluid.

On a sterndrive, the engine trim reservoir is located in the engine compartment, sometimes on the engine and sometimes near it. On an outboard, it's located on the motor mount, against the transom (back) of the boat. The reservoir should be labeled "trim fluid" or something similar. Check the clear reservoir for the proper level of fluid. If it's low or empty, you can assume there's a leak in the system that needs repairing. Adjust your price for the boat accordingly.

Trim tab fluid

Your boat may be equipped with trim tabs that jut from the transom (rear) of your boat on either side of the gear case. The hydraulic fluid for these tabs is inside the engine compartment or bilge, and the reservoir for them is usually mounted near the spot on the inside of the transom opposite where the tabs are mounted.

Check the clear reservoir for the proper level of fluid. If it's low or empty, you can assume there's a leak in the system that needs repairing. Adjust your price for the boat accordingly.

Power steering fluid

The power steering fluid reservoir is mounted on the engine on sterndrive boats. On newer engines, the reservoir cap is yellow and easy to spot. Unscrew it and check the dipstick on the cap to be sure the reservoir has the proper level of fluid. Low levels indicate problems that need further examination by a mechanic.

Operate All Engine Devices

Even if the boat's engine runs and shifts and the propeller turns, if the drive trim and trim tabs don't work properly, the boat won't run properly. So before you sign on the dotted line, make sure these work. Here's how:

- ✔ **Drive trim:** Operating this switch, which is located on the gearshift or throttle, raises or lowers the drive unit. Cycle the switch and make sure it works. If it doesn't, get a mechanic's opinion on the reason.

- ✔ **Trim tabs:** If your prospective boat is equipped with tabs, run the switches on the helm station and make sure the tabs go up and down.

Check the Engine Belt

A serpentine belt is mounted between pulleys on the front of all sterndrive engines and on the top of some outboard engines, under the cowl. A worn belt may be frayed around the edges and may actually be missing chunks of rubber. A belt in this condition needs to be replaced before it breaks and results in a repair with a surprisingly high price tag.

Examine All Engine Instruments

Many auto drivers ignore the instrument panel aside from the fuel gauge and the speedometer. Most people don't even know what their oil pressure gauges or tachometers are telling them. In boats, however, if the engine stops, you can't walk to a service station for help, so you can't afford to be so *laissez faire* about the functions of the instruments.

On boats, I've figured out which gauges I can ignore and which ones I should never ignore. Here's what I look for to make sure the instrument panel gives me the proper information:

- ✔ **The fuel gauge:** On boats, this gauge is notoriously fickle. On pre-owned boats, it often malfunctions, but you won't know if it works until you put fuel in the tank — and you may not want to do that until you buy the boat. So, reserve the right to do so just prior to finalizing the sale, and adjust the price if 10 gallons of fuel doesn't nudge the meter, because it's a sign that you'll need to replace it.

- ✔ **Tachometer:** This dial tells you how fast the engine is running by way of the number of RPMs. Engine problems often are first exhibited in a loss of RPMs, so without a functioning tachometer, you may not even be aware that your engine is increasingly sick until it stops. If the tachometer needle doesn't move up or down as you throttle the engine, it needs repairing or replacing. You should allow for that expense when you make an offer on the boat.

- ✔ **Speedometer:** On a boat, this gauge hardly ever works for long — even on a new boat. I've learned to disregard speedometers in boats and rely instead on my GPS unit for speed info. If the speedometer doesn't work, it's probably not worth replacing, but you could negotiate for a replacement anyway.

- ✔ **Oil pressure gauge:** This gauge tells you how well oil is circulating in the engine. Oil pumps rarely fail these days, so a gauge that doesn't work is most likely simply a faulty gauge, not an actual oil problem. But the consequences of being wrong in that assumption are so expensive that you should have a mechanic check the system if the gauge doesn't function properly.

- ✔ **Voltage meter:** This meter tells you if the engine alternator is charging the battery. It should read between 12 and 14 volts. If it doesn't, you're dealing with a bad gauge, a bad alternator, or a bad connection in the system. Don't ignore this. Get a mechanic to determine that it works, or get a repair estimate to negotiate into the offer.

Test All Electric Devices

When evaluating a boat, turn everything on and off to see if everything works. Here's a list of things to operate:

- ✔ **Navigation lights:** Make sure the boat has red and green bow lights and an all-around white light. It's unsafe and illegal to operate a boat without them (see Chapter 9).

- ✔ **Interior lights:** These lights are handy but not mandatory for operating a boat. Still, make sure they work.

- ✔ **Dash lights:** If dash lights don't function, you can't read your instruments at night. If you're inspecting the boat in the daytime, block the sunlight from the dash to see if these lights operate when you turn on the navigation lights. Sometimes switching on the boat's ignition turns them on, too.

- ✔ **Stereo:** Turn on the boat's stereo system, and put your ear to each speaker to make sure they all work. Put a CD in the CD player disc slot to make sure that works as well.

- ✔ **Freshwater system:** If the boat has a freshwater system, examine the freshwater reservoir (usually found in the engine compartment) to make sure there's no black mold inside. If the system is empty, fill it with water to make sure it's watertight, and run the freshwater pump to be sure it works, too.

- ✔ **Raw water pump:** This device draws from the surrounding water to spray on the boat for rough cleanups. These pumps are notoriously fickle, so make sure it runs and pumps water.

- ✔ **Electrical switches:** Every switch should do its job. Cycle through them all, and double-check their functions.

Check the Drive System Alignment

In sterndrive engines, a common cause for drive system failure is misalignment between the sterndrive and the engine. This often happens as the boat ages and the engine mounts compress over time, causing the engine and sterndrive to shift in relationship to each other. Drive system alignment isn't an easy check for an amateur, but it shouldn't be any trouble for a mechanic. Have one check this alignment before you buy the boat.

Check for a Sound Deck and Hull

I once rode a brand-new boat that had a stringer system loose inside it. *Stringers* are long beams that give strength to the boat from its stern to its bow. As we crested each wave, you could feel the stringer knocking up and down between the hull and deck. The manufacturer took this boat back to the factory and disassembled it completely to make the repair. That's an enormous job with enormous expense.

Something like a loose stringer system is extremely uncommon in new or pre-owned boats, but as boats age, things do begin to weaken, soften, or sometimes rot. Whether the boat you're considering is new or pre-owned, head off potential deck and hull repairs.

- ✔ **Soft spots on the deck:** Take baby steps all over the deck of the boat. If it sags anywhere to the point that you can feel it, count on serious structural problems. Take the boat off your list of possibilities, or adjust the price after getting a repair estimate.

- ✔ **Hull problems:** Loose stringers or other structural problems are detected only by driving the boat over waves and wakes, because the defects often cause the boat to make cracking or thumping noises in such conditions. You can tell if stringers are rotting by unscrewing one of the engine mount bolts. If it comes out wet, or if the stringers are squished out of shape under the engine, the boat probably has rotting stringers. Drive the boat. Does it thump or creak excessively in a way you can feel more than hear? If so, cross it off your list and find another potential buy.

Ferret Out Trailer Troubles

Without a trailer, your new-to-you boat won't be much use unless you plan to dock it for good at your lakeside cabin or at a marina — which are totally viable options. But if you're planning to keep your boat elsewhere and transport it to the water when you're ready for an outing, here are some common weak points to check for when purchasing a pre-owned boat trailer:

- ✔ **Wheel bearings:** Jack up the trailer and spin the wheels. They should turn smoothly and silently. If they don't, count on having to change bearings and hubs — an expensive proposition. Get an estimate for this job, and adjust your offer accordingly.

- ✔ **Lights:** Hook up your tow vehicle to the trailer's lights and make sure they all work. It's unsafe and illegal to tow a trailer without proper brake and signal lights.

- ✔ **Brakes:** Check the brakes on a trailer, because it's often hard to tell if they're actually working except in an emergency stop, which you don't want to try. But you can make sure the calipers aren't excessively rusted, and you can check the brake fluid at the reservoir located on the tongue of the trailer. Just pop off the black cap with a screwdriver and look at the fluid level inside. A low level indicates a leak somewhere in the line. Get an estimate for this job, and adjust your offer accordingly.

- ✔ **Tires:** Oftentimes, boaters finally get around to selling their boats after they've been sitting on their trailers for at least a year (and often several years). Being parked for a long period of time causes trailer tires to delaminate. Look for signs that the boat hasn't been moved in a while, such as tall grass on the outside of the wheels and dead grass under the boat. If it has been sitting in the same place for more than a year, you can bet on impending trailer tire failure. Adjust your price to accommodate mounting new tires.

Index

• Z •